SOCIAL WORK PRACTICE WITH MINORITIES

second edition

by

David R. Burgest

The Scarecrow Press, Inc.
Metuchen, N.J., & London
1989

British Library Cataloguing-in-Publication data available

Library of Congress Cataloging-in-Publication Data

Social work practice with minorities / [edited by] David R. Burgest.—
    2nd ed.
        p.   cm.
    ISBN 0-8108-2207-5
    1. Social work with minorities—United States.   I. Burgest, David
R., 1943-   .
HV3176.S35 1989
362.84'0973—dc20   89-32068

Dedicated

to

Loretta, Juanita, Angela, Dave, and Paul

CONTENTS

PREFACE

The second edition of any book should be easier to complete than the first. However, my experience is that this second edition required more time, work, and energy. I took care to see to it that "no stones were left unturned" in making this book a quality production. As a result, I am certain that educators and students alike will find this text resourceful, beneficial, and rewarding to the learning experience.

In revising this book, I attempted to respond to the constructive input from students in my classes as well as from critics, colleagues, and friends across the country. The study of racial and ethnic concerns in relationships is not designed to terminate at a specified point when our world "gets it right"; rather, it is the continuous study and explanation of such subject matter that will facilitate better relations. In that regard, this second edition is dedicated to the spirit of continuous study and better relations and interactions.

D. R. B.

INTRODUCTION

I have had to rethink certain aspects of this book since the first
edition. In a few areas, I have modified my intellectual and philosophical posture to a position I did not previously hold. It is the
primary focus of this second edition to bridge the relationship
between new and innovative concepts in the field and the author's
professional contribution.

Heretofore, I have referred to racial and ethnic grouping in
America as *minorities*, which is the title of the text. However,
further discourse and intellectual discovery led me to the conclusion that the concept *minorities* is commonly used to denote
cross-cultural, multi-ethnic, multi-racial, People of Color, as well
as *females, disadvantaged*, and the *handicapped*. Therefore,
there is much confusion about the definition of this term. In social
work education and practice, the problem of terminology and
conceptualization is a critical concern to scholars, practitioners,
and students.

The concept *cross-cultural* has been used in social work education and practice to include everything from social class and
economic stratification within a particular racial or ethnic composition to the strict division of class, and social differences between different races. America is dominated by European ethnic
groups; therefore, there are those who perceive cross-cultural dynamics only on the basis of white interaction with People of Color.
Interaction between People of Color, such as Puerto Ricans and
Mexican-Americans, Blacks and Native Americans, is seldom if
ever explored or analyzed from a cross-cultural or multi-ra-
cial/multi-ethnic perspective to facilitate direct services.

In this collection of readings, such terms as *Third World,
Minorities, minority, ethnicity*, and *racial groups* will be used
by the contributors to denote People of Color. The concept *People
of Color* more accurately reflects the make-up of non-European
racial/ethnic compositions as opposed to the concepts of

minorities, Third World, multi-ethnic, multi-racial, and *cross-cultural.* However, in the context of this text, the term *minority* will be used as a characterization of all groupings of individuals based on racial and ethnic distinction without regard for racial or national origin.

As far as the concept *Third World* is concerned, the reference is made to populations in the developing nations of Africa, Asia, and South America. Therefore, individuals who are indigenous to those nations and cultures residing in America are considered *Third World.* There is a direct correlation between the racial and ethnic make-up of People of Color and Third World. People of Color make up the Third World populations. Nonetheless, the concept *Third World* is broadly contested due to the fact that the definition is imposed upon People of Color by the Western World. The terms *multi-ethnic* and *multi-racial* have been used to denote everything from divisions within the composition of People of Color, such as Blacks and Puerto Ricans, to the division between racial compositions, such as Blacks and white ethnics. The concept *cross-cultural* is used to imply everything from social class and economic stratification within a particular racial and ethnic composition (such as Blacks and Mexican-Americans) to a stratification of class and social differences between different races (such as Blacks and Whites). Therefore, such concepts lack an authentic and genuine reflection of the dynamics relating to race and ethnicity.

Ethnicity may be defined as a heterogenous population of people who are of the same or different nationalities but are bound together by a common history, geography, customs, and way of life. In the context of People of Color and European ethnics, the Native Americans and Hispanics make up various ethnic groups of diverse cultures and there are diverse cultures within the Native American and Puerto Rican cultures. In terms of skin color, humankind can be divided into two distinct racial groups consisting of the dark people of the world, or "People of Color," and the White complexioned people of the world, or European ethnics. Anthropologists have divided humankind into basically three distinctive racial groups: Caucasoid (European/White), Negroid (African/Black), and Mongoloids (Asians/Yellow). Caucasians consist primarily of European ethnics and they are light complexioned with straight hair. The Negroid characteristics consist of dark complexioned skin and Mongoloids are tan to dark complexion with straight hair. The Mongoloid and Negroid races make up People of Color and the Third World.

The term *minorities* has encountered resistance by the National Association of Black Social Workers (1980) and other racial and ethnic groups because the concept is viewed as inaccurate in its description. The major contention has been that People of Color are viewed as minorities when, in fact, such groups make up a larger racial percentage of the world's population; the concept *minority* tends to minimize the numerical composition of People of Color and perpetuates a sense of powerlessness. Many People of Color in America see their lives as being intricately tied into the lives of other People of Color in other parts of the world on a political and cultural level. There are those who view the use of the term *minorities* as a political and ideological maneuver by European ethnics to narrow the political perspectives of Blacks and other People of Color in America within the context of the United States.

The conceptualization of terms is further complicated by the designation of the concept *minorities* to denote difference in race, ethnicity, and cultures. Therefore, there has been a recent change in terminology by some scholars to refer to Blacks, Puerto Ricans, Native Americans, Chicanos, Mexican-Americans, Orientals, and Asians in America as People of Color or Third World. It is the intention of this revised edition to focus on the Black Americans, Puerto Ricans, Native Americans and Mexican-Americans as well as all other components of the ethnic and racial society existing in America as minorities. This edition will provide the reader with a framework for viewing the culture or minorities in America along with its implications for education and direct practice skills in an inter-racial and inter-ethnic society.

The readers will be enabled to identify, analyze, and evaluate the various components of education and practice skills for multi-ethnic and multi-racial direct services. The initial steps for social work educators in planning the academic curriculum for cross-cultural, multi-ethnic, and multi-racial practice is the development of clear definitions of concepts and terminologies. This process must begin with clarification of the many definitions and usage of the words *cross-cultural, multi-racial, multi-ethnic* and *People of Color* in social work practice. *Multi-racial* and *multi-ethnic* refer to the inter-racial and inter-ethnic interaction.

Secondly, this manuscript provides social work educators with specific objectives needed for social work education and practice skills with multi-racial and multi-ethnic minorities. The educational and professional objectives provided may serve as a guide for social work students, educators, and practitioners who may be developing a systematic approach for social work delivery with a multi-ethnic and multi-racial clientele. Most of all, educators and practitioners should clearly define the concept *minorities* in addressing Blacks, Puerto Ricans, Native Americans, Mexican-Americans, Orientals, Asians, and European ethnics.

Finally, the objectives below will serve as a knowledge-base for the text:

- assist students in acquiring more comprehension of the literature and resources on social work practice as related to race, ethnicity, and the therapeutic relationship;

- comprehension of the different manifestations of prejudice, racism, and cultural conflict existing in the therapeutic relationship along with the effects of the socio-cultural and ethnic differences upon therapeutic relationship;

- comprehension of the tactics, strategies, and techniques provided by minority scholars and practitioner experts on the practice of human services with minorities;

- ability to identify and recognize the inadequacies in self, the profession, and theoretical orientations which may handicap the therapeutic relationship with minorities;

- an ability to adopt a systematic mode of discriminating between the techniques to employ with individuals, groups and communities of different racial and ethnic groups;

- a sensitivity to those who are different in ethnic background in helping clients of different racial and ethnic backgrounds;

• finally, a willingness and readiness to continuously assess
the Human Service professions and institutions to alleviate
the myths, stereotypes and assumptions which block the
professional relationship between worker and client.

For purposes of clarity, sequence, and synthesis, this an-
thology has been divided into the following topics:

1) Interviewing: Principles and techniques;
2) Observation of culture;
3) Interethnic and interracial intervention;
4) Relationship in therapy;
5) Transference/counter-transference;
6) Implication for ethnic and racial awareness.

David R. Burgest, Ph.D.
Professor of Social Work
Governors State University
University Park, IL 60466

I. INTERVIEWING: PRINCIPLES AND TECHNIQUES

Effective communication is necessary for successful social work and counseling intervention strategies. Effective communication encompasses a comprehensive sensitivity and appreciation of racial, ethnic and cultural differences. Most of all, effective communication requires knowledge of the unique cultural components with People of Color along with an understanding of the dynamics involved in Social Work Practice with minorities. It is the integration and synthesis of the knowledge, understanding and appreciation of minorities with the mastery of appropriate skill for intervention that is the ultimate formula for effectiveness.

This section is designed to identify, explore and analyze the unique racial, ethnic and cultural variables as they may affect the dialogue, interviews and interaction with minorities. In addition to providing data on the relevance of the racial, ethnic and cultural factors in communication, the content in this section will analyze the linguistic issues in communication with minorities as well as use of communication in developing rapport, trust and confidence. The recent and highly selective articles focusing on race, ethnicity, culture and communications in this text are arranged and synthesized to provide practitioners, educators and students with a generic but refined perspective on the subject matter.

This section begins by addressing the primary competencies necessary for establishing a beginning relationship with minorities. For effective communication to take place, the worker must understand the integral relationship between race, ethnicity and culture. Social work and counseling rely almost exclusively on the use of language as a form of communication. Therefore, Burgest's articles on racism and language address the salient parameters on the relevance of language and culture in the interview process and the relationship between language differences and barriers in communication.

The importance of language in work with ethnic and racial minorities cannot be underestimated for language is a primary transmitter of culture. Culture is the spoken and unspoken way of life of a people passed on from generation to generation. Language is more than a communicative device for one who possesses a language also possesses the world view expressed and implied by that language. Moreover, Burgest explains this language influence on thought and behavior. There is a direct correlation between language and culture. Linguists argue as to whether language influences language or if there is a reciprocal process. Yet, all authorities agree that there is an indispensable relationship between language and culture. Therefore, the worker's lack of sensitivity to the unique language of minority cultures may be viewed by the consumers of service as a blatant attack on his/her identity.

Although, language and culture are spoken of in definitive and absolute terms, it must be understood that culture is not fixed but dynamic in a state of constant change. The worker should not look at an individual as a "carrier of culture" but utilize the medium of culture, race, and ethnicity as a tool of assessment in the interview. The overall framework of this section includes these themes:

- Race, ethnicity, and culture are important variables in social intervention with minorities during the interview process.

- Traditional interviewing strategies are ineffective with People of Color.

- Social work practitioners must not be colorblind to the culture, race and ethnicity of minorities.

- New and innovative conceptual frame of references are needed for interviewing strategies with minorities.

- The unique socio-cultural, political, economic and ecological lifestyles of minorities cannot be disregarded in social work practice.

The process of interviewing is the primary tool utilized in social work practice to achieve the necessary goals of therapy and gathering social data. This is the medium for developing rapport, establishing trust, putting the client at ease, and establishing a therapeutic relationship. Communication is not limited to a verbal exchange between worker and client but the non-verbal communication of a client is often as significant as his verbal discussion, if not more so; consequently, it is the responsibility of a worker to listen to the client's words as well as interpret the hidden meaning implicit in the client's language and observe the client's non-verbal communication. Needless to say, difficulties may arise when the worker and client are of different racial and ethnic minority groups but problems also may develop when the worker and client are of the same ethnic and racial group—particularly when the worker refuses to address his/her cultural/racial/ethnic dimension. When the worker and client are of different ethnic and/or racial groups, an obvious difficulty is the language barrier even though the worker and client may speak the same language, the cultural interpretation may differ. In addition, there is the problem of cliche, idioms, and slang from a given minority culture which may not be understood by a worker. At the same time, a worker's interpretation of the minority client's non-verbal communication may be misconstrued, for non-verbal communication is influenced by culture. In the same sense that there may be a communication which is influenced by culture in the same way that language is influenced by culture. In the same sense that there may be a communication barrier on the part of a worker in understanding the minority client, the same problem exists with the minority client attempting to understand the worker.

The literature in this section will analyze the impact of the minority worker relationship with the minority client during the initial interview as well as the ongoing interview. At the same time, there will be a focus on the minority clients as well as European ethnics worker/client relationship. Even though the worker and client may be of the same minority group, there may be problems in communication. First of all, the minority worker is often educated in the language of the European ethnic culture as well as the values of the European ethnic worker; therefore, the minority worker may require that the minority client express himself or herself in the language of the European ethnics. At the same time, the minority worker may apply learned standards to the interpretation of minority non-verbal communication even though that interpretation conflicts with the realities of the client's culture.

This body of knowledge on interviewing attempts to provide a framework for interviewing principles and techniques which are appropriate and applicable to different racial and ethnic minorities. In some instances, the interviewing principles and strategies discussed are limited to a specific ethnic or racial group given the unique cultural identity of the minority concerned. On the other hand, the principles and strategies may be generic to all minorities. Consequently, there are articles covering one specific minority group while other articles are generic to all.

RACISM IN EVERYDAY SPEECH AND SOCIAL WORK JARGON*

David R. Burgest

Social work education places heavy emphasis on interviewing skills, listening skills, case recordings, "listening with the third ear," and understanding nonverbal communication; yet social workers are often deaf to the racist implications in everyday language. Indeed, there is racism in social work's own technical jargon, where it exerts a special influence on the thoughts and policies that affect black people's lives. This article uncovers a few instances of it.

Racism may be defined as the conscious and/or unconscious desire on the part of whites to destroy, castrate, and exploit black people both physically and psychologically. This desire arises from feelings of superiority. Consciously or unconsciously, language can be used to destroy and exploit black people psychologically by (1) attaching inferior, subordinate, and negative connotations to the word *black*, and applying them to black people as well; (2) attaching positive, favorable, and superior connotations to the word *white*, and applying them to white people as well; (3) expressing a world view from which all the characteristics of black culture and the black way of life are seen as inferior; and (4) expressing a world view from which all the culture and way of life of white Americans are seen as superior.

The racism in such terms as *nigger, spook, kite, darky* is obvious to everyone, but it takes some work with the dictionary to

*Copyright 1973, National Association of Social Workers,Inc. Reprinted with permission from *Social Work*, Vol. 18, No. 4 (July, 1973) pp. 20–25.

appreciate the range of connotations associated with *black* and *white*. Davis has found that

> The word *whiteness* has 134 synonyms; 44 of which are favorable
> and pleasing to contemplate, i.e., purity, cleanness, clear, chaste,
> unblemished, unsullied, innocent, honorable, upright, just, straight,
> forward, fair, genuine, trustworthy (a white man's colloquialism).
> Only ten synonyms for *whiteness* appear to me to have negative
> implications—and these only in the mildest sense—gloss-over,
> whitewash, gray, wan, pale, ashen, etc.
>
> The word *blackness* has 126 synonyms, 60 of which are distinctly
> unfavorable and none of them mildly positive. Among the offending
> 60 were such words as: blot, smut, smudge, sully, begrime, soot,
> becloud, obscure, dingy, murky, low-toned, threatening, frowning,
> foreboding, forbidden, sinister, wicked, malignant, deadly, unclean,
> dirty, unwashed, etc. . . . Not to mention 20 synonyms directly relat-
> ed to race, such as Negro, Negress, nigger, darky, blackamoor, etc.[1]

Terms formed by combination with *black* also have negative connotations. *Webster's Collegiate Dictionary* provides the following samples:

> *blackball:* a small ball for use as a negative vote in the ballot
> box. An adverse vote especially against admitting someone to mem-
> bership in an organization
> *black book:* a book containing a blacklist
> *black death:* a form of plague epidemic in Europe and Asia in
> the 14th century
> *black flag:* a pirate's flag
> *black hand:* a lawless Sicilian or Italian-American secret soci-
> ety engaged in crime (as terrorism or extortion)
> *blacklist:* a list of persons who are disapproved of or are to be
> punished or boycotted
> *black magic:* witchcraft
> *blackmail:* extortion by threats especially of public exposure
> *black market:* illicit trade in goods in violation of official
> regulations
> *black sheep:* a discreditable member of an otherwise respect-
> able group (white sheep being the otherwise "respectable" group)[2]

To claim that there is a relationship between these terms and such concrete types of racism as job discrimination and lynching is not, of course, to say which one influences the other. Either one may be the causal agent; both may be the effects of a common cause; or there may be a mutual causal action. It would be difficult, however, to doubt that there is a relationship of some sort. "White only" water fountains, hotels, and dining halls, for example, and "colored entrances" to movie theaters, stores, and lunch counters were designed to keep the purity and cleanliness of whites from being contaminated and soiled by blacks. As Podair has written:

> Language as a potent force of our society goes beyond being merely a communicative device. Language not only expresses ideas and concepts but may actually shape them. Often the process is completely unconscious, with the individual unaware of the influence of the spoken or written expression upon his thought process.[3]

A United Nations committee has urged a "sweeping of the terminology used by teachers, mass media, and others dealing with race." Words such as *Negro, primitive, savage, backward, colored, bushman* would be banned as contemptuous, unjust, or inadequate. They were described as aftereffects of colonialism.[4]

It is not enough, however, to take notice of the racism in a few words. Yabura argues that the entire world view of the Euro-American culture as expressed through its language holds life in contempt and worships private property, favors individualism, and promotes racism and the economic and political exploitation of other human beings.[5] A few illustrations of this world view are given here.

EVERYDAY CONCEPTS

When historians refer to the period of exploitation and oppression by white captors of African captives, they use such terms as *slaves* and *masters*. These terms are racist, and accepting them tends to promote the exploitation and destruction of Africans. Consider how a statement about a master raping his slave differs from one about a white captor raping an African woman held in captivity. The master-slave concept implies ownership of the slave by the master; in raping his slave, the master merely abuses his property. The slave concept makes the captive person into a mere thing, so that the rape of African women by white captors seems tolerable. Only if the concept "slave women" gives way to the true concept "African women in captivity," and the concept "master" gives way to "white American captor," can a statement on the subject be nonracist.

When Columbus arrived in America in 1492, the continent was already inhabited. Columbus is nevertheless said to have *discovered* America. This concept implies that the discoverer is entitled to take what he finds and do with it as he pleases. If a person exploring an unfamiliar part of town stumbles onto a bank he did not know was there, by the same token he ought to be able to take whatever he finds in it. But if this is not what is meant, then it must be that only someone white could discover America—that the native inhabitants were not real people.

When white men set about exploiting and destroying the inhabitants of this continent, their military successes were hailed as *victories*, but whenever the Indians temporarily succeeded in preventing their homes, families, and culture from being destroyed by the white invaders, it was called a *massacre*.

When the African fight for freedom and independence is being discussed, the term *rebellion* is usually used. Implicit in this term is the image of a child opposing the desires of parents; here again, whites are seen as superior and Africans inferior. The fight between the white Europeans in the Colonies and England, however, is called a revolution. *Revolution* connotes the struggle of patriotic men who are willing to give their lives for freedom.

During the mid-1950s and early 1960s many African-Americans adopted nonviolence as a tactic intended to achieve integration. (It was believed then that integration would lead to liberation.) Before long, however, they realized that they were operating under a racist concept. They had resolved never to be violent under any circumstances, thus giving their oppressors the option of being abusive, brutal, and violent with impunity. The blacks participating in that movement under the white concept of nonviolence had agreed in advance to their own inferiority. Eventually, blacks came to understand nonviolence as a reciprocal concept: they would be submissive and passive only as long as whites were submissive and passive. Whites quickly labeled this concept racist.

The concept most frequently used in thinking about race relations is *equality*. While America's version of this concept is racist, because it implies that blacks should become more like whites— that is, more nearly equal to whites, who start out being superior.

As a practical consequence of this concept, whites advocate compensatory education and job training to bring African-Americans up to the level of the whites. But why should African-Americans want to be equal to white Americans if it entails taking on white Euro-American characteristics? A nonracist version of the concept of equality would suggest the survival and coexistence of whites and blacks. It would recognize the specific qualities of each and imply that these are simply differences, not marks of superiority or inferiority. It would not suggest that differences ought to be eliminated or that anybody should accept values other than his own. As Killens says: "When we advocate freedom we mean freedom for us to be black or brown, and you to be white, and yet live together in a free and equal society."[6]

SOCIAL WORK JARGON

Nobody expects everyday words and concepts to be completely free of bias, but a degree of objectivity is expected of technical terminology such as that used in social work. For example, social workers frequently use the term *cultural lag.* They apply it to the inability of a black family to use the services of an institution in resolving its problems. Surely, however, the lag in such a situation is the institution's, not the family's. With all its technical and professional resources, the institution should be able to reach a family that is exploited and consequently unfamiliar with the institution's services.

Culturally disadvantaged and *culturally deprived* are two more terms that have been fashionable in social work discourse; they are generally applied to the workers' black clientele. Yet these terms imply that black people do not have a culture or that the culture of black people is not valuable. Differences from the white cultural norms are automatically inferior, subordinate, or deficient. White universities set up special programs for the "culturally" and "educationally disadvantaged" in order to make blacks into whites. They can hardly do otherwise, because they use the same evaluative tools to assess and direct the behavior of black youngsters as they use for white youngsters. This inevitably turns the specific qualities of black children into inferiority.

Social workers often refer to people of African descent and

other dark people as *nonwhite*. Yet more of the world's peoples are black than white, and the majority should be the norm. It would make better sense to refer to black people as *black* and whites as *nonblack*. The term *nonwhite* can only be seen as a projection of white supremacy.

Many social workers once adopted an attitude of color-blindness in an effort to escape the negative myths, stereotypes, and assumptions that may have been affecting their work with black clients. They tried to take color as an unimportant factor in the worker-client relationship. But this strategy proved unsatisfactory. As Pettit wrote:

> A number of them [social workers], seeking to make allowance for the effects of discriminatory practices, have attempted to obliterate any differences between Negroes and whites. Because of a belief that to identify a Negro as Negro would imply discrimination, some unsound practices have taken place.[7]

The colorblindness approach tended to separate the black person's internal problems from his color. Many white social workers wished to deny that the core of the black man's problem was his being black in white America, because the social worker himself was a product of white America and did not like to believe he was an accessory to racism. Once this was recognized, social workers were glad to start using the word *black* and show off their liberalism. Inside their conceptual system, however, it still meant the same thing.

But white people are not the only ones for whom this word has negative connotations. One commonly hears blacks referring to themselves or other blacks as "happening to be black," particularly if the person is a prominent member of society. The expression dissociates the person's accomplishment from his blackness, as though nothing especially valuable would normally be black. This point is confirmed by nonblacks, who never speak of themselves as "happening to be white" unless it is to express shame at the atrocities whites have perpetrated against blacks. "He happens to be black" is also sometimes used in reference to a black derelict, prostitute, or other unsavory character. In this case, blacks would like to have the offender excommunicated from the race. They fear that such characters will reflect on the entire black race in the eyes of whites.

Table 1
**The Language of European Antihumanism as Compared
to the Language of African Humanism**

European Antihumanism and the White Perspective	African Humanism and the Black Perspective
Race	Ethnicity, color of skin, culture, nationality
Negro, Negroid, colored	African or Africanoid
Nonwhite	Black, brown, yellow, red
Indians	Native Americans
Primitive, uncouth, backward	Culturally different
Savages	Warriors
Tribes	Ethnic groups, nations
Nappy or kinky hair	Naturally curly hair
Slavery	Imprisonment and forced labor
Integration	European domination or supremacy
Emancipation Proclamation	Neoimprisonment
Master, Great White Father	Oppressor, exploiter, colonizer
White blood, Indian blood	Blood
White lie	Lie
Red China	China
Illegitimate babies	Babies
Maladjustment, bad attitude, resistance	Behavior that is compatible with the reality of the oppressed rather than of the oppressor
White backlash	White racism
Law and order	Call for even more repressive measures against Africans
Silent majority	Implacable white majority
"No-knock," "quick entry" provision of 1970 District of Columbia crime bill	Government-sanctioned genocide
Black separatism, racism, supremacy	Black self-determination, restoration, redemption, pride
Economic deprivation	Economic exploitation
Normal behavior	Behavior which has adjusted to a sick, antihuman society

(continued)

Table 1   (*Continued*)

European Antihumanism and the White Perspective	African Humanism and the Black Perspective
Culturally disadvantaged	Culturally dispossessed
Educationally disadvantaged	Educationally oppressed
I.Q.	Equal ability-potential, barring prenatal or postnatal injury
You people, those people, these people	People
Squaw	Female native American
Indian buck	Male native American
Tarzan	Samori, Chaka, El-Hajj Umar, or Mansa Musa
Amos and Andy	Nat Turner
The Lone Ranger and Tonto	Custer and Sitting Bull

Source: Lloyd Yabura, "Towards a Language of Humanism: A Tool for Black Liberation," *Rhythm Magazine*, 1 (Summer 1971), pp. 31–32.

One often hears of universities seeking *qualified black* students and agencies looking for *qualified black* employees. Why is it necessary to stipulate that the black be qualified? If a white student or employee were being sought, it would be taken for granted that he had to be qualified.

The growth of black pride, black awareness, black identity, and black unity has stimulated blacks to seek ways to make use of the resources in their own community for their advantage. Many whites call this development *black separatism*. Meanwhile, however,

> . . . the Negro population [in the nation's cities] grew by 2.4 million while the white decreased by 2.1 million (the balance is made up of other races). During the last two years, the white "escape rate" from the central cities has tripled to an annual rate of nearly 500,000 per year.[8]

Statistics like these raise the question of who is separating from whom.

Table 1 (p. 11) is a start at purging social work terminology and everyday speech of racism. This task is long overdue; if it is not taken up soon, the helping profession may be doomed in the black community. Careful study of the table will reveal that in many cases the differences between a racist term (European anti-humanism and the white perspective) and its nonracist counterpart (African humanism and the black perspective) is a matter of where the phenomenon is supposed to come from. The racist term implies that something is wrong inside the individual—see *maladjustment*, for example—whereas the nonracist term finds the source of the problem in the oppression of the individual. A social worker, of course, may not be in a position to do much against his client's oppressors and exploiters, but he is doing something against the client if he pretends that oppressors and exploiters are not real.

Notes and References

1. Ossie Davis, "The English Language is My Enemy," in Neil Postman, Charles Weingartner, and Terrence P. Moran, eds., *Language in America* (New York: Western Publishing Co., 1969), p. 74.
2. *Webster's Seventh New Collegiate Dictionary* (Springfield, Mass., G. & C. Merriam Co., 1963), p. 88.
3. Simon Podair, "How Bigotry Builds Through Language," *Negro Digest*, 16 (March 1967), p. 39.
4. See "U.N. Group Urges Dropping of Words with Racist Tinge," *New York Times*, September 1968.
5. Lloyd Yabura, "Towards a Language of Humanism: A Tool for Black Liberation," *Rhythm Magazine*, 1 (Summer 1971), p. 29.
6. John O. Killens, *Black Man's Burden* (New York: Pocket Books, 1965), p. 19.
7. Lois Pettit, "Some Observations on the Negro Culture in the United States," *Social Work*, 5 (July 1960), p. 105.
8. Richard Scammon, "The Demographic Profile and Where It Points," *Newsweek* (30 June 1969), p. 18.

ATTITUDES OF BLACKS TOWARD MENTAL HEALTH AGENCIES AND COUNSELORS*

Woodrow M. Parker and Roderick J. McDavis

Mental health workers hold several beliefs regarding the attitudes of Black people toward mental health agencies and services. One belief is that Blacks lack basic knowledge about mental health agencies and services. That is, many counselors are of the opinion that Black people do not know where mental health agencies are located; they do not know what services are offered; they are unaware of the nature of counseling; and in general, they are unaware of the standard operating procedures of these agencies. A second belief is that Black people hold negative attitudes and perceptions about mental health agencies and services that might account for their low utilization of these agencies and services.

Some of these attitudes and perceptions are that mental health agencies are useless; Blacks only want to be seen by Black counselors; White counselors are not interested in helping Black clients; only crazy people use mental health services; Black people are ashamed to use counseling services; Black counselors are not viewed as professionals; and Blacks believe their problems are better handled by the family, relatives, friends, or ministers, rather than by counselors.

Although some of these beliefs about Blacks' attitudes and perceptions of mental health may be mythological or stereotypical, recent literature supports some of the views stated above. In reference to Blacks' knowledge about counseling, Vontress (1969) reported that Blacks were unfamiliar with counseling, and that their unfamiliarity was a major barrier in the counseling relationship. Koegler and Williamson (1973) reported that Mexican-Americans in the Los Angeles area believed that people contact a psychiatrist only if they were "crazy."

Schauble, Parker, Altmier, and Probert (1979) reported that, students in general and minority students in particular, may not be aware of the nature of counseling and may not see such a resource as appropriate for their needs. These writers also reported that minority students from their setting (the university counseling center) expressed fear that their heads might literally be "shrunk" if they became involved in the counseling process. These same authors reported that Black students compared the atmosphere of the university counseling center to that of a funeral home.

Harrison (1975) reviewed 29 studies and found 15 that indicated race makes a significant difference in the counseling relationship. The other 14 studies maintained that race may be a factor in the counseling relationship, but other variables such as sex, therapeutic orientation, and empathic understanding were more important. Some of the researchers who advocate the "same race counselor/client relationship" believe it is too difficult to establish a therapeutic relationship when the counselor and client are of different races (Grantham, 1973; Vontress, 1971; Wolkon, Moriwaki & Williams, 1973).

Several social scientists believe many minority persons see counselors as "handmaidens of the status quo" (Halleck, 1971; Tedeschi & O'Donovan, 1971). Szasz (1970) compares psychiatrists to slave masters using therapy to control people whose ideas, beliefs, and behaviors are different from those of the dominant society.

There is a need for community health workers in local communities to examine the knowledge of and attitudes of Black people toward mental health agencies and counselors. Although local studies are limited in their abilities to generalize, they have the advantage of providing direct and specific information about a specific population. A study of Black's knowledge of and attitudes toward mental health agencies and counselors is also needed in order to better understand the immediate problem of underutilization, to determine if there is a need for programs to educate Black people about community health services, and to identify strategies to better deliver mental health services to Black communities. This article describes a study conducted to determine Blacks' knowledge of and attitudes toward mental health agencies and counselors.

METHODOLOGY

Sample and Procedures

The sample consisted of 80 subjects (40 males and 40 females) from the Black communities of Gainesville, Florida, a small university town with a population of approximately 81,000; 15,000 of whom are Black. A systematic random sample procedure was used to select the participants. Participants were randomly selected from the four major sections of the Black community through churches, barbershops, and beauty salons. Every fifth person who came into the barbershops or beauty salons was asked to fill out a questionnaire. Every tenth person on the church roster was asked to respond to the questionnaire. Barbers, beauticians, and ministers administered the questionnaires to control for experimenter bias. Selecting participants in this manner increased the chance for obtaining a representative sample, because Black people across different socioeconomic levels in Gainesville visit the same barber or beauty shops and attend the same churches.

Instrument

An 18-item questionnaire was administered to the 80 participants. The questionnaire measured three categories of information. The first category consisted of items that measured participants' knowledge about mental health agencies and counselors. The second category consisted of items that measured participants' attitudes toward mental health agencies and counselors. The third portion of the instrument consisted of an open-ended question that asked participants to recommend strategies to better deliver mental health services to the Black community. The categories of information used in the development of the questionnaire were derived from interviews in the Black community with a small sample of residents and community leaders.

A random sample of 25 Black persons from the four Black communities participated in the pilot testing of the instrument. In addition, eight practicing counselors from community mental health centers were asked to examine the questionnaire for clarity and content. These counselors rated the questionnaire high on content validity. The participants in the pilot test reported the items were clear and understandable.

RESULTS

Table 1 contains percentages of participants' responses to the questionnaire knowledge items. The data in Table 1 (p. 18) show that 66% of the participants knew the locations of some mental health agencies, 50% were familiar with the services provided by these agencies, and 90% of the participants had never used any of the mental health agencies. The data in Table 1 also show that 70% of the male participants and 63% of the females knew the locations of some mental health agencies. More males (57%) were familiar with the services provided by these agencies than females (43%). Ninety percent of both female and male participants had never used any of the agencies.

Table 2 (p. 20) contains percentages of participants' responses to the questionnaire-attitude items. The results in Table 2 indicate that 81% of the participants believed mental health agencies provide helpful services, and 90% believed one purpose of counseling was self-understanding. Eighty-three percent of the participants did not believe only "crazy" people use mental health services, and 95% believed Black counselors were as capable of doing their jobs as other counselors. Seventy-four percent believed counselors could help them in ways that their families, friends, or ministers could not.

The results in Table 2 also indicate that 86% of the male participants believed mental health agencies provide helpful services, and 78% of the females believed these agencies provide helpful services. Ninety-six percent of the female participants and 85% of the males believed one purpose of counseling was self-understanding. Eighty-five percent of the males and 80% of the

Table 1
Relative Frequency Distribution of Participants' Responses
to the Questionnaire Knowledge Items

Items	% Female[a]			% Males[b]			% Total[c]		
	Yes	No	DK*	Yes	No	DK	Yes	No	DK
1. Do you know the location of any of the mental health agencies in your county?	63	57	0	70	30	0	66	34	0
2. Are you familiar with the services provided by the mental health agencies in your county?	43	57	0	57	43	0	50	50	0
3. Have you ever used any of the mental health agencies in your county?	10	90	0	10	90	0	10	90	0
4. Is there a charge for the mental health services in your county?	20	37	43	30	40	30	25	39	36
5. Do you know anyone who has used any of the mental health agencies in your county?	47	53	0	50	50	0	49	51	0

*DK = Don't know.   [a]$n = 40$.   [b]$n = 40$.   [c]$n = 80$.

females did not believe only "crazy" people use mental health services. Ninety-six percent of the female participants and 93% of the males believed Black counselors were as capable of doing their job as other counselors. More males (81%) than females (67%) believed counselors could help them in ways their families, friends, or ministers could not help them.

In summary, Black people in this study were knowledgeable of mental health agencies, and they had positive attitudes toward mental health agencies, counselors, and counseling. Black males had more knowledge of mental health agencies than females, and males had more positive attitudes toward counselors and counseling than females. Black females, more than Black males, believed that White counselors could understand their problems. Although Black people had knowledge of mental health agencies and had positive attitudes toward agencies, counselors, and counseling, the results of this study clearly indicate that Black people were not utilizing mental health agencies and services.

DISCUSSION

The findings in this study suggest Black people know the locations of some mental health agencies, and they are familiar with some of the services provided by these agencies. These findings contradict previous assertions that Black people lack knowledge of mental health agencies and services (Tucker, 1979; Vontress, 1971). Apparently, Black people have become more knowledgeable of mental health agencies and services in recent years. Effective public relations programs implemented by mental health agencies may account for some of this increased knowledge.

It was interesting to find 90% of the Black people in this study had never used any of the mental health agencies. This finding supports contentions that Blacks' underutilize mental health agencies and services (Tucker, 1979; Vontress, 1974). It seems that having knowledge of mental health agencies and services is not enough to increase Blacks' use of these agencies and services. This finding suggests there is a need for new strategies to encourage Black people to use mental health agencies and services.

The findings of this study also show more Black males than females know the locations of some mental health agencies, and they are more familiar with the services provided by these agencies. The fact that Black males were more knowledgeable of the locations and services, however, did not increase their use of these agencies and services. Most of the males and females in this study (90%) had never used any of the mental health agencies. This finding indicates neither Black males nor Black females are using mental health agencies.

Table 2

Relative Frequency Distribution of Participants' Responses to the Questionnaire Attitude Items

Items	% Females[a]					% Males[b]					% Total[c]				
	SA	A	U	D	SD	SA	A	U	D	SD	SA	A	U	D	SD
1. Mental health agencies provide helpful services.	28	50	22	0	0	43	43	12	2	0	35	46	18	1	0
2. One purpose of counseling is to help you understand yourself better.	43	53	2.0	2.0	0	45	40	10	5.0	0	44	46	6.0	4.0	0
3. I would go to a mental health agency if I could see a Black counselor.	7.0	22	43	15	13	25	23	28	12	12	16	23	35	14	12
4. White counselors cannot understand my problems.	7.0	7.0	33	43	10	10	10	38	25	17	9.0	9.0	35	34	13
5. Counseling is all talk and no action.	5.0	7.0	10	55	23	2.0	7.0	13	53	25	4.0	7.0	11	54	24
6. Counselors in mental health agencies want to help Black people with their problems.	10	35	53	2.0	0	17	47	23	13	0	14	41	38	7.0	0
7. Only crazy people use mental health services.	0	7.0	13	45	35	0	5.0	10	45	40	0	6.0	11	45	38

Statement															
8. The fact that I am Black causes most of my problems, therefore counseling cannot help me.	2.0	8.0	5.0	45	40	0	5.0	13	42	40	1.0	6.0	9.0	44	60
9. Black counselors are as capable of doing their jobs as other counselors.	68	28	2.0	0	2.0	63	30	2.0	5.0	0	66	29	2.0	10	1.0
10. It is okay for my friends to know that I am seeing a counselor.	17	53	17	13	0	23	42	25	8.0	20	48	21	10		1.0
11. I would not be ashamed for a Black counselor to know that I have problems.	30	55	10	5.0	0	30	48	10	10	30	52	10	7.0		1.0
12. There is nothing a counselor can do for me that my family, friends or minister cannot do.	6.0	10	17	50	17	2.0	2.0	15	53	28	4.0	6.0	16	51	23
13. In counseling, you still have to solve your own problems.	22	30	20	22	6.0	25	45	15	15	0	24	38	17	19	2.0

$^a n = 40.$ $^b n = 40.$ $^c n = 80.$

Black people in this study believe mental health agencies provide helpful services, and that "normal" people use these services. These findings mean Black people have positive attitudes toward mental health agencies and the people who use the agencies. It seems that Blacks believe mental health agencies can provide helpful services to a broad range of people. These findings contradict other reports that Black people have negative attitudes toward mental health agencies and stereotypic views of the people who utilize these agencies (Tucker, 1979; Vontress, 1974).

The results also indicate Black people in this study believe counselors want to help them with their problems, and that counselors can help them in ways their families, friends, and ministers cannot. It seems that Black people believe counselors can help them with problems, and that counselors are important alternatives to talking with family members, friends, or ministers about problems. These findings do not support contentions that Black people have negative attitudes toward counselors, and that Blacks generally believe counselors cannot help them more than families, friends, and ministers (Tucker, 1979; Vontress, 1971).

Black people in this study believe Black and White counselors can understand their problems, and that Black counselors are as competent as other counselors. These results mean Black people believe all counselors are capable of helping them with their problems. Apparently, the race of counselors is not a factor in the Blacks' underutilization of mental health agencies. In other words, Black people have positive attitudes toward Black and White counselors but still are not using the services provided by these counselors. These findings contradict those who believe that the counselor's race is a significant variable in Blacks' use of mental health agencies (Grantham, 1973; Kincaid, 1969).

The results also show Black people in this study believe self-understanding is one purpose of counseling; counseling is more than talking; and that they still have to solve their problems in counseling. These findings indicate Black people understand the purpose and process of counseling and their responsibilities as clients. It seems that Black people know counseling can help them with their problems, and that they must eventually solve their problems in counseling.

More Black males than females in this study believe counselors want to help them with their problems, and that counselors can help them in ways families, friends, and ministers cannot help them. These findings indicate more Black males than females have more confidence in counselors' abilities to help them. Black males also would probably talk with counselors rather than significant others more frequently than females. These findings refute assertions that Black males are reluctant to discuss their problems with counselors (Vontress, 1970).

More Black females than males in this study believe White counselors can understand their problems. This finding means Black females are more likely to believe White counselors can help them than males. Perhaps the counselor's race is less of a factor with females than males. In other words, Black females are as comfortable with White counselors as they are with Black counselors. This result also suggests that Black males may prefer to see Black counselors. It may be less difficult for Black males to trust Black counselors than White counselors.

In this study, more Black males than Black females believe they have to solve their problems in counseling. Apparently, Black males are more likely to seek solutions to their problems in counseling than females. This finding means Black males may respond to nondirective counseling approaches better than females. Black females, on the other hand, may respond to directive counseling approaches better than males. This finding also could mean Black males have less faith than females that counseling actually works.

SUGGESTIONS

The participants in this study offered five suggestions that mental health agencies and counselors can employ to increase Blacks' use of mental health agencies and services. One suggestion was to use the media (television, radio, newspapers, and magazines) to provide more publicity and advertising of mental health agencies and services. Media in local communities could be asked to air or print public services announcements (PSAs) submitted by mental health agencies. Since most Black people have access to some form of media, mental health agencies and counselors could use PSAs as one method of delivering their messages to Black people.

The second suggestion was to present information about mental health agencies and services to Black people in schools, churches, social club meetings, and community organization meetings. Schools, churches, and organizations in the Black community provide direct access to Black people. Many Blacks prefer personal contact with counselors from mental health agencies before they will use the services. Making presentations in schools, churches, social clubs, and community organizations in the Black community would offer mental health counselors opportunities to disseminate information and establish rapport with a wide variety of Black people. As a result of these personal presentations, more Blacks may utilize mental health agencies and services.

Another suggestion was to reduce the amount of "red tape" in mental health agencies. In other words, decrease the number of forms people must complete when they visit mental health agencies. Black people are willing to verbally discuss their problems, but apparently they are less willing to answer the questions on mental health agency forms. Eliminating a lot of the forms and other paperwork in mental health agencies may increase Blacks' usage of these agencies.

The fourth suggestion was to hire more Black counselors to work in mental health agencies. Some Black people would visit mental health agencies if they could see a Black counselor. The best response to this need is to recruit and hire Black counselors. Names of Black counselors could be obtained from a professional organization such as the Association for Non-White Concerns in Personnel and Guidance and from the Minority Mental Health Data Bank, located in the counseling center at the University of Maryland. Announcements could be sent to these Black counselors informing them of available counseling positions.

The last suggestion was to establish mental health agencies in Black communities. It seems that Black people are more likely to use mental health agencies and services if they are located within walking distances of their homes. Satellite mental health offices and services could be housed in schools and churches in Black communities. These satellite offices would provide visibility for mental health agencies in Black communities. The offices also may stimulate more Black people to use the services.

REFERENCES

Grantham, R. Effects of counselor sex, race, and language style on Black students in initial interviews. *Journal of Counseling Psychology*, 1973, *20*, 553–559.

Harrison, D. Race as a counselor-client variable in counseling and psychotherapy: A review of the research. *The Counseling Psychologist*, 1975, *5*, 124–132.

Halleck, S. Therapy is the handmaiden of the status quo. *Psychology Today*, April 1971, 30–34, 98–100.

Kincaid, M. Identity and therapy in the black community. *Personnel and Guidance Journal*, 1969, *47*, 884–890.

Koegler, R., & Williamson, E. A group approach to helping emotionally disturbed Spanish-speaking patients. *Hospital and Community Psychiatry*, 1973, *24*, 334–337.

Schauble, P., Parker, W., Altmier, B., & Probert, B. Taking counseling to minority students: The classroom as a delivery vehicle. *Personnel and Guidance Journal*, 1979, *58*, 176–185.

Szasz, T. The crime of commitment. *Readings in Clinical Psychology Today*. Del Mar, Calif.: CRM Books, 1970.

Tedeschi, J., & O'Donovan, D. Social power and the psychologist. *Professional Psychology*, 1971, *2*, 59–64.

Tucker, C. Underutilization of mental health services by Blacks: strategies for change. In W. Parker & P. Schauble (Eds.), *Counseling blacks: Issues and strategies 3*. Gainesville: University of Florida Psychological and Vocational Counseling Center, Monograph Series, 1979.

Vontress, C. Cultural barriers in the counseling relationship. *Personnel and Guidance Journal*, 1969, *48*, 11–17.

Vontress, C. Counseling blacks. *Personnel and Guidance Journal*, 1970, *48*, 713–719.

Vontress, C. Racial differences: Impediments to rapport. *Journal of Counseling Psychology*, 1971, 18, 7–13.

Vontress, C. Barriers in cross-cultural counseling. *Counseling and Values*, 1974, *18*, 160–165.

Wolkon, G., Moriwaki, S., & Williams, K. Race and social class as factors in the orientation toward psychotherapy. *Journal of Counseling Psychology*, 1973, *20*, 312–316.

THE RACIST USE OF THE ENGLISH LANGUAGE*

David R. Burgest and Lloyd Yabura

By language, I am referring to more than oral or written expressions, phrases, sentences and words:

> Language as a potent force of our society goes beyond being merely a communicative device. Language not only expresses ideas and concepts, but may actually shape them. Often the process is completely unconscious with the individual concerned unaware of the influence of the spoken or written expression upon his thought process.[1]

Thus, in assimilating a language one inherits the symbols, definitions and way of life expressed by that culture—for language communicates all of the values, mores and folkways of its culture. Fanon expresses it this way:

> To speak means to be in a position to use a certain syntax, to grasp the morphology of this or that language, but it means above all to assume a culture, to support the weight of a civilization (for) a man who has a language consequently possesses the world expressed and implied by that language.[2]

To further support the inter-relationship between culture and language Paul Henle states:

> To claim a causal relationship between language and culture is not, of course to say which influences the other. Either may be the

---

*Reprinted by permission from *The Black Scholar*, September 1973, pp. 37–45.

causal agent, both may be effects of a common cause, or there may be mutual causal action (but the fact remains that there is a definite indispensable relationship between language and culture).[3]

Having given a brief synopsis of the literature supporting the inter-relationship between culture and language, I would like to summarize by saying that the white American culture is racist (pro-white—anti-black). Documentation of racism in the American culture has been covered by too many federal documents, sociologists and social scientists' research and through popular literature to attempt to cover that in this publication. Since language is a primary transmitter of culture; the English language is, therefore, racist.

Racism is defined by this author as the conscious and/or unconscious desire manifesting itself in whites to destroy, castrate and exploit black people both psychologically and physically due to inherent feelings of white superiority. In the context of racism in the English language, the definition implies that the language is designed either consciously and/or unconsciously to destroy and exploit black people psychologically by transmitting the racist culture through the language. Examples of this are, (1) defining "black" as inferior, subordinate and negative, and transferring the definition to black people; (2) defining "white" in a positive, favorable and superior manner and transferring such definitions to white people; (3) perpetuating a world-view through the language which denotes all of the characteristics of black culture and way of life as inferior; and (4) expressing a world-view through the language which defines all of the culture and way of life of white America as being superior.

The psychological destruction of the African-American takes place through his acceptance of the white American inferior definition of black which is transmitted through the language and the superior definition of white. Thus, many blacks hate their blackness and their culture because in the context in which they survive black is seen unfavorably and they identify with the racist conception of whiteness and the white culture. Physical destruction follows because in the African-American's attempt to identify with the qualities attributed to whiteness they use every mechanism and device possible to destroy the existence of blackness. Evidence of this is seen in the high proportion of homicide perpetuated by blacks on blacks. The white system has succeeded in destroying blacks without overt participation in the act. In other words, blacks have been caught up in using a device created by whites for black self-destruction.

*   *   *

There have been a few scholars who have recognized racism in the English language from the perspective of certain specific terms. There are those who have designated English terms such as "nigger" and "spook" as being racist, and there are those who attempt to show how the racist synonyms and definitions of the word black (devil, evil, dirty) have been transferred to black people and at the same time correlating the racist positive and favorable definitions and synonyms in the word white (angel, virginity, cleanliness) which have been transferred to white people.

Ossie Davis' critical analysis of racism in the term black was illustrated in "The English Language is My Enemy." According to Ossie:

> The word *whiteness* has 134 synonyms; 44 of which are favorable and pleasing to contemplate, i.e. purity, cleanness, clear, chaste, unblemished, unsullied, innocent, honorable, upright, just, straight, forward, fair, genuine, trustworthy (a white man's colloquialism). Only ten synonyms for whiteness appear to me to have negative implications—and these only in the mildest sense; glossover, whitewash, gray, wan, pale, ashen, etc.[4]

In contrast to the supremacy and superiority characteristics of the definition of whiteness, the term black is described in the following manner:

> The word *blackness* has 126 synonyms 60 of which are distinctly unfavorable and none of them mildly positive. Among the offending 60 were such words as: blot, smut, smudge, sully, begrime, soot, becloud, obscure, dingy, murky, low-toned, threatening, frowning, foreboding, forbidden, sinister, wicked, malignant, deadly, unclean, dirty, unwashed, etc. . . . Not to mention 20 synonyms directly related to race such as Negro, Negress, nigger, darky, blackamoor, etc.[5]

Upon a quick review of the word *black* in any *Webster* dictionary, one will find that concepts or words hyphenated with the term black have a racist connotation. The following words and definitions were taken from the *Webster Collegiate Dictionary:*

> 1–Blackball—a small ball for use as a negative vote in the ballot box. An adverse vote especially against admitting someone to membership in an organization.
> 2–blackbook—a book containing a blacklist.
> 3–blacklist—a list of persons who are disapproved of or are to be punished or boycotted.
> 4–black death—a form of plague epidemic in Europe and Asia in the 14th century (also black plague).
> 5–black flag—pirate's flag.
> 6–black hand—a lawless Sicilian or Italian-American secret society, engaged in crime (as terrorism or extortion).
> 7–black magic—witchcraft.
> 8–blackmail—extortion by threats especially of public exposure, the payment extorted.
> 9–black market—illicit trade in goods in violation of official regulations.
> 10–black sheep—a discreditable member of an otherwise respectable group (white sheep being the "otherwise" respectable group).

In contrast to the above, *Webster* defines *white* as "silvery, made of silver, being a member of a group or race characterized by reduced pigmentation consisting of white people, not intended to do harm, free from moral impurity, innocent." Thus, white hyphenated words take on positive characteristics (white lie, white flag—peace, white angel food).

The United Nations urged a "sweeping of the terminology used by teachers, mass media, and others dealing with race. Words such as Negro, primitive, savage, backward, colored, bushman would be banned as either 'contemptuous, unjust, or inadequate.' They were described as after-effects of colonialism."[6]

However, to limit racism in the English language to the negativism in the word black which has been transferred to black people and specific terms such as Negro and nigger is highly inadequate. The world-view of the Euro-American culture as expressed through the language is marked by a disrespect for life and a profound adulation of private property, individualism, racism and economic and political exploitation of other human beings.

TERMS DEFINED: RACIST PERSPECTIVE

When historians refer to the systematic exploitation and oppression of white captors over African captives, they use such terms as "slaves" and "masters." Those terms are racist and the mental acceptance of those terms are exploitive and destructive to African survival. First of all, the psychological impact of a statement referring to a "master" raping his "slave" is different from the impact of a statement about the white "captors" raping an "African woman" held in captivity. Implicit in the English usage of the "master-slave" concept is ownership of the "slave" by the "master," therefore, the "master" is merely abusing his property (slave).

In reality, the captives (slave) were African individuals with human worth, rights and dignity and the term "slave" denounces that human quality thereby making the mass rape of African women by white captors more acceptable in the minds of people and setting a mental frame of reference for legitimizing the atrocities perpetuated against African people. When the term "slave woman" is changed to denote its true quality, "African women in captivity" and the term "master" defined from its proper perspective, "white American captor," then the terms are non-racist for the definition of "slavery" was based on superiority, exploitation, industry and business.

Another illustration of "the terms defined" from a racist perspective is the white American's historical account of his episode with the "American" Indians, the inhabitants of this western continent. According to American history, Columbus discovered America in 1492. Yet, this continent was occupied with inhabitants before Columbus arrived. Thus, it doesn't take much logic to understand it is geometrically logistically impossible for anyone to "discover" something already occupied. It would be as though I walked into the Chase Manhattan Bank of New York City and said I "discovered" it; therefore, I am entitled to all of the resources within it. The racist implication in the term "discover" relates to the white perception that only someone white could discover this continent thereby affirming his notion of supremacy and superiority.

Further racist definitions were applied to terms to describe the white man's exploitation and destruction of the inhabitants of this continent. The term "victory" was applied when the whites assassinated and killed, winning a battle, and "massacre" was applied when the Indians were successful in preventing their homes, family and culture from being destroyed. "Victory" in the authentic traditional non-racist perspective is attributed to individuals and groups who succeed in defending their life and property against invaders; while "massacre" is attributed to groups or individuals who maliciously set out to destroy a people or community by taking what belongs to that group of people.

The racist Euro-American language did not escape the description of the historical account of the early confrontation with African-Americans. The term "rebellion" is used in describing the African fight and struggle for freedom and independence. Implicit in the term rebellion is a child rebuking the wishes and desires of parents; again, whites placing themselves in a superior position and Africans in an inferior position. Nevertheless, the fight between the white Europeans of this western culture and their mother country in 1776 was termed "revolution." "Revolution" denotes actions by men who are patriotic and willing to give their lives for freedom.

Brother John O. Killens best summed up the perpetuation of racism in English language when he stated:

> All nonwhites throughout the world become "niggers" and therefore proper material for "civilizing" and "christianizing" (cruel euphemisms for colonization, exploitation, genocide and slavery). . . .[7]

AFRICAN-AMERICANS AND THE ENGLISH LANGUAGE

Invariably, blacks preface their introduction of other blacks by saying,

> Race prejudice and discrimination compelled Negroes to identify themselves as being of African descent, yet because the white conception of Negro inferiority and African savagery were absorbed by many Negroes, they displayed embarrassment over the allegedly primitive culture of the ancestral continent (*thereby* accepting the white racist definition of themselves as an "American Negro.")[8]

Probably the most detrimental subordination of Africans through the racist European language was the categorization of Africans as "Negroes." All other ethnic or racial groups of people are referred to by geographical origin, religion, culture or language, and the term "Negro" meets neither category. In essence, the figment of the white American's imagination became a reality when Africans accepted the category "Negro" with all of the inherent values, symbols and definitions implicit in the term.

Nekros is Greek, meaning death; Nigrus-a-um is Latin for black and in Spanish and Portuguese we have Negro. Nig(g)ard(e) existed in early middle English (11th century) meaning slovenly. It was not until the English (Britainers) became aware of slavery expeditions to Africa by the Portuguese that there appeared to be a semantic development where Nigard and Negro began to mean the same thing, or close to it. Thus, the term "Negro" has a historical development equivalent to the word "black" with the same negative, denigrating, conceptual characteristics.

The next atrocity for African-Americans was being deprived of their mother language. Historians, anthropologists, and sociologists place little emphasis on Africans being deprived of their language. Dividing the African families, raping and molesting African children, beating and abusing African captives were truly detrimental, but being raped of a language was severer because it required Africans accepting white definitions. Consequently, the Africans' psychological and cultural destruction could be perpetuated without much physical coercion for the Africans' view of himself was dictated by the oppressor.

Many scholars would probably say that it was imperative for Africans to accept the language in order to survive in their new environment. However, Africans were not taught the English language as a means for survival and self-actualization. Rather, they learned the language in the process of trying to obey the primitive commands of their white captors. In addition to that, Africans were colonized for the support and survival of whites and the communication of the captor was limited to verbal commands which reinforced white superiority and black inferiority.

It is possible that the survival of an African language would have resulted in the liberation of Africans. Efforts to alleviate that possibility manifested itself in the captors separating Africans who spoke the same language. The African languages gave Africans the protection of speaking with each other without the captor's knowledge of their communication; the languages were symbolic of a peoplehood and brotherhood which exceeded the commonality of bondage and assured the maintenance of African identity, personality and culture. The commonality of language strengthened the commonality of color, bondage and culture, and finally there would have been little room for "Uncle Tomism" with communication being a barrier between captor and captive.

*   *   *

Today the commonality of color and oppression provides the necessary bond for brotherly relationships between African-Americans, but identification with the language has caused certain problems. For example, the "Negro" has historically seen himself as being proportionately "whiter" and closer to being human in direct ratio to his mastery of the English language. As expressed by Fanon in reference to the blacks who speak French:

> The Negro of the Antilles will be proportionately whiter—that is, he will become closer to being a real human being—in direct ratio to his mastery of the French language.[9]

In essence, "speaking good and proper English" becomes equivalent to "light skinned," and "good (straight like whites') hair." It is not foreign for blacks to have suffered condescension from other blacks for not being able to "master the King's English." By the same token, it is in the experiences of the "good (white) English user" to have received "compliments" from whites like, "you don't talk like the rest of them," insinuating that you are different and "better" because you speak more like whites. The inability to master the language becomes equated with being "uneducated," "deprived," "disadvantaged." In other words, black as defined from its racist perspective.

Thus, many Africans do not recognize the phenomenon which takes place in their not being able to speak the English language properly. That is, the African's struggle to survive the racist language may be seen as psychological rejection and resistance to mastering the language in the same way that there are physiological antibiotics which work to prevent the admission of foreign and harmful viruses into the body. In other words, many Africans have a psyche-apparatus which prevents the admission of the foreign racist destructive language from entering into their system.

Many Africans did not sit passively by while they were being raped of a language and culture. Africans found ways to nurture and preserve much of their folkways and mores despite the total destruction of their language. They developed unique methods of communicating using the English language in a way that could communicate without the captor's knowledge of the content.

Such songs as "Swing Low, Sweet Chariot," "Nobody Knows the Trouble I've Seen," "Go Down Moses," etc. were often warnings, signals and messages to other Africans:

> Much of the communication relating to fugitive slaves was in a guarded language. Special signals, whispered conversations, passwords, and messages couched in figurative phrases were the common modes of conveying information about underground passengers or about parties in pursuit of fugitives. These modes of communication constituted what abolitionists knew as the grapevine telegraph.[10]

Even today African-Americans communicate in black cultural dialect which is foreign to whites.

TERMS DEFINED: AFRICAN PERSPECTIVE

Fanon's solution to the problem of racism in the language is that blacks bend the language to new requirements. According to Fanon, ". . . the days of colonized laurates are over. An ex-native, French speaking, bends that language to new requirements, makes use of it and speaks to the colonized only."[11]

The prevalence of today's statement "I am an African people," is an indication that the blacks in America are denouncing the white created "Negro," re-establishing their cultural identity.

Other indications that Africans in America are liberating themselves from the racist use of the English language is seen in their redefinition of terminology. "Black is beautiful" refutes all of the negative, unfavorable racist definitions created by whites. The rejection of "integration" as defined by whites (blacks being required to reject their culture and identity and assimilate white values, culture, etc.) is another indication. Africans in America recognize that such a definition of "integration" places white culture in a superior position and black culture in an inferior position. Thus, African-Americans refer to authentic non-racist integration as being a reciprocal process where both entities maintain their ideas but share culture, thereby whites would go to a predominantly African populated school and vice versa.

During the mid-fifties and early sixties many African-Americans adopted a tactic of "non-violence" as a means for integration which was assumed at that time to be a method for liberation. However, it was not long before they realized that they were operating within a racist definition. That is, black people in America subjugating themselves humbly to the supreme, superior, white being with hat-in-hand, weak and submissively begging for freedom. At the same time, the "supreme" and "omnipotent" being had the option of being abusive, brutal and punitive without retaliation. The ultimate of inferiority was dramatized by blacks in America who participated in that movement under the white definition of nonviolence.

Later, however, when "nonviolence" was defined in black terms which denoted reciprocity, that is, blacks would be submissive and passive as long as whites remained submissive and passive, which is authentic, "equal" and non-racist. Whites, however, defined the behavior of blacks as being racist.

The most popular, yet racist terminology used in referring to race relations is "equality." Implicit in white America's use of the word "equality" is the notion that they are superior and blacks should become "equal to" them. Their synonym for equality is "to be like"; consequently, compensatory education and job training is needed for African-Americans to reach the level of whites.

TOWARD A LANGUAGE OF HUMANISM:
A TOOL FOR BLACK LIBERATION

There are two warring levels of political consciousness (cultural modalities) in the world. One is Western Anti-Humanism of which the Euro-American world-view, characterized by racism and fascism, is a cultural variant. The second is Eastern Humanism of which African Humanism is a cultural variant. Western (European) Anti-Humanism is a world-view that is more characteristic of the West than the East and of Europe than Africa. The European world-view is marked by several cultural modalities which reflect a profound disrespect for life and a correspondingly profound adulation of private property, individualism and economic and political exploitation of other human beings. On the other hand, Eastern (African) Humanism is a world-view that places the utmost significance on fostering life and living in harmony with nature.

The world-view that one uses to determine what is right and wrong, good and bad, beautiful and ugly, and human and non-human is a product of the culture in which one is formally and informally socialized. Language is a fundamental part of culture; it reflects one's culture and is the indispensable vehicle for the transmission of culture. People through language and other forms of communication are carriers of cultural standards of beauty, love, art, music, childrearing, funeral practices, eating, and so on. People are carriers of cultural standards just as a mosquito can be a carrier of malaria.

Europeans and their cultural descendants, Americans, may be viewed as being carriers of a world-view which is dangerous and inimical to the interests of the rest of mankind because it is inherently anti-human, racist and exploitative.

The European world-view predates the European invasion and rape of the manpower and natural resources of Africa. It can perhaps best be grappled with and understood by examining the meaning of blackness in western culture. Winthrop Jordan in *White Over Black*, comments on this meaning.

> Long before they found that some men were black, Englishmen found in the idea of blackness a way of expressing some of their most ingrained values. No other color except white conveyed so much emotional impact. As described by the Oxford English Dictionary, the meaning of black before the sixteenth century included: 'Deeply stained with dirt, soiled, dirty, foul . . . having dark or deadly purposes, malignant, pertaining to or involving death, deadly; baneful, disastrous, sinister . . . iniquitous, atrocious, horribly wicked . . . indicating disgrace, censure, liability to punishment, etc.' Black was an emotionally partisan color, the handmaid and symbol of baseness and evil, a sign of danger and repulsion.[12]

The European world-view contains what Kwesi Manza has labeled a devilview of blackness that is usually expressed in oppositional terms. In the form of a chart, it looks something like this:

The European God/Devil View of Blackness and Whiteness	
European Godview of Whiteness	European Godview of Blackness
God	Devil
Superiority	Inferiority
Intelligence	Stupidity
Beauty	Ugliness
Progress	Retrogress
Cultured	Uncultured
Freedom	Slavery
Just	Unjust
Success	Failure
Christianity	Heathenism
Happiness	Sadness
Goodness	Evil
War	Peace

Needless to say the European devilview of blackness is a distortion and a perversion of reality and is completely inimical to the interests of African people. The universal subscription of Europeans to this worldview is indicative of a sickness which is found in far greater proportions among Europeans than Africans. In terms of the analysis being attempted in this paper, Europeans are best viewed as carriers of a deathly, contagious, cultural sickness which poisons and contaminates everything and everyone they encounter. In thinking about this European sickness, I have found it useful to conceptualize it as a mental illness which I have tentatively labeled as a "delusional psychosis." Europeans, then, are carriers of the dreaded disease—delusional psychosis. Because of the contagious nature of this disease, it should be noted for programmatic as well as analytical purposes that to the extent that black people use Europeans as models of how to live, thereby absorbing the disharmonies and destructive values of western culture, our perceptive power also becomes corroded, corrupted and distorted.

What do I mean by the label delusional psychosis? A delusion is a false belief that is persistent in the face of evidence to the contrary. A psychosis, on the other hand, is a mental disorder in which a person's ability to meet the ordinary demands of living in harmony with other people and with nature is impaired. Thus, a delusional psychosis as a disease indigenous to European culture is a persistently false and distorted conception of reality (in this instance, blackness) and an inability to live in harmony with other men (Africans and other Third World peoples) and with nature (as witnessed in their destruction and pollution of the environment in their quest for profit). This, then, is the dreaded, contagious disease that Europeans carry wherever they go.

*   *   *

We have already seen how language is a fundamental part of culture and is an indispensable vehicle for the transmission of culture. We have also attempted to convey how western definitions of blackness are at variance with African well-being. Any African who consciously or unconsciously absorbs the European world-view and its dangerous devilview on blackness is absorbing his own non-being—his own death.

The English language as well as other European languages have words, concepts, symbols and forms of imagery that are destructive to black health, black unity and to black well-being—both collective and personal. European languages when used without an awareness that language is political in that it either fosters group strength and cohesion or spreads confusion and disunity, convey non-being and death for Africans everywhere. European languages convey orientations to reality that are foreign to African culture and humanism. The foreigner's sense of reality is oft-times cold, detached, individualistic, harsh and mechanical; while words, even foreign ones, used in the perspective of African humanism would be warm, involved, group-oriented, accepting and natural.

One of the most fundamental needs of our struggle against the beast-like qualities of western culture (e.g., anti-humanism, racism, militarism, and economic exploitation) is a language of

African Humanism. Such a language would serve at least two major purposes: 1—It would provide us with a much needed alternative to the vicious and destructive language of European Anti-Humanism; 2—It would enable us to free our minds from the control of foreign standards and definitions of reality.

In other words, one of the most meaningful steps that we could make in preparing ourselves and more importantly our children for meaningful participation in the struggle of our people's restoration and liberation is to purge from our minds concepts that represent European definitions of who we are as a people. In the words of El-Hajj Malik El Shabazz, "(our task is to) revamp our entire thinking and redirect our learning trends so that we can put forth a confident identity and wipe out the false image built up (and sustained) by an oppressor." The restorative and liberative struggle of our people is of necessity a physical struggle. But our physical struggle must also be accompanied by a struggle on another level—mental—involving the way we look upon, and interact with each other and the way we interpret our experience *vis-à-vis* the forces of European anti-humanism and exploitation.

Language is political and can be used to foster group strength and cohesion or to spread confusion and disunity. Language can be used to develop human potential or to stultify its development. Words are not merely idle symbols, they can be just as dangerous, repressive and controlling as a policeman with a gun. The language the people use can be analyzed to determine whether or not it is supportive of European Anti-Humanism or of African Humanism.

Examples of statements from the African-Humanism perspective versus the European anti-humanism perspective can best be illustrated by the sentences in the chart on page 40.

The implication of the above sentences from the European anti-humanism and African humanism perspective as they may guide policy and influence behavior is very clear. To speak of black people as "primitive," "savage," or categorize infants into "legitimate" or "illegitimate babies" serves as a justification and rationale for forming cohesive groups—that is for including some persons in the group and for excluding others, which is done through stigmatizing and dehumanizing the individuals or groups intended to be isolated. Terms such as "primitive" and "savage" were described earlier as aftereffects of colonialism. In other in-

Euro-American Anti-Humanism	African Humanism
1) "The blacks of Africa are primitive."	"The blacks of Africa are culturally different."
2) "The African savages attacked the white christian missionaries."	"The African warriors attacked the white christian missionaries."
3) "Statistics show that 50% of the infants in this community are illegitimate."	"Statistics show that babies are 25% of the population in this community."
4) "The 'No-Knock' Act is being contested by 'Negro' community leaders."	"The government-sanctioned genocide act is being contested by delegated African-American leaders."
5) "A new program is being developed for the culturally deprived and economic disadvantaged youth of this city."	"A new program is being developed for the culturally dispossessed and economically exploited youth of this city."

stances, terms such as "No Knock" became euphemisms for "government sanctioned genocide against black people."

*   *   *

When the African humanism perspective is used elements of humanistic values are very clear. A new and different program is needed for the "culturally dispossessed," "economically exploited" and "educationally oppressed" because the focus is toward removing the factors and obstacles handicapping the individual as opposed to the European perspective which is ingrained in the Protestant ethic view of the difficulties being inherent in the individual personality and makeup.

It makes a difference as to whether or not future generations of young black children are socialized/educated to the still viable values and wisdom of their African forefathers as opposed to the world-view of European Anti-Humanism and heroes of western imperialism and neo-colonialism. Words are often used as weapons to "put down" young black children. It is important that we ask ourselves what we are doing when we describe the behavior of black children in the diseased, pathological terminology of the oppressor.

What are we doing when we label our children as culturally disadvantaged, slow learners, maladjusted? What are we saying when we tell each other to stop acting like heathens or niggers? What are we saying when we describe one another as being black as sin? Such anti-human references, absorbed from the European world-view, have no place if we take seriously a most important mandate: to rear future generations of black men and women who, confident in the worthiness of their ethnic identity and cultural heritage, can by virtue of having been innoculated with their own cultural legacies, deal with the carriers of European anti-humanism at any level using means that are appropriate to the task and with no fear of being contaminated or of being diverted from working in the interests of African people everywhere.

European-oriented and controlled education and mass media are two of the major institutional enemies of African people. Both are carriers of anti-humanism, racism and death. The magnitude of their destruction of black human potential is inestimable. It is no accident that one of the first priorities of any politically aware nation is to control its educational institutions and its mass media. If any people does not have control over these two institutions, it will always be the victim of the oppressor's propaganda and thereby controlled. We as people must use a language of humanism in reference to each other. We must maintain a constant vigilance over the kinds of oral, visual and aural forms we need to survive and conquer the onslaught of European anti-humanism and propaganda.

Footnotes

1. Simon Podair, "How Bigotry Builds through Language" *Negro Digest* Vol. XVI No. 5. March 1967 p. 39.
2. Frantz Fanon, *Black Skin White Mask* "The Negro and Language" Grove Press, Inc., New York, 1967 pp. 17–18.
3. Paul Henle, *Language, Thought and Action*, University of Michigan Press, Ann Arbor, 1965 p. 5.
4. Ossie Davis, "The English Language is My Enemy," in Neil Postman, Charles Weingartner, and Terrance P. Moran, eds., *Language in America*, New York: Western Publishing Co., 1969.
5. *Ibid.*
6. *New York Times* "U.N. Group Urges Dropping of Words with Racist Tinge" September, 1968.
7. John O. Killens, *Black Man's Burden*, New York: Pocket Books, 1965, p. 19.
8. August Meier and Elliott Rudwick, *From Plantation to Ghetto*, Hill and Wang, New York, 1966, p. 2.
9. Frantz Fanon, *Black Skin White Mask* "The Negro and Language" Grove Press, Inc., New York, 1967, pp. 17–18.
10. Milton Siebert, "The Underground Railroad from Slavery to Freedom" *American Negro: His History and Literature* New York, Arno Press, 1917, p. 9.
11. Frantz Fanon, *The Wretched of the Earth*, Grove Press, Inc., New York, 1963, p. 10.
12. Winthrop Jordan, *White Over Black*, Penguin Books, 1968, p. 7.

THE USE OF SOCIAL SERVICE AGENCIES BY BLACK AMERICANS

Harold W. Neighbors and Robert J. Taylor

Little is known about the factors that influence social service utilization in the general black population. Despite widespread recognition among human service practitioners that social service organizations play an important role in the lives of many low-income blacks, very little help-seeking research has focused on the demographic and situational correlates of social service use.[1] The few articles that do are often concerned with a particular subgroup and may not be representative of black help-seeking behavior in general.[2] This article is concerned with the utilization of human service programs by black Americans. Specifically, it focuses on the identification of important variables that are related to the use of social service and welfare agencies in a large representative data set.

A series of studies conducted by the Institute for Urban Affairs and Research at Howard University provides some of the best available information on help-seeking among blacks. Leo Hendricks, Cleopatra Howard, and Patricia Ceasar asked ninety-five black unmarried fathers who they would go to for help with a problem; 88 percent said "family," 11 percent said "friends," while only 1 percent responded that they would go to a social service agency.[3] Hendricks, Howard, and Larry Gary found that 36 percent of their sample of black urban adults mentioned going to some type of institution (hospital, community mental health center, or

*Reprinted by permission of the publishers of *Social Service Review* 59:2 (June 1985) 258–268; copyright © 1985 by The University of Chicago.

telephone hot line) for help with a personal problem, while 31 percent said they went to a physician or psychiatrist.[4] Demographic comparisons showed that those most likely to contact an institutional setting were in the lower socioeconomic groups.

While these studies yield valuable information on the use of professional help by blacks, their findings are somewhat ambiguous. For example, the findings from the Hendricks, Howard, and Ceasar study of unmarried adolescent fathers are very specific to that group.[5] Consequently, generalizations from the finding that only 1 percent of that sample would contact a social service agency for help are problematic. The hypothetical nature of the question wording is also of concern. That is, their study asked respondents where they would go for help if they had a problem. It is not known to what extent these respondents do use social service agencies, since their actual help-seeking behavior was not investigated. The Hendricks, Howard, and Gary study is a substantial improvement over the first since it focused on actual help seeking and had a larger, more representative sample. Yet the fact that institutional sources of contact (such as mental health centers and hospitals) were grouped together does not permit an estimation of the relative rates of use among these professional resources. Furthermore, social services were not one of the specific institutional sources mentioned in the Hendricks, Howard, and Gary study.[6] While these studies represent some of the best investigations of black help-seeking available, they clearly leave many questions unanswered.

There are additional reasons for the general lack of information with respect to blacks and social service utilization. First, most of the help-seeking and professional health resource information on blacks focuses on the use of traditional health services such as physicians and hospitals.[7] Little quantitative research focuses specifically on the use of human service agencies. A few articles describe the effect of race on the use of community mental health centers, but these studies rarely explore how and why blacks use social services.[8]

Another reason for the lack of information about the use of social services by blacks concerns a more general shortcoming of most help-seeking studies. The majority of utilization research operates from a sociodemographic framework.[9] Such studies only compare different demographic subgroups (young vs. old, male vs. female) as to whether they sought some type of help. No attempt is made to explain why a gender or age difference in help seeking might exist. Help-seeking studies that operate primarily from a demographic perspective usually do not include the kinds of variables that would be helpful in explaining what it is about being female that makes certain types of professional services more accessible to women, or in clarifying the characteristics associated with being male that impede access to professional help.

The preoccupation with race comparisons in help-seeking research is a more specific example of the general problem with the demographic approach outlined above. Blacks and whites are compared on any number of illness responses, but little is concluded except that the two groups vary in their help-seeking behavior. A more serious criticism of these racial comparisons is that they say virtually nothing about the heterogeneity of illness behavior within the black population. Due to the small numbers of blacks included in cross-sectional surveys, analyses that differentiate among important subgroups within the black population are not possible. As a result, these studies mistakenly imply that all blacks respond in essentially the same manner to stressful circumstances.

The data utilized in this analysis do not have these limitations. The data come from a study entitled the National Survey of Black Americans (NSBA) conducted in 1979–80. One major advantage of the NSBA is its large sample size. This data set allows a degree of differentiation among various population subgroups in a manner unavailable in previous analyses. Statements can be made about more precise target groups such as "low-income black women" or "older, black, unmarried males." Another advantage of having a large sample is that the strength of relationships between variables can be tested by statistically controlling for several variables simultaneously. As a result of utilizing multivariate analysis techniques, more confident statements can be made about the relationship of one variable to another. Similarly, multivariate analyses also permit one to specify the precise nature of a relationship by detecting the presence of interactions. If low-income blacks are more likely than upper-income blacks to use social services, it may be the case that this is only true for certain types of problems (economic, for example). The large sample size of the NSBA data set makes such clarifications of relationships possible.

Finally, the data to be analyzed here are superior to many previous investigations because this study was not limited to a demographic approach. The NSBA also included a number of important social-psychological variables shown to be important predictors of help-seeking behavior.[10] In the analysis to follow, the effect of differential problem definition (problem type) is included along with demographic variables in order to provide a more complete picture of why certain groups within the black community are more or less likely to use social services.

Previous research utilizing data from the National Survey of Black Americans presents some of the more detailed information on the help-seeking behavior of adult blacks. Two out of three (63.6 percent) blacks indicated having experienced a serious personal problem at some time during their life. Of those, about half (48.7 percent) sought some type of professional assistance, and almost nine out of ten (87.2 percent) sought help from at least one member of their informal network. Females, younger respondents, and those with lower incomes were more likely to utilize informal helpers than their counterparts. In addition, females and older respondents had a greater tendency to utilize formal sources. Analyses of the combined pattern of formal and informal help seeking revealed that of the respondents who had a personal problem, 44 percent sought only informal help, 4 percent sought professional assistance only, and 9 percent sought no help at all. An examination of the specific professional help sources utilized revealed that respondents were more likely to contact private physicians, ministers, or hospitals than social service agencies.

The particular research questions to be addressed in this paper are as follows: What proportion of blacks facing a stressful problem turn to social service agencies for help? What types of personal problems do blacks in distress take to social service agencies? Are certain types of problems (e.g., economic, emotional) more likely than others to be referred to social service agencies? Are particular demographic groups more likely to use social service agencies, or are all groups of blacks equally prone to seek such help? Finally, are certain groups of blacks more likely to use social services only for particular types of problems?

METHOD

Sample

The analyses were conducted on a nationally representative cross-section sample of the adult (eighteen years old and older) black population living in the continental United States. The sample was drawn according to a multistage, area probability procedure designed to insure that every black household had the same probability of selection. A total of seventy-six primary areas were selected for interviewing based on the 1970 census distribution of the black population. These sites were stratified according to racial composition, and smaller geographical areas ("clusters") were randomly chosen. Next, professionally trained interviewers listed the habitable households in each cluster. Since correct identification of eligible dwelling units was critical, special screening procedures were developed for finding black households in low-density black areas. Finally, within each selected black-occupied household a single person was randomly chosen from the list of eligible adults to be interviewed. These sampling and interviewing procedures resulted in 2,107 completed interviews conducted in 1979 and 1980, representing a response rate of 67 percent.

Instrument

The section of the questionnaire designed to study help-seeking issues was organized around the concept of a "stressful episode." Respondents were asked to report a personal problem they had experienced in their lives that had caused them a significant amount of distress. If a person had such an experience, they were asked to describe the specific nature of the problem. They were also asked a series of questions designed to elicit information on how they adapted to this stressful event. A total of 1,322 respondents reported experiencing a serious personal problem, but only 48.7 percent of that group sought professional help. The present analysis focuses on the 631 respondents who sought professional help for their personal problem.

Problem type.—Every respondent who said they had experienced a problem was asked the following question: "Thinking about the last time you felt this way, what was the problem about?" This question was designed to ascertain how the respondent conceptualized the nature of the distress experienced. The answer to this question represents the specific locus to which the respondent attributed the cause of his or her personal distress. For analytic purposes, responses were categorized into five problem categories: (1) physical health problems, (2) interpersonal difficulties (marital problems, problems with the opposite sex, and interpersonal relationships in general), (3) emotional problems, (4) death of a loved one, and (5) economic difficulties.

Professional help utilization.—Respondents who had experienced a problem were presented with a list of professional helping facilities and asked if they had gone to any of the places listed for help. That list included the following professional help sources: hospital emergency room, social services, mental health center, private mental health therapist (i.e., psychiatrist/psychologist), doctor's office, minister, lawyer, police, school, employment agency. The term "social services" was self-defined by the respondent. An examination of the data revealed, however, that the majority of respondents were referring to a not-for-profit, public human services agency. In the present report, the use of social services is explored through the use of log-linear models. Professional help utilization is operationalized by a dichotomous variable indicating the number of respondents with a problem who sought help from a social service or welfare agency across four mentions.[11]

RESULTS

Table 1 shows the sample distribution for the use of social services (among respondents who sought professional help), as well as the bivariate relationships between social service use and selected demographic variables (income, education, age, and gender). Family income is significantly related to social service use (p < .001). Close to 21 percent of those respondents making less than $10,000 sought help, while only 8.4 percent of those with incomes above $10,000 did so. Table 1 also shows that education is related to the use of social services (p < .05). Among respondents with

Table 1
Demographics and the Use of Social Services (%)

Demographics	Used	Did Not Use	N
Univariate	14.4	85.6	631
Income:*			
$0–$9,999	20.9	79.1	287
$10,000 and above	8.4	91.6	261
Education:†			
0–11 years	18.4	81.6	266
12 and above	11.4	88.6	361
Age:‡			
18–34	11.8	88.2	263
35–54	13.8	86.2	225
55+	20.3	79.7	143
Gender:§			
Male	10.9	89.1	183
Female	15.8	84.2	448

*$\chi^2(1) = 16.7, p < .001$; gamma $= .48, p < .001$.
†$\chi^2(1) = 6.2, p < .05$; gamma $= .28, p < .01$.
‡$\chi^2(2) = 5.5, p < .10$; gamma $= -.20, p < .05$.
§$\chi^2(1) = 2.5, p < .15$; gamma $= -.21, p =$ N.S.

less than a high school education, 18.4 percent seek help from social services as compared to 11.4 percent of the group with twelve years or more of education. Neither age nor gender show a relationship to the use of social services using the conventional criterion ($p < .05$), although the gamma for age is significant, indicating a substantial linear trend of increased utilization with increasing age.[12] Finally, although insignificant, 15.8 percent of the females as opposed to 11 percent of the males use social services.

Since several of the demographic variables investigated in Table 1 are interrelated, a multivariate analysis was performed. Table 2 shows the results of that analysis. The preferred model indicates that when the relationship of the demographic variables to social services use is explored, only income has a significant

Table 2
The Effect of Family Income (I) on the Use of Social Services (S)
Controlling for Education (E), Age (A), and Gender (G)
(Log-linear Models)

	Family Income	Odds Ratio
	Low/High	2.5

NOTE.—Preferred model: {SI} {IEAG} $LR_{\chi^2}(22) = 20.6, p = .55$.

effect on use. Respondents making less than $10,000 are two and one-half times more likely than persons making above $10,000 to seek help from social service agencies. Table 2 also shows that this income effect is independent of age, education, and gender.

Table 3 shows the sample distribution for the different types of personal problems respondents experienced (col. 1). It can be seen that the majority of respondents (41.5 percent) mention an interpersonal problem, while the least mentioned is death of a loved one (9 percent). A little more than one of every five re-

Table 3
Problem Type and the Use of Social Services (%)

Problem Type	Univariate	Total N	Used Help	Did Not Use	N
Physical	16.2	194	17.7	82.3	130
Interpersonal	41.5	496	10.4	89.6	240
Emotional	11.9	142	11.7	88.3	60
Death	8.9	100	8.7	91.3	46
Economic	21.6	258	24.1	75.9	116

NOTE.—$\chi^2(4) = 14.4, p < .01$.

spondents (21.6 percent) were upset due to an economic difficulty, 16 percent mentioned a physical health problem, while 12
percent were distressed due to an emotional problem. Column 3
of Table 3 shows the percentage of respondents who use social
services by problem type. The highest percentage of users, 24
percent, comes from the economic problem group. Physical health
problems are next, with almost 18 percent of that group seeking
help from social services. Use for interpersonal and emotional
problems is about the same—10.4 percent and 11.7 percent, respectively. Finally, only 8.7 percent of those respondents who
mentioned death of a loved one as a problem sought help from
social services.[13]

One of the goals of this paper is to specify the conditions
under which certain groups are more or less likely to use social
services. One way to do this is to include differential problem
definition in an analysis, along with one or more demographic
variables. The previous multivariate analysis revealed that income
is the only variable significantly related to utilization when all
other demographics are included. Consequently, it was decided to
explore the income-use relationship, taking problem type into account. If problem type influences the relationship between income
and utilization, it will be reflected by the presence of a three-way
interaction. Since gender is strongly related to family income, it
was also included in this analysis.

Table 4 shows the results of this multivariate analysis. The

Table 4
The Effect of Family Income (I) on the Use of Social Services (S)
Controlling for Gender (G) and Problem Type (P)
(Log-linear Models)

Income	Odds Ratio
Low/High	2.3

NOTE.—Preferred model: {SI} {SP} {IGP} $LR_{\chi^2}(14) = 10.8, p = .70$.

preferred log-linear model indicates that income remains significantly related to social service use even when the effects of problem type and gender are taken into account. Specifically, the lower-income group is 2.3 times more likely than the higher-income group to use social services. This income effect holds for all types of personal problems. This model also states that problem type is significantly related to social service use net of income and gender. The effect of problem type corresponds generally to the effects observed in the bivariate analysis: respondents with economic problems are the most likely to use social services, and people with interpersonal problems are the least likely. Respondents with other types of personal problems use social services at about the same rate as the sample as a whole. The preferred model did not include the three-way interaction of income, problem type, and utilization. Although problem type is significantly related to the use of social services, it does not affect the income-use relationship.

DISCUSSION

The major issue highlighted in these analyses is the strong relationship of family income to the use of social services. When the effects of education, gender, and age were taken into account, low-income blacks were more than twice as likely as high-income blacks to use social services. More important, the low-income group was more than two times as likely to use social services than the higher-income group, even when personal problem type was taken into account. Initial expectations were that problem type would specify the particular conditions under which low-income respondents turn to social services. It is clear that having an economic difficulty increases the likelihood of contacting social services. It is also clear that being low income significantly increases the likelihood of such contact. If we assume that low-income respondents have fewer alternative sources of financial assistance than those in the higher income group, we would expect low-income blacks to be more likely to turn to social services for economic problems only, based on the assumption that social service agencies dispense money as their major means of helping.

This was not the case. Low-income respondents were significantly more likely to use social services regardless of the type of problem.

Speculation on the exact meaning of this finding centers on three ideas. First, the fact that low-income respondents are prone to use social services for all types of problems indicates that such agencies may operate as primary sources of care. That is, social service and welfare agencies may be seen by low-income groups as the initial place to turn when in trouble—any kind of trouble. This could be due to a number of reasons. Low-income blacks may be cut off from sources of help (psychiatrists, mental health centers, marriage counselors, physicians) that are more appropriate for dealing with such things as interpersonal problems, emotional difficulties, death, and physical health. Low-income blacks may not see these sources of assistance as effective in solving problems. In another analysis of these data it was shown that very few blacks in distress utilize the mental health care sector.[14] If it is the case that social service agencies are primary sources of care for low-income blacks, then it is imperative that researchers begin collecting information on the type of help offered to this group (especially for nonfinancial matters) and the quality of that help.

The second idea as to the meaning of these data centers on the notion that social services are not necessarily the first and only place poor blacks turn to for help. Rather, social services may be one of a number of places low-income blacks go for help. If this is true, then it also stands to reason that social services are contacted for a very specific type of help, perhaps financial. Social services may be used by low-income blacks in order to get the financial assistance needed to purchase services from other sources of professional help. Persons with physical health problems who may not be able to afford to go to a doctor or the hospital may turn to a social service agency in order to get the necessary money to then go to the doctor. High-income blacks by definition are less likely to need such help. They have other financial resources at their disposal.

A third possibility is that low-income blacks may use social service agencies as a primary referral source. Many in this group simply may not be aware of the most appropriate professional source of help for their particular problem. They do know, however, that social service agencies are tied to the general human service network. Thus, they may go to such places for referral to another agency that might be better able to assist them.

Overall, few respondents sought help from social services (14.4 percent of those who went for professional help). The highest number sought help for economic problems (24 percent); and the percentage on utilization for physical health problems is not much lower (18 percent). The rate of usage for seemingly inappropriate types of problems (interpersonal, emotional, death) is quite low. Thus, the fact that low-income respondents are more likely to use social services for all types of problems may not be a major cause for concern because so few people with non-economic problems contact such places.

Many of the questions concerning how blacks use social services have been answered by the analyses presented here. Yet many more questions are raised by these data. For example, how many of the respondents who contacted a social service agency used that source of help exclusively? An answer to this question would help clarify the issue of whether social services are primary help sources or one place among many turned to for help. An exploration of the type of help offered by social service agencies for different types of problems would also help to clarify this issue. It would also be informative to estimate how many respondents who used social services turned to that place first, and then went on to other professional help sources. Fortunately, the National Survey of Black Americans data set contains items that bear directly on these questions. More in-depth analyses of these data should help to clarify why poor blacks are so inclined to use social services.

Notes

An earlier version of this paper was presented at the 16th Annual Conference of the National Association of Black Social Workers held in Detroit, April 18, 1984. The preparation of this article was supported by a grant from the National Institute of Mental Health's Division of Prevention and Special Mental Health Programs (Center for Minority Group Mental Health). The authors would like to thank Tom Weiser and Mary Randall for typing.

1. Murray Gruber, "Inequality in the Social Services," *Social Service Review* 54 (1980): 59–75.
2. Jeanne Marsh, "Help Seeking among Addicted and Nonaddicted Women of Low Socioeconomic Status," *Social Service Review* 54 (1980): 239–48; Charles Mindel and Roosevelt Wright, Jr., "The Use of Social Services by Black and White Elderly: The Role of Social Support Systems," *Journal of Gerontological Social Work* 4 (1982): 107–25.
3. Leo Hendricks, Cleopatra Howard, and Patricia Ceasar, "Help-seeking Behavior among Select Populations of Unmarried Adolescent Fathers: Implications for Human Service Agencies," *American Journal of Public Health* 71 (1981): 733–35.
4. Leo Hendricks, Cleopatra Howard, and Lawrence Gary, "Help Seeking Behavior among Urban Black Adults," *Social Work* 26 (1978): 161–63.
5. Hendricks, Howard, and Ceasar.
6. Hendricks, Howard, and Gary.
7. Ann Brunswick, "Who Sees the Doctor? A Study of Urban Black Adolescents," *Social Science and Medicine* 13 (1979): 45–56; Diane Dutton, "Explaining the Low Use of Health Services by the Poor: Costs, Attitudes or Delivery Systems?" *American Sociological Review* 43 (1978): 348–68; Horatio Fabrega and Robert Roberts, "Social Psychological Correlates of Physician Use by Economically Disadvantaged Negro Urban Residents," *Medical Care* 10 (1972): 215–33; Gary Shannon, Rashid Bashshur, and Carl Spurlock, "The Search for Medical Care: An Exploration of Urban Black Behavior," *International Journal of Health Services* 8 (1978): 519–30.
8. Charles Windle, "Correlates of Community Mental Health Center Underservice to Non-Whites," *Journal of Community Psychology* 8 (1980): 140–46; Stanley Sue and Herman McKinney, "Delivery of Community Mental Health Services to Black and White Clients," *Journal of Consulting and Clinical Psychology* 42 (1974): 794–801; Dennis Andrulis, "Ethnicity as a Variable in the Utilization and Referral Patterns of a Comprehensive Mental Health Center," *Journal of Community Psychology* 5 (1977): 231–37; Brian Weiss and David Kupfer, "The Black Patient and Research in a Community Mental Health Center: Where Have All the Subjects Gone?" *American Journal of Psychiatry* 131 (1974): 415–18.
9. John McKinlay, "Some Approaches and Problems in the Study of the Use of Services—an Overview," *Journal of Health and Social Behavior* 13 (1972): 115–52.
10. Harold Neighbors, James Jackson, Phillip Bowman, and Gerald Gurin, "Stress, Coping and Black Mental Health: Preliminary Findings from a National Study," *Prevention in Human Services* 2 (1982): 5–29; Harold Neighbors and James Jackson, "The Use of Informal and Formal Help: Four Patterns of Illness Behavior in the Black Community," *American Journal of Community Psychology* 12 (1984): 629–44.
11. Persons who indicated that they had sought professional help were allowed to mention as many places contacted up to a limit of four. As

a result, the analysis combines multiple mentions if a particular respondent had indeed contacted more than one professional help source. Thus, a respondent is coded as using social services regardless of whether social services was mentioned first, second, third, or fourth. Any respondent mentioning the use of social services more than once (across the four mentions) was counted only once in the category indicating use of help. It was felt that by creating a dichotomous variable that takes into account multiple mentions, a more complete description of help seeking could be given than would be possible had the utilization variable been based on the first mention only.

12. In fact, a closer inspection of Table 1 suggests that the age fifty-five and above group is significantly more likely than the two younger groups to utilize social services. As a result of this possibility, it was decided to collapse the two younger groups and compare their help seeking to those age fifty-five and above. This table did show a significant difference between the oldest group and the two younger groups ($p < .05$). While 20.3 percent of those fifty-five years old and older use social services, only 12.7 percent of those respondents below fifty-five years of age did so.

13. An exploration of the difference between the expected and observed call frequencies for this 5×2 table revealed that the major contributions to the significant χ^2 value come from persons with interpersonal problems being less likely than would be expected to use social services and respondents with economic problems being more likely than would be expected to seek help from social services.

14. Harold Neighbors, "Seeking Professional Help for Personal Problems: Black Americans' Use of Health and Mental Health Services," *Community Mental Health Journal* (in press).

II. OBSERVATION OF CULTURE

There is no doubt that the culture of a particular minority member is of crucial significance to the practice of social work and other helping professions for the culture of a people determines its language, lifestyles, folkways, marriage, habits, customs, religion, art, how they view themselves, their relationship to family structure, and peer group interaction, as well as how they view the notion of receiving help and their role as client. All of the above is significant if the worker is going to be effective in helping a client gain a perspective on the problem presented. Even though minority clients may have (successfully) assimilated into what is considered to be mainstream society and have divorced themselves from their culture, the relevance and importance of the individual's culture still plays a key role in determining the dynamics involved.

The observation of culture is not a phenomenon which should be unique to European-ethnic practitioners, educators, and students but all practitioners and educators must be made aware of the implication of culture on behavior. It is also important to note that all ethnic and racial minorities have a unique culture even though there may be similarities in the cultures. Consequently, the study of one minority group may have implication for other minorities. This is true especially when we address the issue of making one sensitive to a culture other than one's own by destroying the negative myths, stereotypes, and assumptions about minority cultures and looking at culture as being *different* from, and not necessarily superior or inferior to, other cultures.

Once the culture is understood and free of prejudicial stereotypes, myths, and assumptions, then the worker can adequately address the problems and concerns of the client. Behavior which may be considered pathological in white middle-class social-work-oriented values may be healthy in a particular culture. Thus, the idea of social work practice is not to make minority clients into middle-class white Americans but to understand the client in the context of his or her culture and assist the client in resolving any conflicts which may exist due to cultural orientation. All minority clients may not bring a problem which has cultural implication to an agency but all problems should be considered from a cultural perspective if the person is to be understood. Consequently, the necessity for observation of culture is relevant.

Some of the cultural realities which practitioners must be aware of if their practice is with Blacks, Native Americans, Puerto Ricans, and Mexican Americans are as follows:

AMERICAN NATIVES

Some of the cultural realities of the Native American culture may be identified as follows:

The inherent value of sharing with others.

Circular concept of time based on the moon, sun, seasons as opposed to linear in the western culture which is divided in minutes, seconds, hours, days, weeks, months, and years. The matters of life are more important than being somewhere on time.[1]

The view of self as an integral part of nature working and living in harmony with nature as opposed to being separate from nature which is the western philosophy. Therefore, the Native Americans do not "kill animals for sport", "pollute the water for technological advancement." (They never took more from nature than they could consume.)[2]

Value and respect for the elderly as extended family.[3]

The Native American value system includes the extended family in terms of living arrangements and help.[4]

There is a value of cooperation with others rather than competitiveness.[5] Family needs are first priority.[6]

A circular concept of space and time in viewing the past, present and future as part of a whole rather than evaluating on progressive scale.[7]

A strong belief in the influence of a Supreme Being having an impact on life rather than the cause-effect phenomenon perpetuated in the Western society.[8]

A view of good and bad as being part of a whole rather than separate entities. Therefore, there is the notion of acceptance of the ill effects on life as natural and expected which should be accepted in the same manner as the joys of life.[9]

Emphasis on the importance of human relation over materialism and harmony with nature over technological advancement if the two should conflict.[10]

PUERTO-RICAN CULTURAL REALITIES

Strong extended family relationships which involves godparents.[11]

A high value placed on individualism and/or personalism. These concepts are not defined in the competitive sense as operationalized in the United States but safeguarding the inner integrity against group pressure and acquiring identity, self-confidence from the family.[12]

Deference to Authority figures.[13]

Patriarchal society with women playing a significant role as counselor in the personal lives of their children.[14]

Emphasis on the machismo male image where the male is regarded as assertive, aggressive and responsible for the well being of the family while the female is the housekeeper and supporter of the male.[15]

The inherent qualities of the male stature not attached to status in life.[16]

A strong belief in spiritualism, mysticism separated from the cause-effect behavioral interpretation of life events.[17]

In-group cohesion of supporting one's own.[18]

Value of female virginity until marriage.[19]

Strict adherence to social amenities in personal relationships as well as professional contacts.[20]

A humanistic approach to life, both personal and business, with an emphasis on personalism and face-to-face contact.[21]

Avoidance of confrontations with family members and others where one's feelings may be injured.[22]

BLACK AMERICAN CULTURAL REALITIES

Extended family relations as support group.

Ingroup dignity and pride.

Strong belief in the influence of a Supreme Being on their daily lives.

Value of religion as an emotional experience.

Strong value placed on the symbol of mother.

Suspicion of authority figures.

Emphasis on social relations and interactions over formal interactions.

Pro-Black attitude and consciousness.

Strong kinship bonds.

Strong work orientation.

Adaptability of family roles.

High achievement orientations.

MEXICAN-AMERICAN CULTURE REALITIES

Strong extended family relationships.

An acceptance of the Divine Order of things as related to their individual lives and to the fate imparted to time.

Deference to authority figures.

Patriarchal society with the female playing the needed role of housekeeper and support of husband.

Strong belief in spiritualism, mysticism.

Strong emphasis on the machismo male image.

In-group cohesion of supporting one's own.

Adherence to socializing and "getting to know" prior to meaningful discussion.

Loyalty to nationhood.

Strong influence of religion in their lives.

Notes

1–10. Herbert H. Locklear, "Native American Myths," *Social Work*, May 1972; also Ronald G. Lewis and Keong Ho, "Social Work with Native Americans," *Social Work*, September 1975.
11. Sonia Bodillo Ghali, "Culture Sensitivity and the Puerto-Rican Client," *Social Work*, October 1977; also Edward W. Christensen, "When Counseling Puerto-Ricans," *Personnel and Guidance Journal*, March 1977.
12. *Ibid.*
13. Rene A. Ruiz and Amado M. Padilla, "Counseling Latinos," *Personnel and Guidance Journal*, March 1977.
14. Kal Wagenheim, *Puerto-Rico: A Profile*, New York: Praeger, 1970.
15. Rene A. Ruiz and Amado M. Padilla, "Counseling Latinos," *Personnel and Guidance Journal*, March 1977.
16. Kal Wagenheim, *Puerto Rico: A Profile*, Praeger, 1970.
17. *Ibid.*
18. Sonia Badillo Ghali, "Culture Sensitivity and the Puerto-Rican Client," *Social Casework*, October 1977.
19. Melvin Delgado, "Social Work on the Puerto-Rican Community," *Social Casework*, February 1974.
20. Edwardo D. Maldonado Sierra, Richard D. Trent, and Marida, "Neurosis and Traditional Family Beliefs in Puerto Rico," *International Journal of Social Psychiatry*, Vol. 6, 1960.
21. Sonia S. Badillo Ghali, "Culture Sensitivity and the Puerto-Rican Client," *Social Casework*, October 1977.
22. Kal Wagenheim, *Puerto Rico: A Profile*, Praeger, 1970.

WORLDVIEWS: IMPLICATION FOR SOCIAL THEORY AND THIRD WORLD PEOPLE

David R. Burgest

In terms of color, mankind can be divided into two distinct groups of people which consist of whites and the colored people of the world, ranging in complexion from light brown, near white, to dark and near black. Anthropologists have divided mankind into basically three distinctive racial groupings: 1) Caucasoid (Europeans/Whites); 2) Negroid (African/Blacks); and 3) Mongoloids (Asians/yellow). Although Caucasians consist primarily of European whites, they are light-complexioned individuals with light skin and black straight hair. The Negroid characteristics consist of dark-complexioned skin, flat nose, thick lips and woolly hair. The Mongoloids are tan to dark in complexion with straight black hair and usually slanting eyes. Irrespective of the distinctive groupings mankind has been placed in by physical characteristics, color, and hair texture, mankind has also been divided by philosophical and ideological differences with one being the Western world view and the other being the Eastern world view. Eastern and Western world view does not refer to the geographical location of a people on the hemisphere but rather it refers to a uniqueness in a culture and way of life expressed by a people. The Eastern world view and Western world view cut across the ethnic and racial composition as well as the geographical location on the hemisphere in that Asians, Africans, and Indians are a few of the people who make up the Eastern world view but they are not united by race, nationality, or geographical location. The same is true of the Europeans and Egyptians who are Western but are not bound by geographical location, nationalities, and ethnic groups. The only commonality which appears to exist is that the colored people of the world fall in the category of Eastern world view and the white people of the world appear to fall within the Western world view. In addition to the above, the third world people, as defined by the Euro-American, consist primarily of the ethnic and racial compositions of the colored people of the world whereas the terminology does not apply to European people of European origins. The concept of third world, in general, applies to the countries, ethnic groups, and races of mankind who have not advanced, technologically speaking, as have the Euro-Americans.

When we analyze the unique qualities of the Eastern world view and the unique qualities of the Western world view, we will find that the social theory created out of a Western world view ideology may have negative implications for a people whose thought and behavior patterns are rooted in Eastern world view ideology.

It must be understood that the epistemological world view of a people has a reciprocal relationship with culture if in fact the epistemological world view does not determine culture. The relationship between world view and culture is similar in character to the relationship between language and culture in that some authorities see a reciprocal relationship between language and culture while others would have culture determine the language.[1] The only difference in the relationship between world view and culture is that there are only a few authorities who have attempted to make a correlation between "world view" and "culture." One resource puts it this way:

> "Worldview" is an elusive term, but when we speak of someone's world view in any of its senses, we do not mean simply the world impressing itself upon his passive receptors, sensory or intellectual. A person does not receive a world view but rather takes or adopts one. A world view is not a datum, a danne, but something the individual himself or the culture he shares partly constructs.[2]

Epistemology refers to the origin of thought and knowledge as it developed and emerged untold generations ago and gave shape to how men think, feel, behave and view their environment from there throughout today and world view denotes the unique characteristics and dynamics manifested throughout the culture. Culture denotes the customs, traditions, way of life, and beliefs of a people as dramatized in their social, political, religious, and

economical arrangements. It is difficult to say that the epistemological world view determines culture but what men thought
and believed untold generations ago has had a definite impact
upon shaping the lives of archaic man as well as influencing the
behavior, actions, and attitudes of modern man. Historians, social
scientists, and others are partly able to determine the thinking and
behavior patterns of the different world views by analyzing and
interpreting the mythologies of Eastern man and the mythologies
of Western man as well as analyzing the thinking of the Early
Greek philosophers and early African philosophers who also provided a foundation for their respective ideological world views. It
is commonly accepted that Greece is the origin of Western
thought and Africa is the origin of Eastern thought.

The impact of the Eastern world view in shaping the Eastern
culture from the beginning of time to the present, as well as the
impact of the Western world view upon shaping the Western
culture from the beginning of time to the present, must clearly be
delineated if there is going to be any credibility in the notion that
the Western theoretical orientation is antithetical to the Eastern
world view and inadequate for diagnosing Eastern man. It is the
thesis of this document that much of the difficulty social science
and social work have in making appropriate diagnosis and treatment plans for Blacks, Puerto Ricans, Indians, and Mexican Americans in America stems directly from the fact that they are being
analyzed from a theoretical orientation of Western ideology and
not from a theoretical orientation based in Eastern ideology. (To
suggest the above is not to imply rigidity in the different world
views because there has been some cross-assimilation on both
parts.) This can be seen in the number of Eastern religions which
have infiltrated the Western world and the number of Western
religions which have infiltrated the Eastern world. By the same
token, the political and economic style of Western man has infiltrated the Eastern world. Nonetheless, there still exists a distinctive and unique character to the culture of the Western world
and the character of the Eastern world which has its roots in the
origin of man.

EASTERN WORLD VIEW/WESTERN WORLD
VIEW:AN ANALYSIS

The unique qualities and characteristics which make up the Euro-

pean epistemological conception of their universe and their relationship to man, God, and nature can best be characterized as
linear (Eurolinear*) while the Eastern world view's conception of
man, God, nature, and the universe can best be described as circular (Afrocircolor*). Eurolinear logic is rooted in looking at matters, materials, forces, and entities in the universe in terms of a
hierarchy separated into compartments, segments, divisions, dichotomies, and conflict. It is as though everything is separated
into divisions and segments on a scale or continuum visualized on
a horizontal or vertical line. There is the view that the forces
which are divided into oppositions and categories are at odds,
strife, and in conflict with each other, between man/nature,
God/devil, cause/effect, organic/inorganic, mind/body, good/evil
and Black/white (plus others). This vertical or horizontal line
which best describes the Western/European thought carries with
it the attachment of opposites such as negatives and positives,
with positive value attached to the upper position on a continuum
and a negative value attached to the lower position. It is apparent
that the Greek society's separation of man from nature was a
break from tradition, based in the mythologies of Greek society.
There are those who suggest that such a decision was politically
motivated. According to Cedric Clarke:

> The Greek political state was a slave state. Even the most noble of
> the Greek thinkers, Aristotle, saw fit to justify the existence of
> slaves in Greek society . . . in separating themselves from other
> men, the Greeks, of necessity, separated themselves from nature as
> well as from man . . . for man was . . . even in the early Greek leg-
> ends, considered to be an integral part of nature. One could not
> divorce himself from other men and still maintain a personal in-
> volvement with nature. But such a divorce did take place in the
> minds of the influential Greek thinkers and such a division is the
> cornerstone of contemporary Western (societies) scientific
> thinking.[3]

First of all, the author above supports the view that the Western world view of the universe is based on dichotomy and separation. At the same time, he is illustrating the reciprocal relationship

---

*See Burgest, David, "Eurolinear/Afrocircolor Worldview: Black and White Cultur-
al Values." (unpublished)

between world view and culture as they influence each other. Finally, the author is suggesting that the motivation and rationale of early Greeks to separate man from nature has deep political overtones. Regardless of the motivation and rationale, the fact remains that such an epistemological orientation has great implications for man's relationship to man.

Another key aspect to the existence of dichotomies, oppositions, and conflict is seen in the negative and unfavorable definition of the concept Black (Blackness) and the positive, favorable definition of the concept White (Whiteness) which has concomitantly transferred to Black people and White people. As one author puts it:

> Long before they found that men were Black, Englishmen found in the idea of blackness a way of expressing some of their most ingrained values. No color except white converged so much emotional impact.[4]

Most lay people as well as social scientists have attributed the origin of the notion of white supremacy with the enslavement of Blacks and other colored people of the world (Indians) for economic expediency[5] while others have spoken about the psychogenetics of white supremacy based on the notion of color deficiency and numerical inadequacy of the European.[6] Many students of history and anthropology still feel that the notion of supremacy and inferiority was generated after observation of the African culture by the European, a culture which was uniquely different from their own. The fact of the matter is that the European world view based in opposition and dichotomy between Black/white and man/nature, is responsible for the notion of supremacy of white and inferiority of nonwhites or the colored people of the world. According to John O. Killens:

> All nonwhites throughout the world become "niggers" and therefore, proper material for "civilizing" and "Christianizing" (cruel euphemism for colonization, exploitation, genocide, and slavery).[7]

There is the underlying assumption that European's subordination of Black and other nonwhite cultures is evidence of the superiority of whites and the inferiority of nonwhites, but a closer look will reveal that a conflict in world views (Eastern/Western) was more responsible for the ultimate oppression of dark people rather than some inherent deficiencies in the dark man's psyche. The epistemological world view of Eastern man is quite different. On the continent of traditional Eastern man, he maintained a belief in the essential unity of all things material and immaterial and fostered the maintenance of a harmonious relationship between God, men, nature, and the universe. There was no separation, dichotomy, or division between matters, materials, forces, and entities within the universe. There was not a view of strife, odds, or conflict between good/evil, man/nature, cause/effect, mind/body, and others. In fact, the Eastern societies see harmony and unity between all forces and entities in the culture and society. This concept of oneness, unity, togetherness, cohesion, and harmony can best be described as a whole, symbolized by a circle in a physical sense. In the words of Charles Frye:

> The most ancient symbol known to man is the black circle or disc. This symbol represents the source of all life, knowledge, understanding and truth. The black circle is the womb, the Great Mother, the container of all that has ever been, is now and ever will be. The black circle symbolizes the undifferentiated state of spirit and matter, light and darkness, good and evil, male and female and all other so-called opposites.[8]

Early African philosophers and thinkers who laid the foundations for Eastern thought in the same way that the early Greek philosophers laid the foundation for Western thought and ideology looked at the universe in this way:

> On the continent of Africa, scholars very much retained their belief in the essential unity of the most highly developed of the African sciences (i.e., Alchemy) [and] insisted that spiritual forces (e.g., incantation) were just as much a part of reality as were the chemicals which they were working. In the northern part of Africa, man saw his observation of the heavens, tied up with forest and rivers. In both cases, as well as in many parts of the Eastern and Southern American world, man did not see himself separated from nature and significantly from other men.[9]

The two distinctively different world views have had an impact on the philosophical outlook on the universe as well as on the social, political, educational, economical, religious, and physical design of their environment. As Clarke puts it:

It is not therefore, by accident that the Polar igloos, South Sea grass
huts, American plains "Indian" lodges, Chinese pagodas and Con-
golese mud huts all share basically the same similarities and all the
social, political and economic institutions erected by traditional
man reflect the symmetry ever present in nature. . . . All Eastern
culture is highly symmetrical.[10]

It is thus not accidental that in the Western world the physical
design of their buildings is horizontal and vertical and the shape of
the Eastern physical world is as it is. By the same token, it is not
accidental that the Africans, Indians, and other Eastern cultures
sat in circles, danced in circles, and conducted their ceremonies in
circles. In traditional Africa, decision-making is conducted by the
elders of the community who sit and argue until they agree and
reach consensus. At the same time, it is not accidental that the
physical arrangement of chairs in classrooms, churches, and meeting places in the Western culture are arranged vertically or hori-
zontally, with everyone facing the speaker. There is a dichotomy
between the individual providing the knowledge and the recipients of that knowledge. In contemporary America, it is considered to be more humane to conduct classes and seminars with the
chairs arranged in a circle because everyone is able to have face-
to-face contact and the "authority" of the speaker is lessened.
    In the Western world the structure of the bureaucracy and
decision-making is linear. The work force is broken up into ap-
prentice, master craftsman, worker, supervisor, director, and president with the line of communication being such that the person at
the lower end of the continuum cannot communicate directly with
the individual at the top of the hierarchy. Instead, communication
must be directed through the hierarchy at every level. In terms of
decision-making, we find that within the hierarchy of the linear
structure the greatest power rests with the person highest on the
scale and each person in descending order possesses a lesser
degree of power. In traditional Eastern culture power generally
rested in the hands of the elders and continuously revolved (circular) from one generation to the next with everyone having the
opportunity to be a decision-maker. On the other hand, the concept of majority rule is placed at the top of the hierarchy in the
Western culture while minority concerns are secondary. This is
different in the Eastern culture, where the concept of consensus,

unity, and oneness in decision-making prevails and is circular in dimension. The concept of majority is placed high on the linear scale while the concerns of the minority are minimized.

Even though the concept of slavery existed in African cultures and Africans oftentimes sold African slaves to Europeans, the concept of "slavery" in Swahili (Utumwa)[11] is defined as "sent, prisoner of war" and the so-called slaves were seen as members of a family with property and religious rights as well as human rights. In the case of Europeans, the slaves were defined as property with no rights under the assumption of white supremacy and Black inferiority.

The Eastern/African philosophical statement which best captures its ideology is "I am because we are, therefore I am" as opposed to the European/Western ideology of "I think therefore I am." The implication of the statement "I am because we are, therefore I am" suggests unity, cohesion, and oneness. It further suggests that the survival of an individual is intricately tied into the lives of other members of the society—those who have gone before and those who are yet to come. On the other hand, "I think therefore I am" places the individual at the height of the linear scale with "individuality" at the top, and all other forces, entities, and matters at the bottom. This statement suggests that man can survive alone without human contact or reinforcement from other humans and we know that not to be true.

Although ethnic and racial groups such as Puerto Ricans, Mexican Americans, Indians, and Black Americans have been dominated by Western cultures for generations, they continue to maintain a unique cultural similarity based in the Eastern world view tradition, even though there are distinctive characteristics of each culture which differ in some degree one from the other. The commonalities which are unique to the Eastern world view are as follows:[12]

> Each culture places a high regard and respect for the elders of their communities, often as mentors and decision-makers in their families. This is an extension of early tradition where the elders played significant roles in the community.
>
> Each culture maintains an extended family relationship which includes family members as well as nonfamily members as an incorporation of the value "I am because we are, therefore I am."

Each culture continues to maintain a belief in the workings of supernatural forces in their lives which causes evil as well as good in their day-to-day lives. They have not completely separated the spiritual from the material in that at times they see certain rituals as being able to resolve the misfortune they face.

Each culture has not significantly separated man from other men (nature) in that there is a more humanistic tolerance and acceptance of other ethnic groups and races (including whites). Interracial children and interracial marriages as well as individual whites are more accepted in a minority community than minorities in white communities.

In some form or fashion minority group members from the Eastern world view perspective have adopted the circular logic of "what goes around comes around" and "you are going to reap what you sow" as the philosophy which guides their behavior and teach those principles to their children. Inherent in the notion of "what goes around comes around" is the view that you better be careful how you treat other people in the circle of men because the same treatment may revolve back to you. The same principles apply in the notion of "you are going to reap what you sow." The notion of individualism in Western society suggests that "only the strong survive" and the dominant force prevails which is linear.

For individuals in the Eastern culture who are destined to follow the linear path, there is a warning in the Eastern culture which says "you better be nice to those on your way up because you may meet them on your way down" and "don't burn down the bridge you cross." In the latter case, the emphasis is on members of the minority culture maintaining a connection with the community of which they are a part. In Western culture, the emphasis is on "getting to the top of the hierarchy the best way you can" even if it means stepping on someone else to do it.

In Eastern cultures and languages, there is no dichotomizing Black and white into superior and inferior positions with white being positive and Black being negative. The upsurge of ethnic and racial awareness and consciousness have oftentimes brought about a notion of Black superiority or Indian superiority but this is merely a reaction to racism.

There may be other similarities between the Eastern cultures but only a few have been mentioned here. The next crucial point is what are the implications of the Western world view for social theory and third world people?

IMPLICATIONS OF WESTERN WORLD VIEW FOR
SOCIAL THEORY AND THIRD WORLD PEOPLE

It has already been pointed out that the concepts Black and white, with their accompanying negative and positive attributes, have been transferred to the Black and colored people of the world. It is also significant to note that the foundation of Western world view social science and social theory pertaining to behavior, is rooted in the outlook of the early thinkers and philosophers. Consequently, it is no wonder that the social science theoretical base is ineffective with third world people. First of all, there is the underlying assumption inherent in social science theory that Euro-Americans are superior to the third world colored people existing in their culture. That is, they are superior socially, intellectually, and spiritually. Such an underlying assumption makes it impossible for social workers, psychologists, and other members of the Euro-American helping professions to establish rapport, a trusting relationship, and empathy with members of the third world due to inherent feelings of condescension, superiority, prejudices, and biases. The same racist factors exist when Euro-American social scientists attempt to investigate and research the colored world cultures and lifestyles. Thus it is easy to see how the evidence gathered reflects a negative correlation with Euro-American culture. It is not that there is something inherently inferior or subordinate about the people and culture of the third world, it is just that the tools and instruments used in the research and investigation by Euro-American social scientists were inadequate and inappropriate—based in a racist orientation.

Secondly the concept of individualism (self-determination) which fosters the idea that nothing is basically right or wrong, but it is all dependent upon the ability or inability of an individual to function adequately in the society. Little emphasis is placed upon family, and the community at large must begin to refocus its attention on third world people and address the welfare of the family and the welfare of the community as primary. There is nothing wrong with treating the person as an individual (who deserves respect and dignity) but it is important to note that this individual is part of a culture with a circular-based logic and this logic should be utilized in helping third world minority cultures overcome their difficulties. Oftentime more dramatic consequences are imposed on an individual, his family, and his community by utilizing the linear logic of individualism in helping the individual than by letting the individual resolve his own difficulties. In addition, there is a prevailing notion in the Euro-American world view that an individual's inability to adapt, adjust, or function adequately in the society is a direct result of internal conflict in the individual, stemming secondarily from family conflict and the community at large.

However, given what we know about the cultures of the Eastern world view, it would seem that a therapist's primary concern would be to focus on the impact of the community at large and the family on the individual's inability to function adequately within society. Much of the difficulties Black, Puerto Ricans, Indians, and Mexican Americans have in adopting and adjusting to Euro-American society may be a direct result of the conflicting and opposing values they must consolidate in order to function in this Western society. When this can be realized and determined it should be the responsibility of the therapist to assist the client in resolving the difficulties, recognizing that the Eastern world view culture of the individual touches on the root of the individual's existence and must not be taken lightly.

There are individuals from the Eastern cultures who may have assimilated well in the Western culture in that they may no longer live in the culture of their community and they may have ascended high on the hierarchical scale of employment, education, status, and position. Some may have gone so far as to divorce themselves mentally, psychologically, and spiritually from their cultural community. Some of these people may not come to the attention of a social agency but if they do the culture under which these individuals were raised is just as important in treatment, if not more so, than the culture they have adopted and assimilated. The culture out of which they came, whether they were born in that culture or not, appears to have implications for the persons concerned, since the epistemological world view of a people appears to permeate their origin and their psychogenetic make-up.

Thirdly, social science and social theory are rooted in the notion of science as prediction and control as opposed to science as understanding. Consequently, nothing is scientific unless it can be measured, observed, and/or repeated, using the same equations and giving the same results. This is not true for most third world people who are in some form or fashion superstitious, intuitive, or rely heavily upon a belief in a Supreme Being as a moderator in their lives. In most instances, the good as well as the bad which occurs in an individual's or a people's life is seen as an act of a Supreme Being who is working for the best in the universe as opposed to the deficits or capabilities of an individual or group behavior based upon some scientific approach or formulas. In the Eastern view, there is no dichotomy between religion and secular affairs or between religion and the State. Religion is a part of everyone's intimate day-to-day activity and touches on every aspect of their daily lives.[12] Their playing the horses and playing the numbers is somehow tied into religion. Religion is not a one-day-Sunday affair where people honor and pay homage to their God; rather, it is based on how they live. A difficult child or conflict with husband or children is seen as an act of God trying to communicate something to the parties involved. This is not to say that all individuals of the third world and Eastern culture are as religious or superstitious as others but when crises arise in their lives they usually revert to the older tradition. Yet, social science theory from the Western perspective is based in the secular world and only chaplains are trained to assist individuals specifically with "religious problems." Nonetheless, it is difficult for a professional therapist to assist any individual of the Eastern world-view culture without putting the impact of religion in its proper perspective. (This is not to suggest, however, that all Eastern problems are of a religious nature.)

The people of Eastern cultures are basically emotional and intuitive—bordering on mysticism. Some individuals of the Eastern cultures may be more orthodox in this approach than others but the factors are present in most members of Eastern cultures in some diluted form. They conduct "reasoning" more by their emotions than they do by their intellect. In other words, they make decisions in their lives based primarily on how they feel about something (intuition, hunch) rather than by the scientific facts which may prevail. On the other hand, third world people are emotional. Some Western oriented people would say that they let their physical emotions get in the way of their reason; rather, they reason by their emotions. In other words, they have not truly separated mind from body to the extent that emotions are physical attributes. In addition to the above, the third world people are basically emotional in the sense that they are highly excitable. They dance with heavy emotion, sing with deep emotions, pray and shout with emotion. In fact one may say that they cathect an idea or object in an extreme fashion. Thus, the murders that take place in the Black, Puerto Rican, or Indian community are usually out of impulse and passion rather than out of a contrived scheme which is based in the intellect. The traditional role of therapist and social scientist has been to try to get the colored people of the world to use their minds and not their emotions. In this way, the Euro-American is attempting to make them Euro-American and in the process is trying to destroy the essence of a people's way of life. The idea should be for Western-oriented therapists to recognize the validity of emotion in thought and help the client to see the fallacy in his thinking rather than attempting to change the individual's whole way of thinking.

Finally, the social theorist should do away with the notions of ethnocentrism and imperialism which dominate the Western-oriented view: that the Western way is the right, proper, developed, and sophisticated way while the ways of other countries which differ from theirs are archaic, outdated, undeveloped, and backward. This notion of classism and racism is detrimental to the welfare of so-called undeveloped people because in their attempt to assimilate the Western point of view as a method of advancement, they oftentimes destroy the essence of their being as they begin to measure their behavior and feelings by Western standards. The Western world has made the claim that it is an authority on human behavior, but has disregarded the fact that there is an Eastern world with a different perspective that guides the actions and behaviors of Eastern people. The Western world view of social theory may be adequate for individuals and a people whose essence permeates the concepts of Western logic but, by the same token, is inadequate for individuals and a people whose logic base is antithetical to the Western world view.

References

1. See Max Picard, *Man and Language, A Gateway*, 1963. p. 41; Harry R. Warfel, *Language: A Science of Human Behavior* (Howard Allen, 1962) pp. 180–197; Simon Podair, "How Bigotry Builds through Language" *Negro Digest* Vol XVI No. 5 (March, 1967), p. 39; Paul Henle, *Language, Thought and Action* (University of Michigan Press, 1965), p. 5.
2. Ong, Walter J., "World As View and World as Event" presented at Wenner-Foundation Burg Wartenstein Symposium no. 41, August 2–11, 1968.
3. Clarke, Cedric, "Black Studies on the Study of Black People," in *Black Psychology*, Reginald Jones (ed). (Harper, 1972), p. 2.
4. Jordon, Winthrop, *White Over Black*. (Penguin Books, 1968), p. 4.
5. See Hugh Butts, "White Racism: Its Origin, Institution and the Implication for Professional Practice for Mental Health," *International Journal of Psychiatry*, vol 8. No. 6. (December 1969), p. 917; Ethel Pearson, "Racism: Evil or Ill," *International Journal of Psychiatry*, vol 8. No. 6 (December 1969), p. 929.
6. Welsing, Frances Cress, M.D., "The Cress Theory of Color Confrontation and Racism (White Supremacy); A Psychogenetic Theory and World Outlook," (Howard University College of Medicine, Department of Pediatrics, Copyright 1970), p. 10.
7. Killens, John O., *Black Man's Burden*. (Pocket Books, 1965), p. 9.
8. Frye, Charles, "The Psychology of the Black Experience: A Jungian Approach," p. 12.
9. Clarke, Cedric, op. cit.
10. Frye, Charles, op. cit.
11. Lee, Robert E., *The Black Expatriates*. Ernest Dunbar (ed). (Pocket Books, 1970), p. 71.
12. See Wagner, Hernandez, Houg, *Chicanos: Social and Psychological Perspectives* second edition. (C. V. Mosby, 1976); also Wogenheim, Kal, *Puerto-Rico: A Profile*. (Praeger Publishers, 1970).
13. See Abraham, W. E., *The Mind of Africa*. (University of Chicago Press, 1962); John S. Mbiti, *African Religions and Philosophy*. (Anchor Books, 1970).

See also: David Landy, *Tropical Childhood: Cultural Transmission and Learning in a Rural Puerto-Rican Village*. (Harper Torch Books, New York 1965); Richard N. Adams, et al., *Social Change in Latin America Today*. (Vintage Press, 1960); Jack O. Waddell and O. Michael Watson (eds), *The American Indian in Urban Society*. (Little, Brown, 1971).

THE ETHNIC AGENCY DEFINED*

Shirley Jenkins

What is an "ethnic agency"? The ethnic organization has been described and classified—there is even a directory for that purpose. Categories include political, fraternal, national, and language; the common denominator is a clear statement of goals and commitment to a defined group. When an organization is called, for example, the "National Association for the Advancement of Colored People," there may be disagreements about its policy but not about its purpose. But if it is called Children's Services, Inc., or the Big Cove Day-Care Center, the matter is not so clear.

The ethnic agency needs to be regarded as both a special form of ethnic organization and a special form of social agency. To be functional it must achieve a balance between both types and find a way to integrate both service and ethnic goals in a single delivery system. Serving the minority client is not a new phenomenon for social agencies. With a disproportionate number of minority people among those in poverty, it would be anticipated that they would also comprise a disproportionate number of agency clients. What is new, however, is the concept of agencies that incorporate ethnic factors, not as "problems" but as positive components of service delivery. The research reported here sought to identify programs and agencies where innovative and constructive work was being done with ethnic clients; to analyze the nature of these activities, including "what worked and what didn't work"; and to operationalize the definition of "ethnic agency." An earlier

*Reprinted by permission of *Social Services Review* 54: 2 (June 1980), 249–261; copyright © 1980 by The University of Chicago.

phase of this research, on attitudes of social workers to ethnic factors in service delivery, has already been reported.[1]

AGENCIES VISITED

For the agency research, target areas in different parts of the United States were selected which had important concentrations of each of the five ethnic groups studied. Child welfare agencies serving Asian Americans were visited in the San Francisco and New York Chinatowns; Blacks in Philadelphia; Puerto Ricans in New York; Mexican Americans in Brownsville, Austin, San Antonio, and four other communities in southern Texas; and Indians in Cherokee, North Carolina, and Phoenix and Sacaton, Arizona. In each area consultants from each of the ethnic groups advised on appropriate programs for field visits. The final sample included fifty-four settings among which were day-care centers, foster care and adoption agencies, residential centers and institutions, mental health centers, services to children in their own homes, youth services, and multipurpose integrated service centers. The auspices of agencies visited were divided, with twenty-five public agencies and nine with private sectarian and twenty with private nonsectarian sponsorship. Although fewer than half were public agencies, over 94 percent received public funds. Their programs served low-income groups; over half had no fee for service, and the remainder had a sliding scale. All but one were ongoing rather than short-term programs. It should be noted that agencies visited were not representative of all programs serving minority children—indeed they were selected not to be representative but because they were innovative, experimental, or creative. The common factor was service to minority clients. Our goal was to develop a typology for service delivery which incorporated ethnic factors and was applicable in cross-cultural settings.

Data to help operationalize the ethnic agency concept were collected in field visits, observations, and extended interviews with agency directors and staff. Areas reviewed included agency characteristics and client composition; program content; and policy, goals, and preferences on ethnic issues in service delivery.

The data on clients served show that almost three-fourths of the agencies served over 95 percent ethnic clients, and no agency served fewer than 50 percent such clients. Ethnic personnel predominated. In thirty-one of the fifty-four agencies visited the director was of the primary ethnic group served. White directors were most frequent in Black and Indian settings. In no case was there a director from an ethnic group other than the primary group served. The ethnic composition of staff was higher than that of directors. In ten agencies all staff was of the primary ethnic group; in twenty-four agencies this was the case for all but a few (under 5 percent). Thus in two-thirds of the agencies, 95 percent of the staff was from the same ethnic group as the primary group served. Furthermore, in about half of the agencies directors reported strong support from their own ethnic community and power structure in furthering agency goals. The only exception was the Asian-American group, where the least support and greatest ambivalence were reported.

PROGRAM CONTENT

The agency interview asked eleven questions on program content which had direct bearing on ethnic orientation, in addition to the questions on bilingualism, which will be discussed separately. In addition, open-ended questions were used to provide descriptive material for qualitative analysis. Among the program-content items are questions on the use of ethnic food, art, music, history, and celebration of holidays, as well as promotion of ethnic awareness, and development of ethnic curriculum. Specific questions were used to obtain the information needed, since most of the program content for children is prescribed. All four-year-olds in a day-care center, regardless of ethnic group, play, nap, eat, toilet, sing, and go outdoors. Given that pattern, what is distinctive about an "ethnic" day-care center, aside from composition of clients and staff?

An official policy to introduce cultural content in agency programs was reported by 63 percent of all agencies but by 89 percent of the Puerto Rican ones. Fewer respondents—26 percent of all, 55 percent of Black agencies—used program content to develop ethnic awareness. There is a significant difference here, with Puerto Rican agencies tending to stress cultural content, and Black ones stressing ethnic awareness or group identity.

Food is often a critical element in cultural differences. Almost one-third of the agency directors said they made regular use of ethnic foods, and another 20 percent said they used it on special occasions. Greatest use was by Mexican-American agencies, which were in less urban areas and had a very homogeneous ethnic clientele. Regular use of ethnic food was noted by about one-third of the Asian agencies, and Indians and Puerto Ricans reported having ethnic dishes on special occasions.

Ethnic music was used in programs by almost three-fourths of the agencies, with highest use in Asian-American, Mexican-American, and Puerto Rican settings. Ethnic art and decorations were used in about two-thirds of the settings, primarily in Asian-American, Mexican-American, and Puerto Rican agencies. The history of the ethnic group was a regular part of the program of only 13 percent of the agencies but was invoked on special occasions by another 44 percent. The Black agencies least used historical material. All groups supported ethnic holidays except the Indians. This may relate to use of the "holiday" terminology rather than "tribal" or "religious" events.

In developing the ethnic study, one of the underlying concepts was that of an ideological continuum in the direction of ethnic commitment. The first level was called "equal rights," as represented by a melting pot ideology. Next came recognition of differences, or "cultural pluralism." The third level, "ethnic identity," is seen in the Black-power and associated movements. In the agency interview, directors were asked which of these three ideological positions their agency supported. Of the fifty-four agencies, 20 percent chose "equal rights," 40 percent chose "cultural pluralism," and 40 percent chose "ethnic identity" as their ideological commitment.

Although not specifically related to ethnicity as such, there were aspects of program content in these ethnic programs that differentiated them from the more traditional child welfare settings. Poverty affected agency clients and made for a more integrated approach to service delivery. Agencies not only reported child welfare programs but met health and dental needs and worked on nutritional problems; a sizeable number gave employment referrals, housing help, and family counseling. Ninety percent reported that support to families was a principal goal. Increasing parental involvement, return of children to natural parents, and helping families assume responsibility for themselves were all stressed. The ethnic agencies were not "child savers"; they saw the ethnic family as the first resource for the minority child, backed up by the ethnic community.

ETHNIC ISSUES

The cumulated figures reported give some measure of agency activities, but anecdotal reports on problems and programs are what really illuminate the ethnic issues. These are responses to the open-ended questions and deal with myths and stereotypes affecting minorities, bilingualism, cultural content, positions on separate institutions, and ethnic issues related to the larger community. Another question which gave wide latitude for response was when agency directors were asked to report on "things that worked and things that didn't work."

There were numerous examples of how sensitive social workers put their knowledge of myths and traditions to good use in delivering services. The concept of "Indian time," for example, was discussed by two therapists on a Cherokee reservation. One therapist, trained in the forty-five-minute-session tradition, expressed frustration and feelings of ineffectiveness in his work because of avowed avoidance of issues by Indian clients and the way in which clients made casual references to important experiences as they left the session. Another therapist, native to the area and empathic to the people, had developed the capacity to "wait it out" and accept the fact that the Indian client would not give fast reactions but when ready was accessible to treatment. She incorporated the concept of "Indian time" in her intervention plan with substantial success.

A second use of tribal knowledge was in relation to the adoption of an out-of-wedlock Navajo infant. Contrary to patterns in some other groups, to give up a baby, born in or out of wedlock, is contrary to tradition, and such an act must be approved by both family and tribe. In the case noted, an Indian social worker in a southwestern city worked with a young Indian mother who desired to give up her baby for adoption but whose family opposed this. The social worker went to the tribal council as well as to the native medicine men to secure support. He organized a "sing" in which the problems and needs were presented to the tribe. The fact that the baby would be adopted by an Indian couple of the same tribe was a strong point in favor of adoption, and tribal consent was secured and the adoption consummated.

For the Asian-American group, the major myth cited in the interviews was that people from Asia comprised a "model minority": docile, hardworking, and not seeking or needing public services. Asian social workers interviewed in agencies gave differing interpretations to this myth and its questionable validity. One response was that there were always problems in the Asian-American community, but in the past they were covered up and handled within the confines of the ethnic institutions. Now people are more free to express needs and even demand services. Another point was that the accustomed Asian-American ways of child rearing—teaching children to be quiet, reserved, and docile—are not functional today. Several Asian-American workers referred to demographic imperatives, such as the increase in recent Asian immigration with new groups entering a restricted labor market, many without marketable skills, and the intragroup conflicts between assimilated Asian-American youth and new arrivals. Perhaps the most trenchant comment was by a Chinese social worker on the West coast, who said, "The Asian community has changed, but it is hard to know what is dispelled myth, and what is the new reality."

Black workers in agencies referred more to negative stereotypes than to traditional myths in describing barriers to effective service delivery. They reported that whites often equated poverty with "blackness," and had lower expectations for Blacks both as clients and as students than they did for whites. White workers were reported as, on the one hand, being afraid of Black children, and on the other, overcompensating by being too permissive. One area of cultural difference reported was family planning and abortion. One Black worker felt that the service system did not comprehend the intensity of antiabortion feeling among many Blacks. For some this negative feeling extended to family planning, which they saw directed particularly to reduce the number of Blacks and other minorities.

Several factors affected use of cultural materials in programs, including age of clients, sensitivity and sophistication of workers, and homogeneity of client groups. Sometimes workers had one idea of appropriate cultural materials and clients another. Client resistance, for example, was reported from teenagers who showed universal devotion to rock music, regardless of ancestry. In some cases it was not the content but the context or frame of reference of the ethnic material that was important. A Japanese group leader, for example, said Japanese youth were very interested in karate lessons. He reported that he had searched for months until he found a karate teacher who was able to teach it with a cultural focus rather than as a destructive martial art. The latter approach was to be avoided so as not to intensify the street fighting which was prevalent in the neighborhood.

In one preschool program studied in Arizona, the Indian director reported on the importance of knowing tribal differences in disciplining children. In her center she had children from ten tribes who were accustomed to very different patterns of discipline at home, due not to family differences but to tribal patterns. In disciplining children for the same offenses some tribes are permissive, some strict, and some practice avoidance. At the center with the children and in parent-education sessions, tribal membership had to be considered in exercising and discussing child-rearing authority. The director had to deal with her own conflicts in the need to be consistent in center policy, while at the same time she had to avoid too wide a gap between practices experienced at home and in school.

BILINGUAL, BICULTURAL SERVICES

The need for bilingual, bicultural service delivery was stressed by both Puerto Rican and Chicano workers. Puerto Ricans in New York stressed the need to make a conscious effort to maintain bilingualism throughout one's life, rather than to have the school experience be a transition from Spanish to English, with attendant dangers of loss of cultural patterns and ethnic identity. School age was the most common time reported for loss of native languages. Mexican-American respondents placed more emphasis on promoting the learning of English in order to succeed in school and as a way to maximize opportunities. The families served in the programs visited in Texas were primarily Spanish speaking, and the rural setting and homogeneous grouping meant that assimilation in the Anglo culture was less of a threat than was total exclusion.

For the Asian-American community, language issues reflected both acculturation and identity issues. For recent immigrants there was strong pressure to enable children to attend school, and parents wanted their children to learn English as soon as possible. In this regard they sometimes came into conflict with culture-oriented workers. In one day-care center in San Francisco, for example, Asian-American social workers were urging recent Filipino immigrants to continue to speak Tagalog at home so that their children would not lose all native language content. The parents, however, were urging Filipino teachers to speak only English in school to help their children adjust to their new life.

The most impressive handling of language differences was observed in a day-care center for newly arrived 4- and 5-year-olds in San Francisco, where children and teachers spoke three Chinese dialects: Mandarin, Cantonese, and Toy san. There was also an American-born Chinese who was to provide a role model as a "nonaccented" English-speaking teacher. Several group discussions were observed, in which each child spoke in his own dialect, was answered in the dialect and English, then responded in English and dialect, with teachers adjusting the extent to which English was used according to individual student capacity.

A second issue arose when Asian-American respondents defined language as an identity question. This resulted in young Asian-American adults whose basic tongue was English returning to school to learn the national languages of their parents.

For the Indian people interviewed, language was a sensitive and important matter. The early official United States policy toward Indian languages, which was one of total obliteration, left scars not easily healed. Several middle-aged Cherokees told of their experiences in boarding schools, to which many Indian children were and still are sent. They were not allowed to speak one word of their native language, and if they did their mouths were washed with soap. This policy has now been changed, but a whole generation has grown up with no knowledge of its mother tongue. Now that they are parents, they are determined that their children should know the tribal speech, and so native languages are being taught in the schools. It is thus the very young and the very old who knew the native Indian languages, while the adults reported feelings of deprivation.

THE LARGER ISSUES

The majority of agency directors expressed interest in "larger issues," but some specified these as "family, not just child," whereas others spoke of poverty as the major problem. For the Asian-American directors, concern with larger social issues was a new phenomenon, reflecting the changing social patterns of their ethnic group. A major issue for the San Francisco Asian-American community, for example, was busing, and Chinese residents took a strong position against having their children bused out of their neighborhoods. Busing was perceived to be a threat to ethnic identity, with the prospect that it would result in fewer rather than more services. Chinese- and Japanese-language classes, Asian studies, and bilingual teachers are provided in schools with high Asian-American enrollment. The result of busing would be to scatter Asian-American students and destroy the base for special services. This is an example of how a larger issue, school desegregation, is viewed differently by different ethnic groups.

Agency directors were about evenly divided on the issue of separate institutions for ethnic minorities. The arguments in favor stressed the need to have decision-making power, the better understanding of "own group" problems, and the value of the ethnic agency in promoting group survival. However, concern was expressed about further polarization of ethnic minorities and the white majority, excessive costs of administrative duplication of services, and possible disservice to their own people by not preparing them to live in a multiracial society. The most reasoned position, expressed by a director of a Black agency, was that there needed to be options—room for both integrated and separated services. He said, "Some Blacks need ethnically solid services, others can benefit from an integrated experience. Both should be available."

In terms of "what worked" and "what didn't work" for minorities, the most enthusiastic support went to bilingual, bicultural programs. Support for families to care for their own children, recruitment of minority parents for adoption and foster care, career training for parents, and leadership development for youth were also noted. There were also several areas of substantial difficulty. Use of groups for teenagers for therapy or other treatment was generally found to be nonproductive. Efforts to have communities accept group homes or deinstitutionalized persons met strong resistance, even in minority neighborhoods. Public grade schools did not follow up on successful preschool bilingual programs, and children lost the gains they had made. There were often conflicts between old and new arrivals or more or less acculturated members of the same group. Finally, there were problems in working out interethnic relationships among different minority groups, and this frequently forestalled united community effort for common goals.

OPERATIONAL DEFINITION OF THE ETHNIC AGENCY

In order to develop the concept of "ethnic agency" so that it can have general validity, it is necessary to go beyond the descriptive and anecdotal material and move to quantitative analysis of the interview data. If a reliable instrument can be developed, it could be applied in a variety of settings and thus contribute to the comparative study of ethnicity and service delivery.

From the extensive data collected and analyzed in the agency interviews, thirty items, drawn from all topical areas, were selected. Each item had specific reference to some question of ethnicity. Responses to the items were tabulated, scored, and factor analyzed to see if there were identifiable components. Although eight rotations were completed, the best groupings were found to occur in factor loadings for the third rotation. Examination of the content of the items led to naming the three factors "culture," "consciousness," and "matching." The factor loadings for each of the items are noted in Table 1.

The next statistical procedure was to test the three sets for validity and reliability. This was done by means of item-criterion correlations, in which each item was tested against the composite index of which it was a part, excluding the item to avoid autocorrelations. Upon inspection of results five items were dropped. New sets of item-criterion correlations were run for each of the

Table 1
Factor Loadings for Instrument Items, by Factors

Item	Item Number	Loading
Culture:		
Ethnicity of director	2	.46
Ethnic composition of staff	3	.55
Ethnicity of board	9	.42
Use of ethnic curriculum	16	.62
Ethnic staff in programming	18	.76
Use of ethnic food	21	.80
Ethnic art	22	.79
Ethnic music	23	.86
Ethnic history	24	.57
Ethnic holidays	25	.59
Consciousness:		
Support ethnic institutions	11	.51
Leadership on ethnic issues	12	.69
Relate to ethnic power structure	13	.52
Relate to ethnic community	14	.53
Train for ethnic awareness	15	.46
Develop pride in ethnic institutions	20	.62
Support group identity	26	.56
Support ethnic ideology in programming	29	.56
Support separate ethnic agencies	30	.55
Matching:		
Percent of nonethnic clients	1	−.49
Preference for ethnic staff	4	−.68
Support matching policy	5	−.45
Prefer workers of same ethnicity as client	6	−.82
Success with ethnic staff	28	−.54

three indexes representing the three factors. Individual items correlated with their respective indexes, and the Cronbach α measure showed sufficient strength to indicate reliability.[2] The reliability for each is shown in Table 2.

Since each of the three factors represented a separate measure of commitment, it was decided to retain three indexes for purposes of analysis rather than to combine them in one composite measure. Thus the operational definition of the "ethnic agency" is the score on all parts of the agency ethnic-commitment instrument.

The three parts of this instrument reflect the three factors which emerged from the statistical analysis of the interview data. Part 1, "culture," has as its core five questions about use of ethnic materials such as foods, art, music, holidays, and history. It also asks about efforts to develop cultural content, about ethnic participation in programming, and about the ethnicity of the director. Part 2, "consciousness," refers to the ideological position of the agency. Eleven items ask about support of ethnic institutions and of ethnic identity, leadership on ethnic issues, development of ethnic consciousness and pride in ethnic culture, encouragement of separate ethnic agencies, support from the ethnic community and the ethnic power structure, and, finally, the level of ideological commitment based on the continuum from "equal rights" to "cultural pluralism" to "ethnic identity." Part 3, "matching," includes six items on the percent of ethnic clients and ethnic staff, ethnic preferences and policies on staff composition, and agency policies and outcome on matching of staff and client.

The scoring plan for each of the twenty-five items gives a potential range for scores from zero to three, the latter being highest on ethnic commitment. For the fifty-four agencies visited, mean scores were as follows: culture, 1.76; consciousness, 1.14; matching, 1.43. Thus agencies visited score higher on ethnic commitment on cultural items, lower on matching, and lowest on consciousness or promotion of ethnic identity. Extensive use of the

Table 2
Reliability of Agency Indexes

Index	Cronbach α
1	847
2	735
3	543

Table 3
Analysis of Variance, Culture Factor
of Agency Ethnic Commitment Index

Groups	M	SD	N	Variance
Index (1)	1.76	.89	54	.80
Asian American	2.11	.78	12	.62
Black	1.31	.94	11	.88
Mexican American	2.41	.51	8	.26
Indian	1.08	.69	14	.48
Puerto Rican	2.31	.37	9	.14

NOTE.—Analysis of variance: among groups—MS = 4.06, df = 4, F-test = 7.38, significance <.001; within groups—MS = .55, df = 49.

scale in many agencies is needed before "lows" and "highs" can be established for scores in general.

An analysis of variance was undertaken to see if there were any significant differences among different ethnic agencies in terms of commitment scores. There were no differences by ethnic group on either parts 2 or 3, but there were highly significant differences on part 1, culture, as shown in Table 3. Ethnic agencies scored significantly higher on the culture part for the three groups whose first spoken language was not English—the Asian Americans, Mexican Americans, and Puerto Ricans. This is of particular interest since there were no specific questions on language among the culture items. The conclusion is that the ethnic agency with the language differential is responding more acutely to cultural issues, whereas consciousness and matching did not differentiate among agencies by ethnic groups.

ETHNICITY AND SERVICE DELIVERY

This empirical approach to developing an operational definition of the ethnic agency is useful for both research and practice. It helps break down the components of ethnic commitment so that each can be measured. It also provides a tool for comparing agencies with each other on each of the identified dimensions. There are also broader implications for social service delivery in calling attention to ethnic commitment in allocating resources and planning for clients.

In the original conceptualization of this study it was hypothesized that the bureaucratization of services which occurred as they moved from self-help groups to the public sector meant that the needs of ethnic minorities were not being met. The growth of the "ethnic agencies" has been seen by the field primarily as a political response to movements for minority rights, but it can also be interpreted as a way of remedying serious deficits in traditional methods of service delivery.

In an unpublished paper, Litwak and Dono put forth a theoretical framework which helps illuminate the phenomenon of ethnicity and service delivery.[3] They suggest that the organizational theory of shared functions, as between primary groups and formal bureaucracies, can be the conceptual base for defining the unique social role of the ethnic group. According to this formulation, ethnic groups can have characteristics of both the primary group and the bureaucratic organization. They state, ". . . what is unique about the ethnic group is in its stress on the in-between group structure; the extension of the primary group demand for non-instrumentality to large numbers of people."[4]

As we examine "what worked" in the ethnic agencies, it is apparent that many of the examples related to primary-group functions. The ethnic agency stressed family supports, encouraging parents to accept responsibility for their own children, maintenance of own languages, career advancement for own clients, accommodations of traditional myths to meet service needs, and recruitment of minority adoptive and foster parents. All of these can be interpreted in terms of extending primary-group goals to large numbers of people. Furthermore, the anecdotal material has numerous examples of meeting unexpected needs and multiple contingencies, characteristics of the primary-group function.

The theoretical approach described extends the concept of the utility of the ethnic agency beyond the interpretation that it is primarily a political response to minority pressures. It suggests that the ethnic component serves to mediate between the primary-group and bureaucratic functions, thus facilitating the task of delivering services. Under this interpretation the ethnic agency becomes the efficient way to deliver services rather than the expedient way.

Notes

Presented at the American Orthopsychiatric Meeting, Washington, D.C., April 2, 1979. This material is part of the study, Ethnicity and Service Delivery, undertaken at the Columbia University School of Social Work and supported by the Children's Bureau, Office of Human Development, U.S. Department of Health, Education and Welfare.

1. Shirley Jenkins and Barbara Morrison, "Ethnicity and Service Delivery," *American Journal of Orthopsychiatry* 48, no. 1 (January 1978): 160–65.
2. For a discussion of the procedures used see G. Bohrnstedt, "A Quick Method for Determining the Reliability and Validity of Multiple-Item Scales," *American Sociological Review* 34 (1969): 542–48.
3. Eugene Litwak and John Dono, "Forms of Ethnic Relations, Organizational Theory and Social Policy in Modern Industrial Society," mimeographed (New York: Columbia University, 1976).
4. *Ibid.*, p. 8.

INCREASING STAFF SENSITIVITY TO THE BLACK CLIENT*

Richard L. Jones

Human service practitioners are often ill prepared for effective work with black people because they too frequently lack an understanding of black culture and the implications this culture has for practice. Some social service agencies have endeavored to make significant inroads on this problem through a variety of approaches, including the provision of day long institutes and the inclusion of content on black people and other people of color in agency sponsored in-service training programs. Eleanor Kautz noted in 1976, however, that her search of the literature revealed that there had been little recording of efforts in this area of training.[1] Since her criticism still holds true today, this article describes an agency sponsored three-year training program and discusses principles and issues that are critical to such in-service training programs on the black family.

PROGRAM RATIONALE

The conducting of agency sponsored staff development programs on the black family is essential to the delivery of responsible, relevant services to the black community. Training or cultural sensitivity programs are needed for a variety of reasons. First,

*Reprinted by permission from *Social Casework: The Journal of Contemporary Social Work* 64: 4 (September 1983) 419–425; copyright © 1983 Family Service America.

many human service practitioners tend to have a very limited knowledge and understanding of the cultural base of black people. Despite the existence of abundant information on the diversity of cultures, pertinent information on problems of minorities and their cultural differences is scarce.[2] Part of the explanation for this problem can be attributed to the nature of the context in which services are rendered. The encounter between the black client and the human service practitioner occurs in the context of American society—its culture, norms, and values. This context is essentially a racist one based on a history of black slavery and oppression within a culture of white dominance and supposed superiority.[3] The standards and values of the majority culture, consequently, are generally used as the normative frame of reference for assessing development, coping strategies, and modes of interaction, while the culture of black people is frequently devalued and greatly misunderstood. In fact, the black family is often viewed strictly as an impoverished version of the American white family, characterized by disorganization and a "tangle of pathologies."[4] The absence of accurate information on black culture leads to inaccurate and incomplete assessments of individual and family functioning, which ultimately affects the kinds of decisions made regarding appropriate intervention strategies. Second, it cannot be assumed that human service practitioners, both professionals and paraprofessionals, have received adequate preparation for work with black people during their formal training in undergraduate and graduate schools of social work. The curricula of most professional schools of social work offer minimal content on blacks in America; that which does get presented is based on a body of literature that contributes to and perpetuates a multitude of myths and stereotypes on black family life.[5]

Robert Washington argues that traditional models of social work practice have emphasized two dimensions of human behavior, the physiological and the psychological. If social work is to respond to the black perspective, however, social work curricula must treat ethnicity and cultural pluralism as integral aspects of human growth and development.[6] Until schools of social work have adopted such a framework, it is incumbent upon social service agencies to develop opportunities and programs which will assist their staffs in acquiring a more accurate and comprehensive understanding of black cultural forms. Black cultural forms, such as the black church and the extended family, are supportive and adaptive functions that should be recognized and utilized by service givers in the black community.[7]

DESCRIPTION OF PROGRAM

In response to a request submitted by members of the counseling staff, the Center for Human Services in Cleveland, Ohio, conducted a three year staff development program on the black family between 1973 and 1976. Program development responsibilities were assigned to a planning committee appointed by the executive director and comprised of staff, administration, and members of the board of trustees. Based on an agency wide survey, information was requested on 115 topics pertinent to American blacks. Subsequently, these topics were grouped into eight major areas. During the first two years of the project, meetings were conducted monthly and involved 130 staff members. A lecture-discussion method was selected for the series with speakers presenting the major content areas and small group discussions following. Information was provided on black cultural forms and institutionalized racism during the first year and on institutional systems and their impact on the black family during the second year. During the third year, the focus shifted to consideration of the application of this information to actual case material. Six study groups comprised of ten staff members each met monthly. Material for these discussions came from members of the study groups, with supplementary materials provided by the planning committee. Funding for the program was made available through the Thomas White Charitable Trust and the Saint Ann Foundation.

From this experience and that of other agencies, it is possible to derive a set of principles and guidelines that are critical to the planning and development of a staff development program on the black family.

PRECONDITIONS FOR PROGRAMS

Three preconditions are essential for agency sponsored programs. The first is the strong commitment of the board of trustees

and the agency's central administration. The support of the trustees and the administration is necessary to the planning, development, and implementation of a program which addresses such a
sensitive topic. For an employee to feel a sense of concern and the
necessity for action, administrators and managers must constructively participate in the sponsorship and implementation processes.[8] At the Center for Human Services, there were times when
some members of the planning committee became concerned that
such commitment was not held by the board or administration. It
was necessary to be reassured that the committee's work was
given the highest priority. Without this commitment, the work of
the committee would have been greatly hampered.

A second prerequisite is involvement of the trustees, the administration, and the staff in preparing for the program and, once
it is in progress, in providing continuous input and feedback.
There needs to be considerable discussion and sharing of information with total staff regarding planning activities and the proposed
content of an in-service training program. This can be accom-
plished through an extensive information campaign circulating
the ideas through management and supervisory personnel, the
employee newsletter, or special brochures.[9] Such activities give
staff members an opportunity to submit their ideas, but more
importantly, they reinforce the perception that such a program is
needed. Kautz[10] concluded that training is more effective for participants who recognize the need for increasing their sensitivity to
black culture.

Continuous input and feedback from the staff, trustees, and
administration are critical. Several mechanisms were developed
by the Center for Human Services planning committee to facilitate
greater staff involvement in the development of the program. One
example was the survey of the total staff to obtain recommendations regarding the specific content of the program. Periodically,
participants were invited to submit written comments on the
speakers and the quality of leadership in the small groups. Based
on this continuous feedback, the planning committee was able to
develop a relevant in-service training program based on the identified needs of staff, as well as to make adjustments in the program
appropriate to those issues that were identified from time to time
by staff.

A clear set of objectives is a third precondition for a successful program. It is important that the consultant or planning committee develop a set of goals and objectives which are readily understood and measurable. This guidance gives the consultant or committee greater opportunity to monitor the program and to make appropriate adjustments when problems arise. Furthermore, a clear set of objectives helps to facilitate greater investment in the task.

There is a variety of ways in which the content of a program can be planned. Some agencies might elect to hire an outside consultant to plan and conduct an in-service training program while others might wish to establish a small staff planning committee. Regardless of the approach, it is important that the core of the program be planned around the needs and interests of staff.

PROGRAM CONTENT

Program content should be organized around a system's perspective and include information on characteristics of black culture and the behaviors of institutional systems that continue to significantly influence the black family. W. E. B. DuBois described the black person in America as possessing two "warring souls." On the one hand, black people are products of their Afro-American heritage and culture. On the other hand, they are shaped by the demands of Euro-American culture. In this article, information is provided on institutional systems and black cultural forms. This is not an exhaustive discussion; hopefully, the information will serve to suggest several starting points for program development.

Institutional Systems

Many social scientists, like Andrew Billingsley, argue that the family must be viewed as a subsystem of the larger society.[11] In other words, it is assumed that the ability of the family to perform its expressive and instrumental functions depends to a great extent upon the economic opportunities and social services provided to its membership by the institutional systems comprising society. Approaching the black family in this manner allows us to widen the scope of our assessment to include the transactions that occur between black people and the systems within and outside their neighborhoods. It also requires that we look not only at the impact of larger systems but at the kinds of systems that have been developed within the black community in the absence of sufficient larger society supports. Denial of societal forces that dramatically impinge upon the minority family is seriously counterproductive and may result in additional harm to the child and the family.[12]

Human service practitioners working in the black community must be prepared to understand that the problems of most of their clients are problems which are products of complex interrelationships between the individual and his or her reference groups and the structure and institutional patterns of society. In other words, most social problems of black clients today are problems which reside not so much in them as in their interaction with forces surrounding them, many of which are forces over which they have no control.[13] Take the economic system, for example. Income is a critical factor in a family's ability to survive and to meet the physical needs of its members through providing food, clothing, shelter, health care, and other material resources. When the incomes of black families are compared with those of white families, what becomes immediately clear is the large gap between them. Two generalizations can be made. First, income in the black community is not as readily available as in other segments of the population. Second, statistical data reveal that there are even fewer dollars available to the increasing number of black families headed by women. This means that many black families lack the kinds of financial resources necessary to maintain a reasonable standard of living or to secure food, housing, clothing, medical care, and other goods and services required for a minimal living standard.

The consequences of institutional patterns can be observed in other areas. With regard to education, most black people who live in central city areas will probably attend schools where the quality of education, in comparison with that offered to other segments of the community, is very poor. In too many schools, achievement levels are three, four, even five years below the average nationwide; high school graduates unable to read, write, or perform mathematical functions at the sixth, seventh, or eighth grade level are in abundance.[14] Finally, institutionalized racism affects all black people and is seen in every facet of their lives, including housing, education, health, and employment.

Culture

Knowledge of the cultural base from which a client is operating is vital for all human service practitioners. In simplest terms, culture consists of those man-made artifacts, symbols, and institutions that man uses to adjust to his environment. According to Gene Lisitzky, "at bottom, cultures are man's own peculiar way of adapting himself to the special conditions of his environment."[15]

A unit on blacks in America should begin with a consideration of their African heritage.[16] This is an important notion since some researchers argue that many black cultural forms are rooted in African traditions. Wade Nobles reported findings that a "Combined continuation of the African value system and its reaction to the cultural imperatives of the wider Anglo-American society . . . forms the root of the special features observed in black family life."[17]

A report completed by the Black Task Force of the Family Service Association of America contains information on several cultural forms that are characteristic of the black community. Much of the following material has been drawn from that report.[18]

Extended Family Relationships. One of the most creative adaptations observed in the black community is the development of extended kin relations to support individual and group needs through the sharing of households, food, money, child care services, and emotional support. The extended family is a supportive structure which is used with varying levels of intensity through the life span of individuals and families. Wilhelmina P. Manns reported that extended family members not only continued to have significant influence in the lives of black people but also for a longer period of time when compared to the white people included in her study.[19]

Family Roles. The constraints encountered historically by black families in securing basic needs from wider societal institutions have promoted egalitarian relationships and responsibilities. Nobles's findings on role performances in black families "attest to the position of black parents that their children, regardless of sex, should be equipped with the pragmatic skills and psychological attitudes to support themselves and their families."[20] Household duties, sibling care, and part-time jobs are encouraged to socialize children toward strong work orientations as well as to develop a sense of cooperation with the family.

The Black Church. The black church continues its viability as a component of black culture in America; it has the capacity to adapt to the changing needs of its members. The strong religious orientation of many black families has been a major sustaining element in the struggle to cope with social realities from the era of slavery to the present. In addition to its satisfaction of spiritual needs and its value-setting function, the church was a focal point of community life where "a series of social, recreational, educa-tion, economic, and political needs of the community were re-flected. . . . It was an assembly hall for protest meetings and other activities which usually dealt with the crucial social issue of the day—slavery. Above all, it was a social welfare agency concerned with the totality of its black membership."[21]

Value System. The sense of "we-ness," the need for interde-pendence and cooperation are major humanistic themes permeat-ing the motivational and behavioral system within black culture.

These are just a few of the cultural characteristics that should be included in any presentation on the black family. It must be recognized that cultural forms also vary from community to com-munity. As was noted by William B. Austin, several an-thropological investigations have uncovered marked cultural pat-terns among a wide range of black ethnic subgroups in various regions and communities across the nation.[22]

PROGRAM FORMAT

In-service training programs are generally structured along two dimensions, the teacher-centered method in combination with small group discussion, and the encounter or experiential method. The teacher-centered orientation so common in most higher edu-cation programs consists of lectures, reading assignments, guest lectures, films, papers, and occasional discussion.[23] It is the most universal teaching-learning approach in higher education. The experiential method, on the other hand, requires greater involvement of the participants. They must take a more active role for their own learning and risk a closer examination of their own culture, attitudes, and values.

Programs have utilized these approaches with varying levels of success. The teacher-centered approach followed by small group discussion served as the principal method utilized by the Center for Human Services. Kautz reported on a racial-awareness program conducted by the Montgomery County Children's Services in Dayton, Ohio, which consisted primarily of encounter sessions. The program was both cognitive and experiential, involving the use of tapes, music, and discussion to develop feeling awareness. In addition to the encounter sessions, other programs available to staff included movies and a discussion series on the black experience, led by a local university professor.

Is the teacher centered small group discussion method more effective than the encounter method? This question will be debated for some time to come. The Center for Human Services administered two attitudinal measures to determine if the participants' attitudes toward black people were changed as a result of their participation in the program; they were used in conjunction with a questionnaire designed to obtain participants' reactions to the group discussions, program format and content, and speakers. Seventy-eight percent of the participants indicated that they gained "some" or a "great deal" of new knowledge from the series. Sixty-nine percent reported that they were much more comfortable and freer in their contact with black consumers; others noted that they tended to be more patient and tolerant. An analysis of the data collected from the attitudinal measures revealed that there were no significant changes. These results have to be interpreted very carefully, because several major changes—including the formation of a new administrative structure—were occurring within the agency during the program. This situation was further complicated by the fact that attendance for the participants was mandatory. In other words, some of the feelings or attitudes indicated on the attitudinal measures reflected staff's reactions to changes occurring within the agency, a factor that must be considered in any analysis of data resulting from such measures.

Don Crompton suggested that the experiential learning model

has a greater potential for achieving the desired objectives. Based on methods used for cross-cultural training in the Peace Corps, Crompton questioned the value of the traditional teacher centered approach, which he labels the information transmission approach. He argued that when this approach was utilized, information was too often incorporated within the trainee's own cultural frame of reference and that little change or modification occurred regarding his world view or his approach to dealing with people or problems outside his own culture.[24] The emphasis of the encounter method is on trainees' becoming more aware of their own feelings and reactions and more analytical, objective, and sensitive to their approach to another culture. A shift to this model, he said, would enable practitioners to more effectively meet the needs and concerns of minority groups. Perhaps, when agencies are interested in achieving attitudinal change, the encounter or experiential method is more appropriate.

The small group is generally used in both the teacher centered and experiential method. There are several principles to be considered when extensive use is made of the small group. First, there must be careful selection of trainers or group leaders. Westphal noted that inexperienced group leaders often produced hostile and defensive attitudes among participants.[25] In order to avoid these problems at the Center for Human Services, consultation and training were provided to the group leaders before the start of the program. The training for group leaders consisted of two half-day workshops under the leadership of a consultant who had considerable experience in conducting groups of various kinds. The first workshop focused on a discussion of the goals and objectives of the program, expectations of the group leaders, and the model which was to be followed during the group discussion. The second workshop was designed to sensitize group leaders to various kinds of group facilitating techniques, especially in relation to warm-ups, the use of role play, and other experiential learning and group techniques. During the in-service training, the group leaders met semi-monthly for discussion, feedback, and mutual support. They reported that the semi-monthly meetings and the task orientation of the model gave direction and control, reduced uncertainty, and offered viable courses of action. While the group process was much strengthened and the support and exchange system went extremely well, the role of the group leader remained stressful. In fact, only a few of the group leaders offered to continue in this role during the program's third year.

The size of the group is another important consideration which cannot be minimized. In the Center for Human Services program, the value of keeping groups small was quickly discovered. During the second and third year of the program, the size of the groups was limited to twelve persons. This allowed for greater discussion among the participants and more control. John De Santo reported on a racial awareness program that was conducted by the Port of New York Authority for a group of supervisors. The groups in that program were too large, and many of the participants strongly recommended that the groups be reduced markedly to twelve or fifteen people to encourage a franker exchange of ideas and opinions.[26]

In summary, there are several critical decisions that must be faced by an agency which is considering developing an in-service training program on the black family. The use of the teacher centered as opposed to the experiential method will in all likelihood yield different results, while decisions regarding the size of discussion groups and the training of group leaders will also be significant in program outcomes.

IMPLICATIONS OF THE PROGRAM

It is almost axiomatic that once an in-service training program on the black family has been implemented, staff will begin to raise important questions regarding the agency's central administration and the service delivery system. During the program conducted by the Center for Human Services, several agency issues arose during the small group discussion. For example, concern was expressed about the limited number of black staff members holding significant administrative positions within the agency, as well as the limited number of black professional counseling staff serving the black community. In order to ensure that these concerns were responded to, a mechanism was established by the planning committee. Group leaders were expected to write up issues as they were identified during the group discussions. These were then presented at regularly scheduled meetings with the executive director and other members of the central administration. In addition, two administrative staff members were given the responsibility of monitoring and reporting on subsequent actions taken once the problem and the appropriate levels of administrative involvement had been identified. The intent of this system was to ensure that a systematic method for collecting, sorting, and responding to staff concerns was established. An inevitable result of effective racial awareness training is conflict with the agency system that infuses all levels of staff. Therefore, it requires an openness on the part of the system to legitimate and support a viable program.[27]

CONTINUING EFFORT

This article has examined several issues and principles that warrant careful consideration by agencies planning in-service training programs on the black family. The provision of such training is considered essential and only a beginning. Changes in attitudes toward black people and the recognition that black people have a culture which should be highly valued will occur very gradually for most staff members, rapidly for some, and not at all for others. The slowness of manifest change often leads to discouragement, and it might be felt that all of the effort invested in the development of a meaningful experience for staff is of minimal value. However, social service agency personnel must appreciate the fact that racism remains an insidious force which continues to significantly influence every aspect of our lives. Agencies must continue to provide staff members with as many opportunities as possible to assist them in obtaining a greater understanding of black culture and its implications for practice, as well as a greater self-awareness.

Notes

1. Eleanor Kautz, "Can Agencies Train for Racial Awareness?" *Child Welfare* 55 (September–October 1976): 547–51.
2. JoAnne Selinske and Isadora Hare, "Culture Responsiveness in Child Protective Services. Information Paper 4" (Washington, DC: National Professional Resource Center on Child Abuse and Neglect, 1978), p. 3.
3. Alex Gitterman and Alice Schaeffer, "The White Professional and the Black Client," *Social Casework* 53 (May 1972): 280–91.

4. Daniel P. Moynihan, *The Negro Family: A Case for National Action* (Washington, DC: U.S. Department of Labor, Office of Policy, Planning and Research, 1965), p. 30.
5. Anita J. Delaney, ed., *The Black Task Force Report* (New York: Family Service Association of America, 1979), p. 21.
6. Robert Washington, "Social Work and the Black Perspective," *Journal of Applied Social Sciences* 3 (Spring/Summer 1979): 149–67.
7. Delaney, *The Black Task Force Report* p. 19.
8. Mary Westphal, "Reaction: Minority Sensitivity Training," *Public Personnel Review* 32 (April 1970): 77.
9. *Ibid.*, p. 77.
10. Kautz, "Can Agencies Train for Racial Awareness?" p. 550.
11. Andrew Billingsley, *Black Families in White America* (Englewood Cliffs, NJ: Prentice-Hall, 1968).
12. Selinske and Hare, "Cultural Responsiveness in Child Protective Services," p. 7.
13. Washington, "Social Work and the Black Perspective," p. 160.
14. Bernard Watson, "Education," in *The State of Black America*, ed. James Williams (New York: National Urban League, 1978), pp. 41–82.
15. Gene Lisitzky, *Four Ways of Being Human* (New York: Viking Press, 1956), p. 14.
16. James Banks, *Teaching the Black Experience* (Belmont, CA: Fearson Publishers, 1970), p. 35.
17. Wade Nobles, "A Formulative and Empirical Study of Black Families," Grant No. 90-C-255 (Washington, D.C.: U.S. Department of Health, Education and Welfare, Office of Child Development, 1974).
18. Delaney, *The Black Task Force Report* p. 9.
19. Wilhelmina P. Manns, "Significant Others in the Lives of Black Social Workers and White Social Workers," (Ph.D. diss., University of Chicago, School of Social Service Administration, 1981).
20. Nobles, "A Formulative and Empirical Study," p. 9.
21. Delaney, *The Black Task Force Report*, p. 11.
22. William B. Austin, "Why Ethnicity is Important to Blacks," *Urban League Review* 1 (Fall 1975): 15.
23. Don Crompton, "Minority Content in Social Work Education—Promise or Pitfall?" *Journal of Education for Social Work* 10 (Winter 1974): 9–18.
24. *Ibid.*, p. 11.
25. Westphal, "Reaction: Minority Sensitivity Training," p. 77.
26. John De Santo, "A Training Seminar for Supervisors of Minority Group Employees," *Public Personnel Review* 32 (April 1971): 71–76.
27. Kautz, "Can Agencies Train for Racial Awareness?" p. 551.

THE INFLUENCE OF MINORITY SOCIAL WORK STUDENTS ON AN AGENCY'S SERVICE METHODS*

Kathleen A. Olmstead

Institutionalized racism is easily detected by members of minority groups, but its manifestations can be difficult for others to recognize. Although it may be surprising to some, subtle forms of racism can be found in the practice of typical social work treatment modes. This becomes apparent when attention is focused on the problem. Borom, for example, has written that

> institutional racism, regardless of the setting, is so pervasive in this country that all of us must become experts earlier on in recognizing the tidal wave as it bears down upon us; and expend/waste excessive amounts of our life energies combating institutional racism— the huge wave that has us gasping and coughing, a wave that threatens to inundate, to drown us. Therefore, none of us need have a diagram drawn in order to recognize institutional racism. It is one of the most pervasive influences in our daily lives. The question of how to deal with it does require extensive study and knowledge of the specific setting in which it occurs if we are to develop effective strategies for dealing with institutional racism.[1]

In 1980, the author coordinated a training project for graduate students in social work who were members of minority groups. The purpose of this project was to promote permanency planning methods, to develop and implement a parent-aid program, and to

*Reprinted by permission of the author and publisher of *Social Work* 28:4 (July–August 1983) 308–312; copyright © 1983 National Association of Social Workers, Inc.

increase the pool of trained minority professionals. The staff of the participating agency, Child and Family Services, Hartford, Connecticut, were especially anxious to find out what the students felt could be done to improve service to minority clients, and they sought the interns' views on a variety of the agency's policies. This article will (1) discuss specific cultural, racial, and other issues that affect practice which were brought to the staff's awareness as a result of the student project, (2) recount efforts that have been made (subsequent to the beginning of the project) to combat inadvertent racism in the agency's treatment programs, and (3) present a case history to illustrate the effects of change in the agency's approach to service delivery as a result of some of the suggestions that were made by students.

THE CONTEXT OF THE PARTICIPATING AGENCY

Child and Family Services is a private child welfare and mental health agency whose history reflects the efforts of leading members of the white middle class and of upper-class philanthropists to address needs of "the less fortunate." Varying categories of the less fortunate are reflected in the different names the agency has had during its history—such names as The Female Beneficent Society, The Hartford Orphan Asylum, and Children's Village. These names indicate the progression in the agency from social concern for the unwed mother to the orphan, to the physically ill, and finally to the emotionally troubled.

The appearance of the agency and its environment resembles progressive institutions of the 1920s. Spacious lawns and attractive cottages are located on the outskirts of Hartford. The trees that border the inner city, however, serve as a symbolic barrier. The inner-city area is overpopulated and run down. Housing is limited, unemployment is high, illegal use of drugs is rampant and other crimes are common, and money for education and recreation is in short supply. The population is largely black and Hispanic, and most of the agency's clients come from this population.

It is easy for a nonminority person to be unaware that a minority person is likely to view the agency warily when walking on the grounds for the first time. One reason for this wariness is that the first people encountered—the security officer, the telephone operator-receptionist, the maintenance staff, and the fee clerks—are all likely to be Anglo. Also, because of loss of qualified minority staff prior to the time of the student project (and despite efforts to replace them), the permanency-planning professional staff, both administrators and practitioners, are white. The students expressed concern that this lack of minority staff at the professional level was a deterrent to the effectiveness of the program because minority staff are likely to remind their colleagues to be constantly aware of cultural and racial issues. The students, as well as minority employees in other departments of the agency, pointed out that the agency's employment of minority persons only in lower level positions appeared to be a reflection of racism. This criticism was taken seriously by the staff, because clients, under the best of circumstances, typically experience anxiety in the initial contact with a social agency. To admit to personal problems and feelings of helplessness is to expose one's greatest vulnerabilities. An accepting, nonjudgmental worker in a neutral setting is therefore essential in forming an alliance with the client.[2] This is obviously more difficult to accomplish if the client is a minority person and the worker is Anglo. As Griffith has said,

> Given the history and current status of black-white relations, a mutually accepting relationship may be difficult to achieve between the white therapist and black client. Cultural differences and ingrained attitudes toward blacks may interfere with the white therapist's ability to convey accurate empathy, respect, and appreciation for the black client. And given the propensity of clients in general toward guardedness in the initial stages of treatment, the black client is likely to be sensitive to all signals that disclose the white therapist's position regarding his racial status.[3]

When the client does not view the setting as neutral and does not trust the worker to be accepting, it is probable that the client's anxiety will be multiplied.[4] The students stressed that acknowledging this anxiety is an important step toward forming an alliance with the client.

It was well into the academic year before the students felt secure enough to disclose their uneasiness about communicating with their supervisors. As a result of this uneasiness, they admitted, they took certain actions on behalf of their clients that had not been discussed with supervisors for fear of disapproval. Examples included promoting a client's involvement in a neighboring minority church and transporting a client to the welfare office. Although these actions were entirely appropriate to case management, the students felt that the supervisors would not be attuned to the cultural basis for actions that the students wanted to take and would therefore criticize them for using poor clinical judgment. This kind of problem is parallel to problems having to do with cultural differences that can arise between workers and clients, and it points up the importance of open discussion with regard to these matters.

OUTREACH

The students judged the agency's outreach program to be weak. To improve it, they suggested that home visits should have a purpose beyond straightforward diagnosis or the convenience of the client or worker. The students stressed, to begin with, the value of understanding and relating to the minority client's culture. To take one example, it is important to know that Puerto Rican culture views the worker's willingness to accept hospitality as an indicator of the trustworthiness of the worker. The following clarifies this concept:

> Unlike the Anglo client, who expects a "professional"—distant yet efficient—therapist, the Puerto Rican client expects a more intimate relationship. The therapist should not be *un*professional in the sense of ethics, of course, but rather adopt a warm and more humanistic style for this group. Clinicians must be willing to go to their homes when invited, partake of refreshment, and answer questions related to personal background.[5]

It became clear after discussions between staff and students that making other community resources (schools, housing authority, and so forth) available to clients works best if negotiations are conducted in person rather than on the telephone, because these resources can appear as ominous as any traditional agency. The students also pointed out that important sources of adjunct services for clients existed beyond the Yellow Pages or the United Way directory; for example, the minister of the neighborhood church may know of a member interested in serving as a Big Brother to a child; the neighborhood grocer may know of odd jobs available for adolescents.

Although the agency has an active board-staff advocacy committee involved in legislative issues concerning outreach and other programs, the students said they were not informed of its activities and did not have access to it. They were not alone: most staff were unacquainted with the significant aspects of outreach in which the agency is involved. After they learned how the agency's outreach program operated, the students suggested some new ideas, such as making a direct effort to find potential clients; that is, to locate people who are not asking for or looking for services but who are clearly in need.

The students also felt that outreach in hiring practices is essential. The search for new staff, they said, should cover larger geographical areas, and advertising should be placed in newspapers and journals that serve minorities.

DIAGNOSTIC ISSUES

The students pointed out that, in their view, environmental factors were not given enough weight by staff when diagnosing clients. These factors often cause clients to receive labels that are negative, inaccurate, and misleading. An example is the label "below average intelligence" that minority children acquire when they have scored below the mean on intelligence tests that were designed without cultural differences taken into account. This kind of labeling will take place even when a particular test is not considered reliable for the purpose of measuring potential.

The students also felt that when inner conflicts are regarded by workers as more important than the environmental situation, treatment plans will reflect this view. More energy will get invested in helping clients to change and find new ways to deal with their situation than in trying to change the situation. There is, in other words, an acquiescence to "unalterable" aspects of the situation. Minority social workers, blacks in particular, view positive change and social growth as goals that *society* must work toward. Accordingly, they place less value on adaptation by an individual client as the solution to a problem.

It also came to the staff's attention that certain diagnoses of clients, especially hysteria and paranoia, are often questionable. Puerto Ricans' culturally conditioned suspicions of the white world, for example, can be defined as reasonable reactions to certain kinds of difficult situations. This problem has been noted previously in the literature:

> The *ataques* reaction is a form of hysteria characterized by hyper-kinetic seizures as a response to acute tensions and anxiety. It is a culturally expected reaction and an ordinary occurrence.[6]

> Grier and Cobbs (1968) suggest that this tendency of black clients [to be paranoid] represents a healthy cultural paranoia, a black norm that white therapists must learn to distinguish from patholog-ical states.[7]

The same cultural conditioning is frequently the reason for a minority child's failure to maintain eye contact, which may have nothing to do with a child's ability to relate to others. It is also important for agency workers to recognize that anger and depression in minority clients often results from privileges denied because of bias, not just as a result of intrapsychic factors.

Another important consideration is that the power structure in a minority family is often more important than it is in an Anglo family. Therapy, for example, will not be accepted if offered without the knowledge and consent of the Puerto Rican father (who may appear to be absent) or of the grandmother who is the head of a black family. Consequently, a diagnosis of resistance may in reality be a failure to engage a family because there has not been consultation with its executive.

The author's minority colleagues suggested that the focus should not be on client pathology. Instead, the competence that the minority client possesses should be emphasized—diagnostic labels should reflect clients' strengths, assets, and strivings and at the same time take into consideration that these clients are coping with a society that is more oppressive to its minority members than to others. Derogatory labels should be reserved for *social* ills, such as poverty, discrimination, unemployment, poor housing, lack of opportunity, and other indicators of oppression.

These concepts lead to an ecological perspective that stresses competence and the importance of a goodness of fit between people and their surroundings. As Maluccio has said,

One promising framework is provided by the ecological perspective and the life model of social work practice that is derived from it. This framework relies on a broad array of knowledge from such disciplines as general systems theory, ecology, evolutional biology, cultural anthropology, social psychology, and ego psychology. It offers a useful way of conceptualizing new directions and programs in child welfare in general, and in practice with parents in particular. For instance, it stresses that the focus on intervention is the family unit in the context of the environment. Professional intervention is addressed not to the child or parents as separate entities, but to the total family constellation as an open, dynamic system, and to the ongoing transaction with the impinging environment.[8]

Although the ecological perspective may be viewed by some as only a different way of stating traditional theory, the shift is new in focus. The person in pain is seen as one whose competence has been threatened by societal inadequacies and lack of supports rather than one who is unable to cope with stress because of personal inadequacy. This new perspective has important implications for treatment.

RETHINKING TREATMENT STRATEGIES

Several recommendations resulting from discussions with the students and staff are being implemented at the agency. For example, the ecological model will be the basis for diagnosis. The initial interview, therefore, will focus on the client's strengths and on promoting an understanding of the systems encountered daily (school, church, workplace) by him or her. Employment opportunities and courses in schools in the client's neighborhood will be explored to discover what is available to him or her. The worker will attend to potential resources in the client's environment, such as social networks and natural helping systems. Information about discrimination will be elicited and the client's feeling of power or powerlessness in dealing with systems will be evaluated. Home visits will be for the purpose of demonstrating a worker's interest in gaining knowledge of the client's situation and because the worker will be aware of the importance of accepting the client's hospitality. Goals will be set with cultural factors in mind, and the environmental approach will address the individual needs of each child.

Workers, acknowledging their lack of knowledge and under-standing of some important areas of the client's life, will invite the client to tell about his or her personal experiences with the welfare system, with discrimination, and with cultural differences. The worker will carefully examine family relationships, separating normal from destructive attachments while looking for inherent strengths of the close family. If these strengths exist, rather than striving for separation and individuation, the worker will attempt to strengthen the individual contributions that enable the family to function as a whole. This is especially important in the Puerto Rican family, where even such informal support systems as botanicas, herbalists, and spiritualists often are considered important resources by the family.[9]

Active intervention in systems affecting the client will be part of the treatment plan. For the client who feels caught in the foster care system, joint interviews with the client and with the public agency will be held. Service agreements spelling out the responsibilities of all parties will be made. Rather than reinforce the client's feeling of helplessness because the state agency has not performed as promised, the state worker—or, if required, his or her supervisor—will be confronted by an agency worker, so as to be certain that the state's efforts are directed toward the best interests of the client.

If a client fails to keep agency appointments, the worker will try to empathize with the client's discomfort with service agencies. The client will be encouraged to bring a friend to interviews if the friend can help interpret unfamiliar language, provide support to the client, or assist in empowering the client who feels helpless.

In permanency planning, the availability of responsible relatives as permanent caretakers for children can be easily overlooked. This is an important alternative to foster care or adoption when a child cannot live with his or her own parents.

Besides recognizing that social problems of minorities are the prime cause of many of their difficulties, workers must be aware that an effective alliance with a client requires that the worker demonstrate concern for larger issues. An active role as advocate at both the agency level and the legislative level will help build trust. Minority clients should be able to expect that the agency advocacy committee is actively working in pursuit of day care facilities for children, for example, and that the worker is aware of and responds to legislative issues of importance to minority people.

CASE HISTORY WITH TWO TREATMENT PLANS

A brief case history will be presented, followed by two alternative diagnostic summaries. One diagnosis reflects a traditional view; the other reflects an ecological orientation. (This case was considered a permanency-planning case because prevention of placement was the major goal.)

> Sandra Sanchez and her two sons, Jamie, age six, and Eddie, age five, were referred for help by the state's Department of Income Maintenance because the boys were having nightmares. Sandra, age twenty, had several siblings and was the child of a black mother and a Puerto Rican father who separated when Sandra was three. At age ten she was placed with an aunt in a neighboring town because her mother was hospitalized with a nervous breakdown, but two years later she ran away and returned to live with her mother. At age thirteen she became pregnant. A year after Jamie's birth, Eddie was born. Sandra and the children's Puerto Rican father married and had a variety of living arrangements, including living with the paternal grandparents, living briefly on their own, and living with the maternal grandmother. The marriage ended when Sandra's husband and her younger sister became lovers.
>
> Sandra entered a new relationship and remarried. She and her new husband, also a Puerto Rican, went to Puerto Rico for an extended visit, leaving the children with the maternal grandmother. They returned, got their own apartment, and assumed care of the children. Then her husband began to abuse her physically, so Sandra separated from him and returned to live with her mother. At the time of referral, Sandra and her two children had just moved to their own apartment in a housing project a few miles from the maternal grandmother's apartment, which was also in a project. The family's problems included, besides the nightmares, the children's reluctance to go out and play because they feared black children, who were the primary residents of the project, and their refusal to accept their mother's rules and discipline.
>
> When Sandra and Eddie came for the second interview, Eddie looked depressed and seemed to be lacking in energy. It was subsequently learned that he had not eaten for two days because there was no money for food. Clearly, Sandra felt isolated; she said she left her apartment only twice a month, when her welfare checks

came and she joined her mother to go grocery shopping. She slept most of the day and watched television at night. Jamie often missed school because Sandra was not awake to get him ready.

Diagnosis and Treatment Plan No. 1: A Traditional Clinical Approach

Sandra Sanchez, an immature young mother whose need for nurturance causes her to depend on relatives, is depressed and unable to function as a responsible parent. It appears that her relationships with men have been motivated by emotional needs rooted in unhappy childhood experiences. And just as her own childhood was fraught with insecurity and lack of nurturance, so Jamie and Eddie have not had the kind of consistent nurturance important to their sense of security. Their night fears may symbolize anxiety about losing what little security they feel. Although Eddie responds in a more openly frightened, unsure, and untrusting manner, Jamie responds with bravado. He sees himself as the strong and powerful head of the house and is afraid of allowing himself to be what he is, a six-year-old boy.

The treatment plan will include weekly individual sessions for Sandra and Jamie, and a psychiatric evaluation will determine Sandra's need for antidepressants. Sandra will be encouraged to join the boys when they go out to play, and she will be instructed in child management techniques. Assistance in budget planning will be provided to Sandra. Jamie will be offered supportive therapy wherein he can be allowed to assume the role of a little boy. If progress is not noted, a referral to protective services might be necessary to assure that the children are not neglected.

Diagnosis and Treatment Plan No. 2: Treatment Based on an Ecological Model

Sandra Sanchez is a young mother who has the capacity to nurture and enjoy her children but who functions best with the support of her extended close-knit family, particularly her mother. Sandra's housing, in a project several miles from her mother, has meant the loss of significant support. Sandra's mother and her mother's neighborhood are familiar and safe to the children, but they find the new neighborhood frightening, particularly because they are Puerto Rican and feel discriminated against by the blacks in the new neighborhood. Sandra's present isolation, which has resulted from her separation from her husband and the move away from her mother, leaves her feeling depressed. This contributes to her inability to care for the children appropriately. Jamie, seeming to recognize the absence of support for his mother, has attempted to take on the role of head of family.

The treatment plan will include assignment of a parent aide to visit Sandra at her apartment twice a week. The parent aide will offer support to Sandra, help her learn new child-management skills, and assist her with budget problems. Also, Sandra needs to learn ways of maintaining contact with relatives through more skillful use of public transportation and to gain support from people other than extended family members so that she will not feel so isolated and depressed when family members are not available. The parent aide will assist Sandra in getting to a health clinic for checkups and to the housing unit to apply for an apartment in the project where her mother lives.

Jamie will be seen individually and will be helped to understand that efforts are being made to have people help his mother so that he can be more appropriately involved in school and play. In individual sessions, Sandra will be helped to think about and plan for herself, Eddie, and Jamie. She will be encouraged to use the support available in her extended family while working on ways to become more independent, such as getting job training and learning homemaking skills. She will be helped to understand Jamie's need to know that she does not want him to be the head of the family. Sandra's mother will be included in an early session, either at the agency or at her apartment, so that she can contribute ideas about Sandra's use of the extended family. A school meeting will be set to explore the possibility of a group experience for Jamie and Eddie, which might help them become more comfortable in their school and in their neighborhood.

CONCLUSION

Since the beginning of the student project, the agency has opened an inner-city outreach office that, unlike other agency services, is staffed primarily by minority professionals who have already generated much enthusiasm in the process of delivering relevant services. For example, they have opened a walk-in service, changed the practice routine by allowing third parties to set up appointments rather than insisting on calls from prospective clients, developed an alliance with another inner-city agency that is involved with a youth job program, acquired offices in the same building that houses the Urban League, and formed community relationships with police and fire department officials. The agency's flexibility in allowing all this to occur has given renewed spirit to the staff. And in designing service delivery that is more acceptable for clients, they have also created a more attractive and rewarding work environment for themselves.

The outcome of the ecological treatment plan that was carried out in the case illustrated was that Sandra, Jamie, and Eddie remained a family unit. Prevention of placement is the most important goal of permanency planning, so the outcome can be considered successful. This case demonstrated how much more constructively an agency can treat a case when the agency is committed to the recognition of the client's unique culture, lifestyle, environmental stresses, inner strengths, and resources in societal networks.

The experience gained from training minority students has led to an approach that includes awareness of minority clients' mistrust of the world beyond the extended family; recognition of the need to provide outreach in an active, positive way; a shift in diagnosis from a pathological orientation to an ecological model that stresses competence; and treatment plans that reflect this orientation.

Incorporating these and other insights into staff training programs, bringing important minority-related issues to the attention of the board and administration, and being open to further changes in service delivery were judged by staff to be essential in improving relations with minority clients. To assure these changes, the following steps have been taken: new case record guidelines have been designed to encourage the worker to view cases from the ecological perspective. A school of social work faculty member is teaching a course at the agency on permanency planning, using the ecological model as the guiding premise. Supervisors, during meetings, stress the importance of using and teaching new approaches.

Also, steps have been taken by the agency to combat any implication of discriminatory hiring practices, with the result that affirmative action goals have been exceeded. There are more minority people serving on the agency's board of directors and in professional positions now than ever before. And workshops are being offered to raise the staff's awareness of minority issues. Thus, the student project has resulted in tangible progress at the agency. Most important, though, is the staff's commitment to continue to learn from minority students and minority clients, as well as from colleagues.

Notes and References

The student project described in this article was supported by Grant No. 5-T-01-MH-15971-02, Mental Health–Social Work Education, the National Institute of Mental Health.

1. Roy Borom, "Institutional Racism in Health Care Settings," in Jerome C. Stevenson, ed., *Black America: Reawakening for the Future* (Baltimore, Md.: National Association of Black Social Workers, 1976), p. 62.
2. Annette Garrett, *Interviewing, Its Principles and Methods* (New York: Family Service Association of America, 1942).
3. Marlin S. Griffith, "The Influence of Race on the Psychotherapeutic Relationship," *Psychiatry*, 40 (February 1977), p. 31.
4. *Ibid.;* Felisha S. Gwyn and Allie C. Kilpatrick, "Family Therapy with Low-Income Blacks: A Tool or Turn-Off?" *Social Casework*, 62 (May 1981), pp. 259–266; and Clifford J. Sager, Thomas L. Brayboy, and Barbara R. Waxenberg, "Black Patient—White Therapist," *American Journal of Orthopsychiatry*, 42 (April 1972), pp. 415–423.
5. Carol Hardy-Fanta and Elizabeth MacMahon-Herrera, "Adapting Family Therapy to the Hispanic Family," *Social Casework*, 62 (March 1981), p. 144.
6. Sonia Badillo Ghali, "Culture Sensitivity and the Puerto Rican Client," *Social Casework*, 58 (October 1977), p. 463.
7. Griffith, *op. cit.*, p. 32.
8. Anthony Maluccio, "An Ecological Perspective on Practice with Parents of Children in Foster Care," in Maluccio and Paula Sinanoglu, eds., *The Challenge of Partnership: Working with Parents of Children in Foster Care* (New York: Child Welfare League of America, 1981), p. 23.
9. Hardy-Fanta and MacMahon-Herrera, *op. cit.*

III. INTER-ETHNIC AND INTERRACIAL INTERVENTION

One cannot properly discuss social work practice with minorities without focusing on the inter-racial and inter-ethnic between relationships. Failure to recognize these variables has been the basis for most of the difficulty existing in the interview and therapeutic process in social work practice with minorities. The problem has been reciprocal: minority workers experience difficulties with European ethnic clients and by the same token non-minority workers experience difficulties with minority clients. Traditionally, more of the problems have existed between European ethnic with people of color rather than in the area where both the worker and client are members of the same ethnic or racial grouping. Therefore, this section is needed to highlight both the difficulties and the strategies and techniques which may be applicable.

This is not to suggest that there are no inherent difficulties in the interaction and relationship when worker and client are members of the same ethnic or racial group. The literature available, however, focuses primarily on the interaction and relationship between European ethnics with people of color. There is a conspicuous absence of literature on the implication of racism upon the European ethnics interaction and relationship with each other. Nonetheless, this is an area which deserves a great deal of further study and observation particularly in relation to the dynamics of racism in the client and worker, or when the client is prejudiced and the worker isn't, or the worker is prejudiced and the client isn't. There must be occasions when racial prejudice is identified in a white client by a white worker or when there may be conflict between the worker's and client's perceptions of other minorities.

In the worker/client relationship, when the worker and client are of different racial or ethnic groups, the problems of prejudice, bias, racism and ethnocentrism often emerge along with language difficulties, lack of insight, insensitivity, and lack of knowledge of the other's culture. The literature addresses many of these issues and proposes techniques and strategies which the worker may employ to mitigate the difficulties. At the same time, there is the reaction of people of color to the European-ethnic worker which may cause problems. Often the client may harbor the same prejudices, bias, racism and ethnocentrism as the worker, even though the European ethnic worker may be sensitive, understanding, and well prepared through observation of the culture, and of therapeutic skills. The worker must assist the client in overcoming his or her prejudices. The unprepared European ethnic worker may never be able to detect the negative attitude of the client, for the minority client need not demonstrate hostility to manifest his/her anger. By the same token, if the European ethnic worker is prepared, he or she must somehow deal with the presenting problem as well as the problem of communication which emerges. The fact is, the client will never be able to get to the underlying problems without first resolving the problem of communication. Nevertheless, the focus on this section of the reader is to analyze and evaluate the dynamics inherent in the relationship and interaction of the worker and client when in the various combinations of the same and/or different racial and ethnic groups. The only exception is that of the dynamics involved in the white worker/white client relationship. In the same manner that there are factors that the therapists must consider in their relationships with all clients around self-awareness, self-insight, growth, and proper utilization of the therapeutic process, additional recognition and understanding is needed in the multi-ethnic dyad. The summation of the acceptable implications for the multi-racial and multi-ethnic practice are as follows:

> Explore openness and willingness of the worker to take a risk by exposing self anxieties about race/ethnicity through exploring pertinent content with the client.

> Worker's exploration of overidentification with client in search of self-awareness.

> Recognition of worker that "I may be part of the problem." Worker becomes the first to confront the differences and conflicts in the worker/client relationship.

Worker's assumption that clients of color can accept the genuine and authentic feelings, actions, and behaviors of social caseworkers.

Worker stimulation and encouragement of negative expressions from clients of color regarding feelings toward the worker.

Worker must feel free to take risks in exposing his/her subjective perceptions in the therapeutic process.

Worker viewing behavior as functional and dysfunctional rather than deviant/normal.

Worker viewing the differences in the culture of People of Color and the white majority culture as real issues but not on which to determine behavior.

Worker looking at culture/ethnicity and race as merely being *different* and not superior or inferior to one another.

Worker recognizing, identifying and acknowledging the cultural, racial and ethnic biases and prejudice which may exist in self and destructive to the social work practice with People of Color. Worker recognizing and accepting the fact that "total freedom" from ethnic, racial and cultural biases is impossible.

Worker doing away with the need to "standardize" behavior as being acceptable only if it falls within norms of majority culture.

IMPLICATION FOR THE BLACK WORKER WITH MULTI-ETHNIC/MULTI-RACIAL CLIENTS

In addition to the general principles and ethics which all workers must employ in multi-ethnic and multi-racial education and practice there are specific concerns that each racial and ethnic group must be aware of in working with their in-group and inter-ethnic/social group. The implications for the Black Worker with multi-ethnic and multi-racial practice are as follows:

The Black therapist must accept and view the non-Black client as a unique individual rather than as a mere reflection or stereotype of the non-Black ethnic and racial group.

The Black therapist should clearly explore and analyze his/her psychic needs in working with non-Black clients in spite of the fact that the therapeutic relationship may be involuntary.

The Black therapist must become familiar with the dynamics of racism on the psyche of non-Black individuals and its implication for the worker/client interaction.

The Black therapist must recognize that he/she is not totally free of prejudice and should not respond to a posture of "prove that you are not prejudiced" and/or "prove your equality." The Black therapist should purge their unconsciousness for stereotypes which automatically associate Black people with everything negative and white people with everything positive.

The Black therapist should recognize that he/she has "power" and "authority" in the worker/client relationship and need not "prove it."

The Black therapist should understand the dynamics of sexual stereotypes and how they may interfere in the transference/counter transference phenomenon with non-Black clients.

The Black therapist must understand the significance that the symbol of color and race may play in the transference and counter-transference phenomenon with non-Black client.

The Black therapist should not be threatened by negative transference when the client may be hostile but recognize the strength in the ability of the client to express such feelings.

The Black therapist should not be misled by positive transference as being an indication that the issue of race may not be a concern in therapy.

IMPLICATION FOR WHITE WORKER WITH
MULTI-ETHNIC/MULTI-RACIAL CLIENTELE

The white worker must be concerned about the implications of multi-ethnic and multi-racial practice both from a self-awareness perspective as well as the fact that oftentimes whites are considered to be "part of the Problem." Therefore, this section explores the implications for white workers with multi-ethnic and multi-racial education and practice.

The white worker must recognize that he/she may never be totally free of racial prejudices and biasness but should avoid the dynamics of trying to "prove that they are free of racial prejudices." The white worker must become familiar with dynamics of white supremacy/Black oppression on the psyche of People of Color as it may affect the interaction with his/her relationship with People of Color.

The white worker must recognize the client's possible assimilation of the values and symbols in the American society as to "what Black isn't" and "what white is" as it may pertain to the dynamics of the white worker/Black client relationship.

The white worker must recognize anger, hostility, and apologetic behavior as possible indications of distrust in non-white clients which may present problems of self disclosure.

The white worker must analyze questions of guilt, over-identification and anti-racial attitudes and emotions which may exist in self.

The white caseworker should not be misled by a positive transference as being an indication that the issue of race is unimportant.

The white worker must recognize guilt, racial insecurities, anxieties, and fears of the unknown as a key cause of the white caseworker's inability to empathize with multi-racial clients.

The white worker should understand the dynamics of sexual stereotypes and how they may interfere in the trans-

ference/counter-transference phenomenon in the multi-ra-
cial/ethnic relationships.

The white worker should do away with the racist stereotypes
which automatically associate Black people with everything
negative and white people with everything positive. The white
worker should understand the significance that symbols of
color and race may play in the transference and countertransference phenomenon with People of Color.

The white worker must recognize that factors of Blackness
and whiteness does not present a problem in Black-white
interactions in a society free of negative attachment of Blackness and positive attachment to whiteness.

The white worker's openness and willingness to take a risk
exposing anxieties in self through exploring unknown territo-
ry with client.

The white therapist should not feel anxiety or threatened for
"not knowing" or "not understanding" but use his/her lack of
understanding to demonstrate a willingness to learn.

The white therapist must be willing to seek clarification and
understanding of the client's experience rather than assuming
the posture of "I understand."

The white worker must accept and view the non-white client
as a unique individual rather than as a mere reflection or
stereotype of the non-white race.

IMPLICATION FOR INTER-ETHNIC/INTER-RACIAL
PRACTICE AND SKILLS

There are a few dynamics which social work practitioners as a
unique member of a particular race or ethnic group must realize in
the therapeutic process with minority clients. In most instances, it
is not important as to whether the worker is a member of the
majority society or whether he/she is a member of the minority
society. The same basic principles and ethics must apply because
of the nature of social work theory and education. Some of these
principles are as follows:

Recognition of the unique cultural traits of each ethnic minority group as it pertains to the delivery of services.

Appreciation and sensitivity of unique cultural traits within each minority group.

Recognition and appreciation of the element of distrust when manifested in contact within each minority client.

Exploration early in the therapeutic process of the meaning of the differences in ethnicity, race, and culture.

Acceptance and acknowledgement of "not knowing it all" when applicable but expression of a willingness to learn and help.

Sensitivity and awareness of the unique conflicts which may exist between your ethnic/racial group and the minority ethnic/racial group being helped.

Recognition and acceptance that the theories of human behavior learned may not be adequate for understanding the behavior of the particular minority group being helped.

Use of the social dynamics and parameters inherent in a specific minority culture to resolve problems of personal adjustment.

Appreciation and willingness to learn the language of the minority culture being helped.

Looking at each minority client as an individual and not as a reflection of what "you might subjectively think" about that specific minority group.

Use and understanding of the minority client's cultural definition and significance of his/her social and psychological problem as a measure of treatment. Awareness and recognition of linguistic interpretation of a minority group's use of symbols and words as they may differ from the dominant society even though the same words may be used.

Recognition that culture is fluent, changing and not static; therefore, there must be a readiness to constantly assess and reassess and not maintain a rigid view of culture in relationship to the therapeutic process.

CROSS-CULTURAL COUNSELING AND PSYCHOTHERAPY: A HISTORICAL PERSPECTIVE, IMPLICATIONS FOR RESEARCH AND TRAINING*

Elaine J. Copeland

Attention to cross-cultural counseling and therapy is a relatively new occurrence. Most of the literature on this topic has appeared within the last 2 decades. Identifying research that addresses the effects of cultural difference between client and counselor and those that examine cultural variables as they relate to appropriate theory and practice is often complex. In many studies cultural variables are confounded with socioeconomic status (SES). The current concern for counseling the culturally different is a product of a number of societal changes. One major influence, the Civil Rights Movement of the 1960s, and a recognition that the United States is a pluralistic rather than a monolithic society raised the consciousness of many professionals. They began to recognize that to be culturally different from the dominant society need not be viewed as being inferior. In order to review the current status of cross-cultural counseling, it is necessary to understand its development. The primary objectives of this article are to: (1) trace the historical development of cross-cultural counseling and therapy, (2) examine relevant theory and research, and (3) discuss implications for cross-cultural counselor training.

*Reprinted with permission from *The Personnel and Guidance Journal* 62:1 (September 1983) 10–15; copyright © 1983 American Association for Counseling and Development. No further reproduction authorized without further permission of AACD.

A HISTORICAL OVERVIEW

American society has as a major cornerstone an individualistic philosophy that values the uniqueness and worth of the individual regardless of race, creed, color, sex, or national origin. Founded on the principles of life, liberty, and the pursuit of happiness for all members of its population as proclaimed in the Declaration of Independence, this country at least in principle supports the concept of individualism, the lack of rigid class lines, the importance of the work ethic and the incentive to exercise one's talents to the best of one's ability (Shertzer & Stone, 1974). It is little wonder that the Counseling and Guidance, Mental Health, and Child Study movements of the early 1900s reflected the lofty ideals of the society.

Counseling is primarily a western creation. According to Sue (1981), all definitions of counseling encompass certain western-oriented philosophical assumptions. Included in these are:

(a) concern and respect for the uniqueness of clients, (b) the worth of the individual, (c) a high priority placed on helping others to attain their own self-determined goals, (d) the freedom and opportunity to explore one's characteristics and to develop one's potential, and (e) a future-oriented promise of a better life. (p. 3)

It seems apparent that the forerunners of counseling and psychotherapy would reflect American philosophy. The impetus for development of the counseling and guidance movement grew in response to this philosophy, societal needs, and pressures to ensure education for the masses. At the turn of the century, the influx of immigrants to this country as well as the migration of racial minorities and other rural dwellers to large urban centers, coupled with the Industrial Revolution, created a need for vocational training and counseling services (Aubrey, 1977).

Educational historians credit Jesse B. Davis with introducing counseling and guidance in educational settings and Frank Parsons with establishing vocational guidance in community agencies. The initial aim of this movement was to match a potential worker with a suitable vocation. Psychometrics and subsequently the adoption of trait-factor psychology gave vocational guidance respectability and a foothold in educational settings. Although formal recognition of counseling did not occur until the early

1940s, the mental health and child study movements as well as the introduction of psychoanalysis to the United States in 1909 all provided a climate for counseling to flourish. The concepts of self-determination and freedom were major factors in changing the direction of guidance to incorporate counseling in the 1940s.

This change in direction was greatly influenced by Carl Roger's client-center counseling, which began to prosper in the 1950s. During the early 1950s, the aim of the profession seemed to be one of assimilation. Group differences were deemphasized and the goal of guidance and counseling was to assist various racial and cultural groups to become members of the larger society. The use of such terms as *disadvantaged* and *culturally deprived* to refer to racial minority populations seem to infer inferiority rather than difference. Professionals were ethnocentric in their orientation and used the western dominant culture as the standard to which all other groups were to aspire. It is interesting to note that equal access to education, housing, and public facilities were still to elude a large segment of America's population.

Only after the 1954 Supreme Court Decision of *Brown vs. the Kansas Board of Education* and the Civil Rights movement that followed nearly a decade later, did some members of the professions begin to recognize the need to devote attention to various cultural groups in the population (Patterson, 1958; Wrenn, 1962). During the same period, a number of questions faced those in the counseling and guidance profession. One of the major issues was whether counseling should deal exclusively with normal development needs or include concerns of a psychological nature. This dichotomy was blurred by the outcries from various groups demanding that counseling be relevant to their particular needs. Initiated primarily by Black professionals, counseling and guidance, especially in educational settings, was singled out as one tool, instrumental in maintaining the status quo. The counseling and guidance movement that philosophically was designed to serve the masses focused on the average homogeneous White student, and various forms of psychotherapy were available primarily to elite segments of society. Since America's educational system was created to serve all of its people, it was singled out as a means of rectifying many inequalities and was attacked for the discrepancies between philosophy and practice. The new wave of discontent and the emphasis on racial pride and cultural identity initiated in the early 1960s served as the impetus for other powerless and disenfranchised groups (i.e., Hispanics, American-Indians, Asian-Americans, women, and more recently the handicapped, veterans, and the elderly), to demand relevant services. No longer was assimilation the desired goal. A recognition of and an appreciation for cultural differences became major objectives.

Psychotherapy, too, is primarily a western creation. Although some forms of therapy are practiced in nonwestern societies, cultural comparison on process, goals, and outcomes cannot readily be made. Prince (1980) has maintained that only very limited segments of the world's population, literate societies, are capable of engaging in the psychotherapeutic process as defined by western standards. Influenced primarily by Freud and his followers and more recently by behaviorists, psychotherapy is a process that assumes a certain level of sophisticated cognitive functioning. Of those studies that have examined mental disorders outside the United States, most have focused on identifying deviant behavior and comparing rates of incidence and symptoms to those found in western cultures. Sundberg (1981) found that most research and practice oriented reports on cross-cultural counseling have focused on white, middle-class English speaking counselors, working with Black or Hispanic clients in the United States or in Great Britain, those exceptions being a few studies dealing with international student populations in the United States (Higginbotham, 1979). Cross-cultural counseling and psychotherapy in this article will be discussed primarily in this context, and it is recognized that some practitioners have transported counseling.

CROSS-CULTURAL COUNSELING: A DEFINITION

Recognizing that there is much overlapping, Draguns (1981) has made a distinction between counseling and therapy. Counseling is viewed as a process that facilitates problem solving, and therapy is described as an activity concerned with changing persons, for instance, their overt behaviors and personalities. The use of the term *cross-cultural counseling* in the literature is a rather new occurrence receiving attention only during the last 2 decades. It is now used to describe various counseling situations. To create further confusion, such terms as *transcultural counseling, inter-*

cultural counseling, and *minority counseling* are frequently used interchangeably in the literature.

Defining culture is an equally difficult task, since Kroeber and Kluckhohn (1952) in reviewing the literature found over 150 different definitions. A global definition first introduced by Herskovits (1955) refers to culture as the human made part of the environment. Different groups of individuals who share a common experience, history, and language or dialect, and who also reside in the same geographic location are referred to as members of a particular cultural group. Although members of a particular nationality may share a common culture, culture should not be equated with nationality or race. Small groups of individuals within a racial group or nationality may represent specific cultural groups, since experiences and patterns of behavior and language may vary among members of a particular race. Of primary significance to those concerned with social interaction are an individual's perception of the environment. To focus on perceptions, Triandis introduced the concept of "subjective culture," which he defined as the perceptions that an individual has regarding the social environment (Triandis, Vassiliou, Vassiliou, Tanaka, & Shanmugam, 1972). Included as variables of subjective culture are norms, roles, belief systems, laws, and values. Cross-cultural counseling then may be defined as a counseling relationship in which two or more of the participants differ with respect to cultural background, values, norms, roles, and life style and methods of communicating (Sue, 1981).

Wohl (1981) has presented a number of situations in which cross-cultural counseling and therapy may occur. These include: (a) situations where the counselor-therapist is a member of the dominant American population and the client is a member of a racial or ethnic minority, (b) where an individual from a western-oriented country transports therapy to a foreign nonwestern country, (c) where counseling services are offered to foreign students in the United States, (d) and where ethnic-racial minority professionals counsel members of the "dominant" culture or members of another subcultural group. He further illustrates how differences in cultural variables, such as in religious beliefs between client and counselor, may justifiably be referred to as cross-cultural counseling. Torrey (1972) has provided a list of active ingredients in counseling-therapy that are necessary for cross-cultural interactions: naming and explaining the problem, fulfilling the need for acceptance and warmth, exercising one's status and prestige, effective communication, and conveying one's understanding. Mendel (1972) has listed a number of universal (etic) variables of all psychotherapeutic relations. He maintains that all therapy involves hope, learning, relationship, and a here-and-now encounter. In behavioral concrete operational terms, he indicates that universally counseling and particularly therapy include confrontation, exploration of the past, exploring new alternative behaviors, and transferring these behaviors to everyday life situations.

THEORY BUILDING

A review of the literature suggests that while many authors have been concerned with needs of specific subcultures, coverage has often been fragmented. Early writers took a provincial view and were generally concerned with one racial-minority group. Recognizing a need for generating relevant theory applicable across cultures, Sue (1977) made a call to the profession to examine cultural dimensions. Much of his recent work has focused on the relevance or lack of relevance of western counseling assumptions as they relate to cultural variations (Sue & Sue, 1977; 1978; 1981).

It is Sue's (1981) contention that the following assumptions have been instrumental in developing counseling theory and in guiding mental health and counseling practices:

1. *Definition of Activity:* Western culture stresses an active modality of doing. A being orientation that emphasized a more passive, contemplative role is the antithesis to American values. . . . Activism is the mode of the problem solving and decision making. Learning is active and American emphasis is on planning behavior.
2. *Definition of Social Relations:* Americans value equality and formality in relating to others. Friendships are many, of short commitment, nonbinding, and shared. Obligations to groups are limited.
3. *Motivation:* Achievement and completion are valued as healthy. The worth of an individual is measured to objective visible and materialistic possessions.

4. *Perception of the World:* The world is viewed distinctive from humankind to be mastered and controlled.
5. *Perception of Self and Individual:* The self is seen as separate from the physical world and others. . . . The importance of a person's identity is reinforced by the educational system. Autonomy is encouraged, and emphasis is placed on solving one's own personal problems, acquiring one's own possessions, and standing up for one's own rights.

Cross-cultural counseling theorists have been concerned with cultural, class, and language differences, differences in cognitive styles, and problems of identity, as well as acculturation of various subcultural groups. In this regard not only have they relied on psychological personality theories but on the works of cultural anthropologists to provide a framework for examining different value orientations. Kluckhohn's classification of values has served as a framework for understanding how a particular subgroup may vary when compared to a western value orientation (Kluckhohn & Strodbeck, 1961).

Trimble (1981) has compared western thinking to that of some American Indian subcultures and has provided an illustration of how conflict may develop between a majority counselor and an Indian client. Differences on value dimensions may create misunderstanding during the counseling process. For example, counseling and psychotherapy have traditionally focused on the intrapsychic worlds of clients rather than on interpsychic factors; counseling-therapy has been future oriented, and some subcultures have been oriented to the past or present; counseling theories have emphasized the ability of the client to make changes in the environment and, yet various cultures rely more heavily on external forces to control their lives. Because self-direction is viewed as a major concept in most counseling theories, Sue (1978) utilizing Rotter's (1966) Locus of Control Theory proposes a variation of the model for understanding the world views of clients who are culturally different for dominant American culture. In this model he includes not only locus of control but locus of responsibility and explains how certain orientations may require different counseling styles and processes. In addition to Sue, the works of Pedersen, Draguns, Lonner, and Trimble (1981); Marsella and Pedersen (1981), and Brislin (1981) have focused on the "cultural inclusiveness of counseling." These authors suggest that influences both within the field of counseling and from other disciplines (i.e., anthropology, cross-cultural psychology, psychiatry and sociology) have led to this development. Most recent publications are now acknowledging the importance of cultural variables, and several authors have compared the cultural differences of racial minority populations in relation to counseling needs from a global perspective (Atkinson, Morten & Sue, 1979; Henderson, 1979; Marsella & Pedersen, 1981; Pedersen et al., 1981; Sue, 1981; Walz & Benjamin, 1979). To these, only Pedersen et al. (1981) and Marsella and Pedersen (1981) have extended their discussion to include international student populations in the United States.

The concepts of racial identity and acculturation have also received attention (Cross, 1972; Jackson, 1975; Vontress, 1971). Although most identity developmental models have primarily been generated by Black theorists, these models provide a framework for examining cultural assimilation of other groups. A comprehensive model, the "Minority Identity Model" is presented by Atkinson et al. (1979).

In summary, those involved in theory building for cross-cultural counseling have moved from a provincial to a more global perspective. Attention is now being given to cultural values and perceptions of various subcultural groups in the United States as well as to international student populations. Although relying heavily on etic (universal) psychological concepts, many theorists are focusing on research conducted to examine emic (cultural) variables of subcultural groups. Although various theories are now being generated to explain how cultural groups respond to the social environment, the ones discussed in this section were selected to focus on several salient issues. Subcultural groups may differ from the dominant culture in the way they view themselves in relation to the world and in the values they hold. Since they function in at least two cultures, they must learn to be bicultural. A major goal for counselors and therapists is to understand how clients respond to the social environment and the identity problems they may encounter. The models described are not all inclusive and should be viewed only as useful examples of developing theory.

A REVIEW OF RESEARCH ON CLIENT-
COUNSELOR/THERAPIST DIFFERENCES

Current literature indicates that a number of researchers have examined the effects of client-counselor difference in relation to the counseling process. Since the effectiveness of counseling and psychotherapy depend primarily upon an interpersonal relationship, many studies have focused on differences in the client and counselor on demographic dimensions (SES, age, sex, and race) and how these differences influence preferences, expectations, goals, and outcomes (Garfield, 1978; Lorion, 1978; Parloff, Waskow & Wolfe, 1978).

Many of the initial studies examined the relationship of client-counselor demographic differences to attrition, type of service received, and expectations but did not explicitly focus on cultural variables (i.e., norms, roles, values). Only recently have client-counselor differences been discussed in the context of culture variations (Lambert, 1981; Marsella & Pedersen, 1981; Sue, 1981). Although the effectiveness of various theoretical approaches (i.e., insight, behavioral and cognitive counseling-therapy) with subcultural groups, primarily those of low SES, has received some attention in the literature, most practitioners who are concerned with cross-cultural counseling suggest that total commitment to any one approach is inappropriate. Rather it is suggested that an eclectic approach, one in which the counselor-therapist alters techniques in order to respond to the needs of individual clients with specific problems is most desirable. This discussion then will be limited to a cursory review of the research on how client-counselor differences effect client-counselor perceptions and interactions.

Parloff et al. (1978) have classified variables that influence client-counselor-therapist interactions into three general categories: (a) counselor-therapist variables independent of the counseling setting (i.e., personality, mental health, sex, SES, experience, and training), (b) second within the counseling setting (therapist style and contribution to the relationship), and (c) third client-counselor variables in combinations such as those alluded to earlier, congruence or incongruence in counselor-client expectations, of the counselor's role, and the perceptions of the function of the counselor process, as well as differences in values, cognitive styles, and both verbal and nonverbal means of communicating. In reviewing the research focusing on client variables, Garfield (1978) found that most studies to date have dealt with the effects of differences in client-counselor demographic variables. It is understandable that since race and SES are significant variables in social interactions in the United States, and many racial minorities are disproportionately represented among the poor and underclass that many researchers would view these as salient variables in the counseling process. Although the results are inconclusive, some studies have revealed that persons of low SES have different expectations both of the counselor's role as well as the goals of counseling when compared to the service provider. Whether this expectation is primarily due to SES or to cultural values, independent-class differences are debatable. Some international student populations have expectations, however, consistent with low SES American clients. That is, they view counselor-therapists as authority figures, advice givers, and resources for obtaining information (Tan, 1967). Some foreign-student populations and low SES-American clients have expected a more directive guidance and nurturant-oriented counselor rather than the participation expectation (i.e., the client assuming an active role in the interaction) held by most middle-SES counselors-therapists.

Further, Garfield (1978) has suggested that while many studies show that such demographic variables as race, sex, and SES affect the attrition rate and type of service received of those seeking service, not enough attention has been paid to the biases of the counselor-therapist. Research examining attributions that the counselor makes about culturally different clients and that clients make regarding the counselor-therapist is one area that needs attention with implications not only for cross-cultural counselor training but for precounseling orientations for culturally different clients. Several authors have suggested (Garfield, 1978; Lambert, 1981; Lorion, 1978; Parloff et al., 1978) that multimethod research both at the subcultural group-level and at the individual level of both client and counselor is needed. In addition to research on client expectancies, preferences, and satisfaction, studies that examine therapist-counselor biases and the impact of cross-cultural counselor training is necessary. Multimethods of evaluation are essential. More research to examine the effects of training should be forthcoming as various methods as those described in the following section are incorporated into traditional counselor education or counseling psychology programs.

APPROACHES TO TRAINING

Various authors have suggested that training programs should include at least four components (Copeland, 1982; Henderson, 1980; Sue, 1981): a consciousness raising, a cognitive understanding, an effective, and a skills component. The consciousness raising component consists of utilizing various activities to assist the counselor in becoming familiar with a particular culture. Not only is the trainee encouraged to explore the history of a cultural group but to be knowledgeable of the present environmental conditions. A second step in training included both cognitive and experiential learning. Henderson (1979) stressed the importance of systematically collecting ethnographic data. General knowledge that includes the geographical location (i.e., region of the country, urban, or rural setting where most of the population resides), socioeconomic status (SES) of most of the members of the group, family structure and socialization patterns, rates of unemployment, level of literacy, and educational attainment is useful.

Henderson (1979) has listed, for example, several major steps that a high school counselor might undertake prior to working with certain subcultural groups: (a) study the history, (b) spend time as a participant observer, (c) examine school achievement and work history, (d) examine self in terms of personal biases, (e) study the attitudes that the majority society has about members of the population. The use of a cultural broker or interpreter of the culture may be useful at this level of training (Brislin, 1981). Although Brislin (1981) recognized the importance of studying the history of a group of people in the context of the society in which they live, he cautioned professionals on the problems inherent in categorizing individuals who are members of a particular subcultural group. Counselors-therapists may form and maintain stereotypes and have difficulty in reacting to individual factors. While consciousness raising, several authors stress the importance of relating learned concepts to skills training (Sue, 1981; Traindis et al., 1972; Triandis, 1977). Pedersen's (1978) triad model illustrates the value of role-playing techniques in skills training. In this simulation activity the counselor in training interacts with a culturally different client as well as an "anticounselor," a person of the same cultural group of the client who injects the conflicts resulting from cultural differences into the interaction. Triandis (1977), while not addressing specifically the training of counselors, has presented an empirically tested model for predicting behavior in interpersonal interactions. His model includes both learned behavior (habits) and behavioral intentions. Behavioral intentions are a function of social, affective, and cognitive influences. The social influences are a function of norm roles, values, and self-concept.

A thorough knowledge of the model and of cross-cultural research on specific subgroups should assist counselor-therapists in understanding which components are more influential in predicting behaviors of their culturally different clients. It is recommended that understanding the dynamics of interpersonal interactions can be achieved by attribution training, sensitivity training, and behavior modification (Triandis, 1977). Other methods include the microcounseling model described by Ivey (1971) and while not developed primarily for counselor training, the use of the cultural assimilator was developed initially by Fielder, Mitchell and Triandis (1971).

Once the trainee has received simulation training, a supervised practicum or intern in an appropriate setting is desirable. This experience should provide direct interpersonal interaction with clients of a different cultural background along with an instructional component that allows feedback from the supervisor as well as others in training.

Those involved in training counseling professionals have suggested various approaches to incorporate content into graduate programs (Copeland, 1982; Sue, 1981). Copeland (1982) while suggesting four basic approaches to training: separate course, interdisciplinary, integration, area of concentration model, recognized the problems inherent in each. She feels that these approaches are complimentary and may be used separately or in combination. Sue (1981) has pointed out that most programs to date have stressed consciousness raising and affective and cognitive training but have not adequately addressed the skills component. The following represent a summary of the types of competencies that should develop in skills-building areas:

1. The counselor-therapist must develop the skills to make "isomorphic attributions" about the client's behavior. He or she must understand how the client perceives the social environment and evaluate the behavior in that context.
2. The counselor must be able to identify the problem of the culturally different client and select appropriate techniques of remediation.
3. The counselor-therapist must be able to determine client expectancies concerning the outcomes of the counseling process.
4. The counselor must have the skills to assist the client in transferring insights and behaviors learned in the counseling setting to everyday situations once counseling-therapy is terminated.
5. Psychological tests have been traditionally used in counseling settings. The therapist must develop skills to determine whether tests developed in a dominant culture are relevant for use with specific subcultural groups. When and if these tests are used, the cultural background and experiences of clients must be considered in the interpretation.
6. The counselor-therapist must also be able to focus on his or her own behavior and understand personal biases.

CONCLUSION

Attention to cross-cultural counseling and therapy should continue to increase. Counseling professionals now seem more aware of differences across cultures and the problems inherent in attempting to serve culturally different clients. This recognition should be helpful in providing services not only to various subcultural populations in the United States but to international student populations. As developing countries institute formal education programs to serve specific segments of their populations, the need for counseling and guidance will become more acute. One would expect that the counseling professional educated in the

United States and other western countries will return to their homelands and begin to develop relevant programs utilizing both etic and emic concepts. The proliferation of literature on cross-cultural counseling and therapy, especially since 1970, indicates that this is a viable and growing field.

References

Atkinson, D. R., Morten, G., & Sue, D. W. *Counseling American minorities: A cross-cultural perspective*. Dubuque, IA: Wm. C. Brown, 1979.

Aubrey, R. F. Historical development of guidance and counseling: Implications for the future. *Personnel and Guidance Journal*, 1977, *55* (6), 228–295.

Brislin, R. W. *Cross-cultural encounters: Face-to-face interaction*. New York: Pergamon Press, 1981.

Copeland, E. J. Minority populations and traditional counseling programs: Some alternatives. *Counselor Education and Supervision*, 1982, *21* (3), 187–193.

Cross, W. E. The Negro-to-black conversion experience. *Black World*, 1971, *20*, 13–27.

Draguns, J. G. Cross-cultural counseling and psychotherapy: History, issues, and current status. In A. J. Marsella & P. B. Pedersen (Eds.), *Cross-cultural counseling and psychotherapy*. New York: Pergamon Press, 1981.

Fielder, F., Mitchell, R., & Triandis, H. The cultural assimilator: An approach to cross-cultural training. *Journal of Applied Psychology*, 1971, *55*, 95–102.

Garfield, S. L. Research on client variables in psychotherapy. In S. L. Garfield & A. E. Bergen (Eds.), *Handbook of psychotherapy and behavior change*. New York: Wiley, 1978.

Henderson, G. *Understanding and counseling ethnic minorities*. Springfield, Ill.: Charles Thomas, 1979.

Herskovits, M. *Cultural Anthropology*. New York: A. A. Knopf, 1955.

Higgingbotham, H. N. Cultural issues in providing psychological service for foreign students in the United States. *International Journal of Intercultural Relations*, 1979, *3*, 49–85.

Ivey, A. E. *Microcounseling: Innovations in interviewing training*. Springfield, Ill.: Charles C. Thomas, 1971.

Jackson, B. Black identity development MEFORM. *Journal of Educational Diversity & Innovation*, 1975, *2*, 19–25.

Kluckhohn, F. R. & Strodbeck, F. L. *Variations in value orientation*. New York: Harper & Row, 1961.

Kroeber, A. L. & Kluckhohn, C. *Culture: A critical review of concepts and definitions*. New York: Vintage Books, 1952.

Lambert, M. J. Evaluating outcomes variables in cross-cultural counseling and psychotherapy. In A. J. Marsella and P. B. Pedersen (Eds.), *Cross-cultural counseling and psychotherapy.* New York: Pergamon Press, 1981.

Lorion, R. P. Research on psychotherapy and behavior change with disadvantaged: Past, present, and future directions. In S. L. Garfield & A. E. Bergin (Eds.), *Handbook of psychotherapy and behavior change.* New York: Wiley, 1978.

Mandel, W. M. Comparative Psychotherapy. *International Journal of Psychoanalytic Psychotherapy*, 1972, *1*, 117–126.

Marsella, A. J. & Pedersen, P. B. *Cross-cultural counseling and psychotherapy.* New York: Pergamon Press, 1981.

Parloff, M. E., Waskow, I. E. & Wolfe, B. E. Research on therapist variables in relation to process and outcome. In S. L. Garfield & A. E. Bergin (Eds.), *Handbook of psychotherapy and behavior change.* New York: John Wiley & Sons, 1978.

Patterson, C. H. The place of values in counseling and psychotherapy. *Journal of Counseling Psychology*, 1958, *5*, 216–223.

Pedersen, P. B. The triad model. *Personnel and Guidance Journal*, 1977, *56*, 94–100.

Pedersen, P. B. Four dimensions of cross-cultural skill in counseling training. *Personnel and Guidance Journal*, 1978, *56*, 480–484.

Pedersen, P. B., Draguns, J. G., Lonner, W. J. & Trimble, J. E. (Eds.). *Counseling across cultures* (2nd ed.). Honolulu: University Press of Hawaii, 1981.

Prince, R. H. Variations in psychotherapeutic procedures. In A. J. Marsella, R. Tharp & T. Ciborowski (Eds.), *Perspective on cross-cultural psychotherapy.* New York: Academic Press, 1980.

Rotter, J. B. Generalized expectancies for internal versus external control of reinforcement. *Psychological Monograph*, 1966, *80*, (whole No.) 609.

Shertzer, B. & Stone, S. *Fundamentals of guidance.* Boston: Houghton Mifflin, 1974.

Sue, D. W. & Sue, D. Barriers to effective cross-cultural counseling. *Journal of Counseling Psychology*, 1977, *24*, 420–429.

Sue, D. W. World views and counseling. *Personnel and Guidance Journal*, 1978, *56*, 458–462.

Sue, D. W. *Counseling the culturally different: Theory and Practice.* New York: John Wiley & Sons, 1981.

Sundberg, N. D. Cross-cultural counseling and psychotherapy: A research overview. In A. J. Marsella & P. B. Pedersen (Eds.), *Cross-cultural counseling and psychotherapy.* New York: Pergamon Press, 1981.

Tan, H. Intercultural study of counseling expectancies. *Journal of Consulting Psychology*, 1967, *14*, 122–30.

Torrey, E. F. *The mind game: Witchdoctors and psychiatrists.* New York: Emerson Hall, 1972.

Triandis, H. C., Vassiliou, V., Vassiliou, G., Tanaka, Y. & Shanmugam, A. V. (Eds.). *The analysis of subjective culture.* New York: John Wiley & Sons, 1972.

Triandis, H. C. *Interpersonal behavior.* Monterrey, CA: Brooks/Cole Publishing Co., 1977.

Trimble, J. G. Value differentials and their importance in counseling American Indians. In P. B. Pedersen, J. G. Draguns, W. J. Lonner & J. Trimble (Eds.), *Counseling across cultures* (2nd ed.). Honolulu: University of Hawaii, 1981.

Vontress, C. E. Racial differences: Impediments to rapport. *Journal of Counseling Psychology,* 1971, *18* (1), 7–13.

Walz, G. R. & Benjamin, L. (Eds.). *Transcultural counseling: Needs, programs and techniques.* New York: Human Sciences Press, 1978.

Wolh, J. Intercultural psychotherapy: Issue, questions, and reflections. In P. B. Pedersen, J. G. Draguns, W. J. Lonner & J. Trimble (Eds.), *Counseling across cultures* (2nd ed.). Honolulu: University of Hawaii, 1981.

Wrenn, G. The encapsulated counselor. *Harvard Educational Review,* 1962, *32* (4), 444–449.

A STUDY OF PSYCHOSOCIAL CASEWORK WITH CHICANOS*

Ernesto Gomez, Louis A. Zurcher, Buford E. Farris, and Roy E. Becker

Evaluating the effectiveness of casework services is one of the most challenging problems facing social work today. Generally, efforts to conduct such investigations have suffered from an absence of vigorous research methodology and have usually yielded ambiguous results.[1] With a few notable exceptions, little research exists to document the results of casework services or the effects of the varied techniques employed in casework.[2]

Despite this scarcity, the literature implies that social casework is irrelevant and that psychosocial casework, in particular, is ineffective with Chicano clients.[3] Proponents of this view, however, have not substantiated their criticism with empirical data. Their presentations tend to be theoretical, based on subjective impressions and assumptions, or to be supported primarily by anecdotal evidence and unsystematic use of case material.[4] Brown, however, suggested that psychosocial therapy can be used successfully with Chicano clients, when therapy is provided within the framework of the Chicano cultural system.[5] But, Brown's discussion, like most others, is theoretically rather than empirically based. In fact, Brown recognized this shortcoming by indicating that a systematic study of the effects of psychosocial casework with Chicanos should be conducted.

*Reprinted by permission of the authors and *Social Work* 30:6 (November–December 1985) 477–482; copyright © 1985, National Association of Social Workers, Inc.

To address the lack of research in this area, the authors conducted an exploratory study to evaluate empirically a model of short-term psychosocially oriented casework with Chicano clients. Although the conceptualization and the application of the psychosocial casework model vary from setting to setting, the model is generally based on a flexible theoretical system that allows it to be used in situations that emphasize the psychological or the social/cultural sphere of human needs.[6] In the study, which was conducted at two community mental health centers, the model of casework described by staff members approximated Hollis's conceptualization.[7] This conceptualization uses the person-in-situation gestalt to designate the whole system of the client in interaction with other people in the immediate milieu and with institutions. The model's intervention strategies focus on the present with frequent examination of the client's history or the etiological aspects of the client's life. Attention to the immediate social milieu within the psychosocial casework model encompasses strategies involving an awareness of culture-oriented behavior.

The study presented here was not a test of psychosocial casework per se. The psychosocial casework model was used to identify the behaviors of workers employing this approach. The data on the outcomes and techniques of psychosocial casework were obtained as the initial phase of a large comparative study examining a newly developed culture-oriented intervention model.[8] The findings reported here address two questions: (1) What are the effects of psychosocially oriented casework with Chicano clients? and (2) What are the behaviors workers exhibit that clients associate with service satisfaction?

METHODOLOGY

Casework services were evaluated using a single-group, pretreatment-post-treatment design applied to short-term treatment (six to eight weeks) at two community mental health centers.[9] Both centers are located in the same large South Texas community and serve primarily Chicano clients. Both centers also have a history of selecting staff and providing staff development according to the principles of cultural compatibility in service delivery.

Sample

The study population consisted of workers and Chicano clients at each center. Twenty-six caseworkers, all of whom provided direct services, volunteered to participate in the study. Exactly half of the volunteers were male. In terms of years of employment at the centers, both the mean (3.4 years) and median (3.2 years) indicated that workers had considerable casework experience in the Chicano community. The majority of caseworkers who volunteered to participate were Chicano (16, or 62 percent); approximately the same number of black (five, or 19 percent) and white (four, or 15 percent) caseworkers volunteered to participate. Only one worker in the sample fell into another ethnic category. Ten of the 26 caseworkers (39 percent) had formal social work training (eight MSWs and two BSWs); an additional 11 had degrees in related disciplines. Only five caseworkers in the sample (19 percent) had no degree. Sixteen (62 percent) of the caseworkers reported using Spanish in the delivery of services to clients.

The client sample was drawn from the pool of persons entering the outpatient services units at each center. They were selected according to several criteria critical to the study and in a fashion preserving routine agency procedures. Clients were considered for inclusion if they were (1) Chicano (responding "Mexican American/Hispanic" to the ethnicity/race item on agency intake forms); (2) 18 years of age or older; (3) experiencing emotional problems not severe enough to require extensive medication; (4) a new admission, a readmission, or a recently transferred client from a different therapist; and (5) willing to participate in six to eight weeks of treatment.

Potential client subjects were identified initially by an "intake specialist" who conducted a preliminary screening using the criteria enumerated above. All persons determined to be possible subjects were randomly assigned to a caseworker participating in the study. The worker then proceeded with the usual processing, which involved a diagnostic interview and case staffing. Once a case had been established and staffed and a treatment plan developed, a project research associate initiated data collection with those clients who agreed to participate in the study.

Of the 58 Chicano clients in the sample, 42 (72 percent) were male. For more than half the clients (55 percent), the current admission was their first to the mental health center. One-third (19) were admitted as a consequence of a court order. On the average, the client sample was 35 years old and had completed 9.7 years of school. Clients ranged in age from 19 to 57 and in educational background from having no formal education to having completed 14 years of school. Most clients were of low socioeconomic backgrounds; 74 percent had incomes below the poverty level and the average income was $3,535. The client sample consisted of 24 (41 percent) married, 19 (33 percent) single, and 15 (26 percent) separated or divorced people.

Instruments

Two types of measures were germane to this report: those that dealt with outcomes and those that measured worker behaviors. In both areas, special efforts were made to identify appropriate instruments and to select those with the greatest validity and reliability. When existing instruments proved inadequate, project personnel developed the measures, and the validation procedures are reported here in considerable detail.

Outcome Measures. Client change is multidimensional and there are numerous ways of reporting such changes.[10] Thus, the study employed multiple measures of outcome: a standardized, global measure of a client's clinical symptoms; individualized change criteria; and a client report on satisfaction with services. Following Herzog's suggestion, both global and individually tailored measures of outcome were used.[11] Effectiveness was measured by clients' satisfaction with the services received and by positive changes in scores on clients' conditions over the course of treatment.[12] Four specific indicators of effectiveness were identified: (1) reduction in the severity of clinical symptoms, (2) reduction in the severity of complaints as reported by clients, (3) reduction in the severity of complaints as reported by workers, and (4) service satisfaction.

Clinical symptoms were assessed by using the SCL-90, a self-report symptoms scale that provides an inventory of the different types of complaints common to psychiatric outpatients.[13] A number of psychiatric studies have established the validity of the SCL-90, and Waskow has shown it to be sensitive to racial and class differences in symptomatology.[14] The Global Severity Index, one of several indexes calculated from the SCL-90, was used to produce a single value indicator of the depth of disorder by combining symptoms and perceived severity values. The index essentially consists of a summation of weighted scores divided by items included.[15]

The study also used the Target Complaint Procedure, a technique for individualizing the measurement of change. Researchers have encountered indirect evidence for the validity of this procedure, finding that the severity of complaints correlated significantly with other outcome measures.[16] The present study applied the scale separately with clients and with workers to determine how severe each considered the complaints targeted for treatment to be. The procedure elicited and rated target complaints on a 13-point severity scale from "not at all" to "couldn't be worse."[17] In the analysis, perceptions of clients and those of workers were treated as two distinct indicators of outcome. The fourth measure of outcome used was the eight-item Client Satisfaction Questionnaire. Scored on a 4-point anchored scale, this questionnaire possessed a high degree of internal consistency and validity.[18]

Worker Behavior Measure. The type and frequency of the different worker behaviors during treatment were measured by the Worker Behavior Interview Schedule (WBIS), an instrument specifically designed for this study and modeled after Shulman's work on the helping process.[19] It was developed in three phases. First, during a series of meetings with the members of the research group, the staff of the mental health centers described the intervention model they currently used. Staff members' perceptions of the casework services they provided were considered crucial, because the perceptions offered the only means for defining the intervention approach being applied. After several lengthy exploratory discussions and after consulting the literature, the researchers prepared a written description of the casework model described by staff members. They then submitted the written description to the staff for discussion and revision.

The revised description of the "psychosocial" casework services used at the mental health centers and a description of the culture-oriented intervention model served as the working documents for the second phase of work: the translation of the two casework models into specific worker behaviors. The worker behaviors identified were then represented by questions that would become the WBIS. A total of 57 behaviors were identified and categorized as either (1) generic to both the psychologically oriented psychosocial model and the culture-oriented model (12 behaviors), (2) specific to psychologically oriented psychosocial intervention (13 behaviors), (3) consistent with culture-oriented intervention (17 behaviors), or (4) indicative of interactionist behaviors adapted from Shulman's Worker Behavior Questionnaire (15 behaviors). The WBIS had to be an instrument that clients could easily understand and that could be self-administered. Clients were to indicate how frequently the worker exhibited the behavior on an ordinal scale: "never" (0), "seldom" (1), "occasionally" (2), or "very often" (3).

The third and final phase of work in developing the WBIS involved an examination of its validity and reliability. The validity issue had to be addressed in the broader context of the larger comparative study. It was necessary to determine how well the items in the WBIS reflected (or sampled) the kinds of worker behaviors appropriate and essential to the psychosocial model and the culture-oriented model.

A panel of experts not associated with the study was provided with the description of the casework models, the WBIS, and material categorizing worker behaviors into the four groups. Panel members were asked to respond to four questions:

1. How would you rate the adequacy of the conceptualization (description) of each of the models being examined?
2. To what extent do questions operationalize the description of each practice model?
3. To what extent does the classification of behaviors agree with your reading of these models?
4. What other crucial behaviors would you include with each of the models?

Based on responses to these questions, the researchers reworded a number of items on the WBIS, added others, and reclassified some in terms of the four categories. All panel members indicated that the description of the models was "very good" and that the WBIS adequately translated each model. The reliability of the WBIS was addressed by focusing on its stability or "time-associated" reliability—that is, whether an interviewee would give the same answer to an item if asked the same question two weeks later.[20]

A test-retest procedure was used to determine the level of confidence in the stability of answers. A pilot study of the WBIS was conducted using Chicano clients participating in casework services at the mental health centers and another community-based multiservice center. As much as possible, clients for the pilot study were selected according to the same criteria used to select the client sample population. The pilot study sample totaled 38 clients, 25 from the multiservice center and 13 from the mental health centers. The sample consisted of 13 males and 25 females. The retest, done by the interviewer who did the initial interview, took place two weeks after the first test.

Eighty-five percent of the responses to the items were identical in both tests. Seventy-seven percent of the responses of clients at the mental health centers were identical, while 92 percent of the client responses at the multiservice center were identical. An item analysis showed that the rate of identical responses for individual items ranged from 71 percent to 95 percent. These results support the WBIS's stability and reliability.

The WBIS was applied at posttreatment to measure the frequency with which each worker behavior occurred during treatment. Although workers at the mental health centers indicated that the psychosocial casework model reflected their primary orientation to treatment, they acknowledged that in actual practice, workers were eclectic in their use of casework skills. These observations are consistent with earlier findings that suggest a certain degree of heterogeneity in the use of casework skills, because there can be no "pure" application of any particular casework model.[21] The workers also pointed out that the mental health centers had, over the course of several years, engaged in numerous inservice and staff-development activities focusing on various aspects of improving mental health services to Chicanos. For these reasons, the examination of worker behaviors was not limited only to those described within the psychosocial category of the WBIS. Instead, as an exploratory feature, clients were asked to report on the workers' use of the entire array of 57 behaviors as a means of operationally describing the services.

RESULTS

The discussion of results addresses the issues involved in outcomes on effectiveness and then examines how one of those outcomes—service satisfaction—relates to worker behaviors. Because the statistical complexities of pretreatment versus posttreatment analysis are beyond the scope of this article, service satisfaction, which can only be measured after treatment, was selected for the correlational analysis with worker behaviors. The effectiveness of casework guided by a psychosocial model is indicated by findings specific to clinical symptoms, target complaints, and service satisfaction.

Clinical Symptoms

Pretreatment means and standard deviations on the nine symptoms measured by the SCL-90 scale, and the Global Severity Index, when compared to scores of a nonpatient normal sample provided by Derogatis, showed that the sample of clients in this study scored well above the "normal" means.[22] The client mean score for the Global Severity Index (84.19) indicates that the number and severity of symptoms and the intensity of perceived stress was quite high at the beginning of treatment. The mean difference in scores (pretest versus posttest) for each of the nine symptoms and the Global Severity Index are shown in Table 1. The t values show that client change was statistically significant at the .05 level for all symptoms except somatization. For seven of the symptoms, as well as for the Global Severity Index score, the mean differences were significant at the .005 level. The Global Severity Index score showed a mean reduction of 22.02 for the total client population. Among the nine symptoms, clients reported the greatest reductions in depression, anxiety, hostility, paranoid ideation, and interpersonal sensitivity.

Target Complaints

The problems identified as complaints were, for descriptive purposes, grouped into general categories. Almost three-quarters (74

Table 1
SCL-90 Symptoms Change Scores

Symptom	Mean Difference	SD	t-Test Values[a]
Somatization	.12	.68	1.30[e]
Obsessive-compulsive behavior	.20	.68	2.21[d]
Interpersonal sensitivity	.26	.70	2.88[b]
Depression	.37	.70	4.05[b]
Anxiety	.25	.66	2.88[b]
Hostility	.25	.71	2.99[b]
Phobic anxiety	.19	.60	2.49[c]
Paranoid ideation	.31	.82	2.87[b]
Psychoticism	.24	.61	2.99[b]
Total Severity	22.02	50.17	3.34[b]

[a]One-tail p values: $df = 57$.
[b]$p \leq .005$
[c]$p \leq .01$
[d]$p \leq .05$
[e]$p \leq .10$

percent) of the clients reported an emotional problem, 46 percent reported a family problem, and over one-third (40 percent) indicated the desire for assistance with a social problem. They also reported problems with substance abuse (35 percent), employment and finances (30 percent), relationships (21 percent), and other areas (9 percent).

Ratings of the severity of client problems were made independently by clients and workers before and after treatment. Figure 1 shows tabulations of the clients' and workers' mean ratings for each of three target complaints. The pretreatment ratings by both clients and workers generally show severity ratings between "very much" and "pretty much." Both clients and workers reported a decrease in the severity of problems after treatment. From pre-treatment to posttreatment, client complaints decreased in severity by an average of 2.9 scale points so that the severity of complaints after treatment generally fell between "pretty much" and "a little." For the same comparisons, worker-rated complaints showed a smaller mean reduction (1.7) and on the average remained in the "very much" to "pretty much" range of severity. The largest decrease in perception of severity was on the first target complaint; on the average, it decreased for clients from 9.2 to 5.9 and for workers from 9.2 to 7.0.

When severity ratings for all complaints are combined and comparisons made of clients' and workers' perceptions before and after treatment, statistically significant differences emerge for clients ($t = 7.03$) and workers ($t = 4.74$) at the .0001 level.

Figure 1
Clients' and Workers' Mean Ratings on Target Complaints before and after Treatment ($N = 58$)

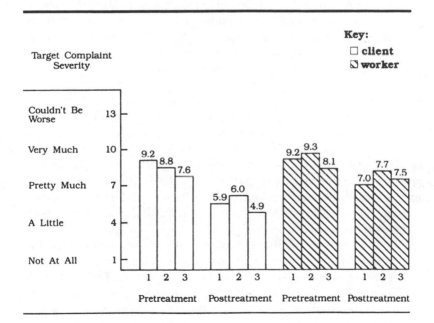

Satisfaction with Services

Possible scores on the Client Satisfaction Questionnaire range from 8 to 32. Among the Chicano clients in this study, this measure showed a mean rating of 26.5 and a standard deviation of 3.6. Categorically, over half of the respondents (or 31, 53 percent) had satisfaction ratings between 27 and 32, while only five (9 percent) had ratings of 19 or 20—the lowest occurring in this sample.

Improvements evidenced by the SCL-90, the target complaint outcomes, and service satisfaction scores lead to the second main issue in this study: What worker behaviors are associated with client service satisfaction? Table 2 provides the correlation coefficients for the 12 worker behaviors that had a positive and statistically significant association ($p < .05$) with service satisfaction.

The culture-oriented category contained the largest number of behaviors showing this relationship (four), while there were three in both the interactionist and generic categories. The behavior showing the highest correlation with service satisfaction (.43) is the reinforcing of positive concepts of self as Mexican American, followed in order by communicating honesty and respect (.40), developing client motivation (.39), and reaching out for information on events that occur between sessions (.36). One behavior emerged from each category to constitute the four that are most highly related to service satisfaction. The two psychosocial behaviors showing significant correlations suggest that some aspects of Freudian theory may prove useful in working with Chicano clients. The skill of developing clients' motivation or overcoming the resistance of involuntary clients is associated with satisfaction. In addition, the skill of exploring how clients feel about experiences in their past is also helpful. The effectiveness of this latter skill supports one of Freud's basic theoretical tenets—that clients' history can help in understanding and dealing with certain problems.

The culture-oriented behavior of developing and reinforcing positive feelings about the clients' ethnic self produced the highest correlation with service satisfaction ($r = .43$). Two behaviors aimed at inquiring about clients' cultural makeup were also correlated with satisfaction: inquiring about the relationship of clients' beliefs to the problem ($r = .31$) and exploring clients' natural helping systems ($r = .22$). Allowing clients to use the language of

Table 2
Correlation Coefficients of Worker Behaviors
with Clients' Satisfaction with Service

Worker Behavior	Pearson's r[a]
Psychosocial	
Assessing and/or assisting in developing client motivation	.39
Exploring client's feelings associated with their past	.23
Culture-Oriented	
Reinforcing positive concepts of self as Mexican American	.43
Inquiring about client's beliefs as they relate to problems being addressed	.31
Allowing clients to use language of preference or need	.29
Exploring natural helping systems	.22
Interactionist	
Reaching for between-sessions data	.36
Supporting client strength	.33
Asking for a review of the learning	.27
Generic	
Communicating honesty and respect	.40
Clarifying roles	.33
Communicating genuine concern	.28

[a]All behaviors significant at .05 level.

their preference (Spanish, English, or a combination of the two) was also associated with client satisfaction ($r = .29$).

Of the interactionist behaviors examined, three produced significant correlations. Shulman's study had found that two behaviors—supporting clients' strengths and reaching out for information on events that occur between sessions—were significantly correlated with helpfulness.[23] In supporting clients' strength, workers project an honest belief in the clients' ability to deal with problems. This display of belief in the clients' potential strengthens their own view of the possibilities in the undertaking. By reaching for data on events from between sessions, workers again recognize the clients' strengths and render the clients as active participants in the helping process. This skill is aimed at giving the clients a sense of an agenda in helping and conveys to them that their agenda is important.[24]

The significant correlation with the third interactionist behavior—asking for a review of the learning—contradicts Shulman's finding concerning this behavior. This technique is part of the process of ending the helping relationship; the workers ask the clients to review and sum up what they have learned in the helping relationship. Such evaluation is thought to augment client learning, being therapeutic in itself.

Three generic behaviors were also significant. The skills of communicating "honesty and respect" ($r = .40$) and demonstrating a "genuine concern" ($r = .28$) for the client were described by Hollis as important elements in developing a helping relationship.[25] Shulman found that the third generic skill—clarifying roles—was also significant in association with helpfulness. His study, however, reported that "clarifying roles" was more closely related to the relationship-building process than to helpfulness, suggesting that the task of discussing purpose and roles can not only precede the engagement in a relationship but can contribute to its development.[26] The correlations of these generic skills with service satisfaction suggest that a helping relationship may be central to client satisfaction.

CONCLUSION

There is good evidence that the Chicano clients in this study experienced considerable improvement in symptoms and complaints and that the casework services they received were highly satisfactory. Coefficients correlating with client satisfaction showed that as workers begin with the clients, they must be conscious of the importance of communicating honesty, showing respect for the clients as people, and demonstrating a genuine concern for the clients. Also, early in the relationship, the workers need to clarify their role for the clients. This will provide clients with a clear sense of what workers can offer and help facilitate the relationship-building process. This should be accompanied with work on developing client motivation or overcoming client resistance, whichever is appropriate.

The data strongly indicate that it is important for workers to explore and employ certain psychocultural data from clients in treatment. The feelings clients associate with past experiences help in the understanding of the clients' current problems. The workers need to help clients explore past experiences and place these in perspective with current problems.[27]

In addition, the workers' consideration of clients' cultural beliefs and natural helping systems serves to bring the cultural dimension into treatment. The most significant culture-oriented skill of workers was the development and the reinforcement of positive feelings about clients' self-concept as Mexican Americans. Associated with these dynamics is the skill of allowing clients to use their preferred language. The use of a familiar and comfortable form of verbal expression can help clients tune in to their concept of self as a Mexican American and facilitate communication.

Through the entire helping process, workers need to support clients' strengths by clearly demonstrating a belief that clients can address their problems. At the start of each session, workers must show that they feel it is important to pursue the clients' sense of an agenda. This technique allows the introduction of new information into the helping process and assists clients in understanding and being a part of the progression of the helping process.

As a means of bringing the helping relationship to a close, workers must help clients evaluate what they learned in the relationship. This evaluation can be therapeutic and helps clients deal with their feelings about ending treatment.

Overall, the study found that the short-term casework services provided had a positive effect on the problems of Chicano clients and that clients were highly satisfied with the services. The reports of clients on the type and frequency of workers' behavior during treatment revealed that workers were eclectic in their use of skills that cut across different modes of intervention. It is important to emphasize that the workers' psychosocial-cultural behaviors, which the findings suggest account for the treatment outcome, are directly associated with each worker's evaluation of the clients' conditions. That is, the particular configuration of skills that each worker used with each client comprised a therapeutic response formulated by each worker to fit the client's situation, although workers shared a general psychosocial-cultural approach. This finding reflects the many combinations of treatment strategies and therapeutic skills embodied in the psychosocial-cultural casework approach.

The findings of this study must be considered in light of the limitations of the research design. Perhaps the most severe limitation is the absence of a control group. Both organizational and ethical constraints against depriving people of needed services restricted the choice of a design. The lack of a control group jeopardizes internal validity by not controlling for the effect of extraneous variables. Because plausible alternative hypotheses might explain the changes in client condition, the findings of this study should be considered tentative although suggestive of the impact that psychosocial-cultural casework can have on Chicano clients and of the therapeutic techniques associated with such results.

Notes and References

The research for this article is based partly on support by ADAMHA Training Grant No. MH 13619 from the Division of Manpower and Training Programs of the National Institute of Mental Health.

1. See J. Fischer, *The Effectiveness of Social Casework* (Springfield, Ill.: Charles C. Thomas, Publisher, 1976); and L. L. Geismar, "Thirteen Evaluative Studies," in E. J. Mullen and J. R. Dumpson, eds., *Evaluation of Social Intervention* (San Francisco: Jossey-Bass, 1972).
2. See L. Shulman, "A Study of Practice Skills," *Social Work*, 23 (July 1978), pp. 274–281; and W. J. Reid and A. W. Shyne, *Brief and Extended Casework* (New York: Columbia University Press, 1969).
3. See R. Mejia, *Culture Conflict Theory: A Culturally Syntonic Theoretical Alternative for La Raza*, monograph on Emerging Perspectives on Chicano Mental Health (Houston: Chicano Training Center, 1975); R. A. Ruiz, "The Delivery of Mental Health and Social Change Services for Chicanos: Analysis and Recommendations," and M. R. Miranda and F. G. Castro, "Cultural Distance and Success in Psychotherapy with Spanish Speaking Clients," in J. L. Martinez, ed., *Chicano Psychology* (New York: Academic Press, 1977).

4. See J. A. Brown, "Clinical Social Work with Chicanos: Some Unwarranted Assumptions," *Clinical Social Work Journal*, 7 (Winter, 1979); and L. A. Santa Cruz, and Dean H. Hepworth, "Effects of Cultural Orientation on Casework," *Social Casework*, 56 (January 1976), pp. 52–57.
5. Brown, "Clinical Social Work with Chicanos," p. 264.
6. F. Hollis, "Social Casework: The Psychosocial Approach," in *Encyclopedia of Social Work* (17th ed.: Washington, D.C.: National Association of Social Work, 1977).
7. *Ibid.*
8. Data on outcomes and techniques of psychosocial casework derive from a larger study in E. Gomez, "An Evaluation of Psychosocial Casework Service to Chicanos: A Study of Process and Outcome." Unpublished Ph.D. thesis, University of Texas at Austin, 1982. See also Gomez, "The San Antonio Model: A Culture-oriented Approach to Social Work Practice," in G. Gibson, ed., *Our Kingdom Stands on Brittle Glass* (Silver Spring, Md.: National Association of Social Workers, 1983).
9. See S. Isaac and W. B. Michael, *Handbook in Research and Evaluation* (San Diego: Edits Publishers, 1979) for a description of this design.
10. See A. E. Bergin and M. J. Lambert, "The Evaluation of Therapeutic Outcomes," in S. L. Garfield and Bergin, eds., *Handbook on Psychotherapy and Behavioral Change* (New York: John Wiley & Sons, 1978).
11. E. Herzog, *Some Guide Lines for Evaluative Research* (Washington, D.C.: U.S. Children's Bureau, 1959).
12. See Fischer, *The Effectiveness of Social Casework*.
13. L. R. Derogatis, R. S. Lipman, and L. Covi, "SCL-90: An Outpatient Psychiatric Rating Scale (preliminary report)," *Psychopharmacology Bulletin*, 9 (January 1973), pp. 13–27.
14. I. E. Waskow, "Selection of a Core Battery," in I. E. Waskow and M. B. Parloff, eds., *Psychotherapy Change Measures, DHEW Publication No. 74-120* (Washington, D.C.: U.S. Government Printing Office, 1975); and L. R. Derogatis, *The SCL-90 Manual I: Scoring, Administration and Procedures for the SCL-90* (Baltimore, Md.: Johns Hopkins University School of Medicine, 1977).
15. Derogatis, *The SCL-90 Manual I*, p. 12.
16. See C. C. Battle et al., "Target Complaints as a Criteria of Improvement," *American Journal of Psychotherapy*, 20 (January 1966), pp. 184–192.
17. Herzog, *Some Guide Lines for Evaluative Research*.
18. See D. L. Larsen et al., "Assessment of Client/Patient Satisfaction," *Evaluation and Program Planning*, 2 (Summer 1979).
19. L. Shulman, "A Study of the Helping Process." Unpublished manuscript, School of Social Work, University of British Columbia, Vancouver, Canada, 1977.
20. See Isaac and Michael, *Handbook in Research and Evaluation*.

21. See Hans H. Strupp, "Psychotherapeutic Technique, Professional Affiliation, and Experience Level," *Journal of Consulting Psychology*, 19 (February, 1977).
22. Derogatis, *The SCL-90 Manual I*, p. 29.
23. See Shulman, "A Study of the Helping Process."
24. Ibid.
25. Hollis, "Social Casework: The Psychosocial Approach."
26. Shulman, "A Study of the Helping Process."
27. Hollis, "Social Casework: The Psychosocial Approach."

PRINCIPLES OF SOCIAL CASEWORK AND THE THIRD WORLD*

David R. Burgest

INTRODUCTION

In all of the academic professions which are involved in the delivery of human services such as Medicine, Law, Psychiatry and Social Work, there is the existence of a philosophical and ideological preamble of ideals divined as principles, oaths, creeds or codes of ethics governing the interaction and relationship between the consumers of services and the worker. In the profession of social work, there are two components. A code of ethics which itemizes the statements of belief and moral conduct and the principles governing casework relationship which provides for fundamental frame of reference for the attitudes, values and judgments the workers must internalize and manifest in their relationship with clients. In this article, we will focus on the principles of the casework relationship as they relate to The Third World worker/client relationships.

Third World has come to be defined as any developing countries in the world. By the same token, there is a direct correlation between the developing countries considered to be Third World and the mankind which make up the Eastern epistemological world-view consisting of the Negroid and Mongoloid races. Although, Third World in contemporary language has become synonymous with "underdeveloped" countries such as those in Africa

*Reprinted by permission of the author and *International Social Work* 26:4 (1983) 7–23; copyright © International Council of Social Welfare.

and Asia, the operational definition of Third World minorities in the manuscript refers to ethnic and racial groups in America whose genetic origins are Negroid, Mongoloid or some ethnic hybrid thereof. More specifically, Third World minorities in this instance refer to individuals and groups whose origin is identified with nations defined as Third World but living outside of this geographical origin in places such as America and Europe. The major focus of this article will be on Third World Minorities in America.

PRINCIPLES OF THE CASEWORK RELATIONSHIP

The seven principles of the casework relationship as composed and defined by Felix Biestek became assimilated, accepted and adopted by the social work profession as the definitive statement to govern the casework relationship. It may appear on first thought that there is no need to elaborate on the seven principles of the casework relationship as they might relate to Third World clients. There may also be the assumption that the principles of the casework relationship as stipulated by Biestek transcends both race and ethnicity and that the generic nature of the principles should be applicable to all individuals regardless of race, ethnicity or culture. None-the-less, the experiences of history in social work practice and education with Third World minority clients in America have demonstrated that the social theory, methods and techniques implemented without specific regards to race, ethnicity and culture have proven ineffective and inadequate as one source puts it:

> Schools of social work have, for the most part, been oblivious to the need for adapting methods of practice to Third World minority groups. Rather they teach practice derived from a generic method that is dictated primarily by the majority. Yet much social work practice is carried out in the United States with minority groups and, too often, social workers apply it by a blanket method supposedly effective with all people
>
> Each Third World minority group has its own problems and personality-derived from long-existing cultural and moral values, language patterns of behavior, socio-economic conditions, ethnic background, and many other factors. Social work practice in a minority community shows that besides the variations that must be

made in the generic method to suit individuals, certain adaptations should be made in applying social work methods to the specific minority group.[1]

One of the most blatant pitfalls in the generic application of social theory, method and practice in social work has been the use of the "color-blindness" approach by social caseworkers in working with clients from different racial groups. The "color-blindness" approach is a simple disregard of color, race, and ethnicity as being relevant in the worker/client relationship. Secondly, social caseworkers operated under the assumption that the Western middle-class standards were universal as a guide to define, analyze and diagnose the behavior of all clients. Thus, it is necessary that specific elaborations, evaluations and dramatizations of the seven principles of the casework relationship be highlighted in relationship to Third World clients. Too often, as described above, the unique dimensions inherent in the worker/client relationship with Third World clients are obscured in the generic application.

The first principle of the casework relationship is *individualization*. The principle is defined as "the recognition and understanding of each client's unique qualities . . . based upon the right of human beings to be individuals and to be treated not just as a human, but *this* human being with his personal differences.[2]

INDIVIDUALIZATION in the worker/client relationships with Third World minorities first and foremost requires that the factors of race and ethnicity must be recognized as being of primary importance during interaction with Third World clients, the emphasis of this social casework principle should be on *this particular human being*, taking under consideration the *race, ethnicity*, and unique cultural *qualities* of the individual. The traditional social work practice approach of denying race and ethnicity as being relevant in the casework process has specifically impeded the casework relationship between white workers and Black clients.

The underlying assumption inherent in the "color-blindness" premise has been that a worker's consideration of race, color and ethnicity of the client in the worker/client relationship may somehow prohibit the factors of individualization in that the recognition of race and ethnicity in a client may serve to the worker. The overriding assumption of the social casework discipline has been that the element of "humanness" or "being human" is separated from race, ethnicity and color. Therefore, the accepted view of the social casework profession has been to simply look at a client *as a client* and a human being as *just a human being* without regard for the race and ethnicity of the client.

In regards to Third World clients, the traditional interpretation of *individualization* provides social workers with a ready-made escape for making allowances for the effects of discriminatory practices and personal prejudices on the part of the worker by obliterating any differences between being "colored" and being "human." Moreover, social caseworkers may be prohibited from developing self-insight by denying prejudices and racism inherent in self under the camouflage of not recognizing race and ethnicity. Implicit in the Western World is a series of negative stereotypes, myths and assumptions regarding Third World cultures and the denial of color by the worker may indicate an acceptance of those negative myths and stereotypes. The denial of color and ethnicity may provide an opportunity for the worker to maintain the negative myths, stereotypes, and assumptions associated with color and ethnicity. If color is considered relevant in the worker client relationship then the worker would be persuaded to confront in his own mind the myths and stereotypes associated with color, race and ethnicity.

Perhaps, the most destructive manifestation of individualization with the Third World populace is the attempt of the worker to separate the race and ethnicity of a client from their "humanness." This approach may be seen as a clear indication of biasness, prejudice and racism practiced by the professional in that it suggests that the social worker could not justifiably view a Third World individual as "human" unless the factors of ethnicity and race were removed. It might be said that white/whiteness and white people are the epitomy of that which is "human" while Third World clients (people of color) are the epitomy of that which is "nonhuman." The educational training in social work has traditionally made it possible through the denial of race and ethnicity for social caseworkers to justify their relationship with Third World clients by unconsciously assigning them the status of being "white" in "color-blindness" approach.

OBSTACLES PRESENTED AND THE ROLE OF THE WORKER

Do away with the "color-blindness" tradition and recognize that color, race and ethnicity of the client as important and relevant factors in the worker/client relationship.

Individualization in social work practice must become sensitive to the fact that race and ethnicity are important and crucial factors to consider in the professional relationship with Third World clients. It has been stated earlier that (1) traditionally social casework practitioners, educators and the social work profession accepted the view that color and race are unimportant and should be disregarded and overlooked in the relationship with Third World clients, (2) during the early sixties American social work educators and scholars began to challenge the "color-blindness" approach of "a client as a client" and racial identity should not be taken under consideration. It was further pointed out that (3) recognition of color implies that some unsound practices have taken place. The alleviation of the color blindness approach of the 1960's have revolutionized the thinking and approaches of casework practitioners in this regard.

Modern day critics of the "unimportance" of race and ethnicity in the individualization process must readily accept the fact that the failure to recognize the most obvious would truly render the caseworker helpless in recognizing the more subtle problems which the client may bring. A basic contradiction in social work practice through the process of individualization has been the recognition of culture as a relevant factor but the avoidance of the recognition of race and ethnicity, yet, race and ethnicity must be associated as an integral part of culture.

Do away with the negative myths, stereotypes and assumptions regarding race, ethnicity and color:

In the Western World, there is an accumulation of negative myths, stereotypes and assumptions regarding various ethnic and racial groups. One of the key inhibiting factors of the negative myths and stereotypes perpetrated is that they may prohibit the worker from looking at factors in self which may block the development of an effective relationship with clients. This principle applies to workers and clients of the same and different racial and ethnic groups in that the worker may see a "client as a client" disregarding ethnicity and race. In an effort to abolish the negative myths, stereotypes and assumptions regarding Third World clients which affect the individualization process, the worker must:

> Identify and analyze the negative assumptions, myths and stereotypes existing in the Western World which may block the development of authentic and effective professional relationship with clients of the same and different racial/ethnic groups.

> Identify the positive assumptions, myths and stereotypes existing in the Western Society regarding Western behavior and analyze its impact upon behavior of social caseworker toward self and Third World client.

> Define, identify and analyze the assumptions needed to facilitate the development of an authentic and effective relationship with a client of the same and/or different racial and/or ethnic group.

> Explore, recognize and identify the assumptions, behavior, and prejudices in self which may block the development of effective social casework relationship with members of the same and/or different racial and ethnic groups.

> Explore, recognize and identify the assumptions, behavior and attitude needed to facilitate an effective, authentic professional relationship with members of the same and/or different racial ethnic groups.

Do away with social work jargon and cliches regarding Third World minorities which mitigate the development of authentic interpersonal professional relationships.

The stereotypical language, cliches and social work jargon used to define and describe Indians, Puerto-Ricans, Mexicans, Africans and others are interwebbed within the socialization of negative myths, stereotypes and assumptions regarding Third World minorities in America. Such prevalently used concepts reflected in social work literature and diagnostic recordings as "culturally deprived", "culturally disadvantaged", "hard-to-reach", "hard core", "underdeveloped" and "cultural lag" are available masks for social casework practitioners who wish to use a shield that prohibits self-inventory and self-insight on the part of the worker. The end results are that the ineffectiveness in therapy is blamed on the client and the social work jargon justifies that perception.

The practitioner may not see the Black, African or Puerto-Rican client as an individual with unique qualities and characteristics rather they only see the symbols hidden behind such concepts as "culturally deprived." Consequently, the caseworker has a built-in escape to avoid the factors in self which may be debilitating in the casework relationship with Third World clients. The caseworker is unable to see the strengths of the client which is a necessary step in affecting change rather they are limited by the symbols in the social work jargon. Hence, there is also the self-fulfilling prophesy of legitimizing the perceptions inherent in the language. As one social work theorist says, the process of relationship building and *individualization* greatly depends on emotional understanding with reciprocity and rapport being crucial; however, "current cliches can be as handicapping to understanding as were past stereotypes."[3] As we summarize the principle of individualization, the following assumptions will provide the foundation and frame of reference for social work practitioners to follow.

ACCEPTANCE

Biestek defines Acceptance as:

> A principle of action wherein the caseworker perceives and deals with the client as he really is, including his strengths and weaknesses; his congenial and uncongenial qualities; his positive and negative feelings; his constructive and destructive attitudes and behavior, maintaining all the while a sense of the client's innate dignity and personal worth.[4]

One of the more devastating, yet, unique qualities inherent in the principle of acceptance with Third World clients is the attachment of negative stereotypes and assumptions of inferiority to the life styles, culture and behavior. The correspondingly attachment of positiveness and superiority to the Western society and their

life styles complicates the dilemma. Kitano points out that there is
a two-track system composed of non-white inferiority and white
superiority which dominates the American society as much as the
Protestant ethnics. This two-track system is seen as ingrained in
the Western World-View tradition as "red, white, and blue." Therefore, it may be difficult for a caseworker to perceive Third World
individuals as having any constructive and positive attitudes and
behaviors, congenial qualities and positive and constructive
qualities. In other words, there may be impediments to the worker
meeting the primary mandate of *acceptance* which is to "see the
client as he really is." This is particularly crucial when all of the
qualities of acceptance such as congenial/noncongenial, construc-
tive/destructive and other attributes are contaminated by the
worker's negative vision of the Third World.

It may be easy for a worker to implement the principle of
acceptance in encouraging the uncongenial and destructive attitudes of a client as long as negative disposition is directed away
from the worker but difficulties may arise when those negative
qualities and feelings of a Third World client are directed toward
the therapist. The negative attitudes and behaviors of a Third
World client directed toward the worker and the therapeutic relationship may create insecurity and discomfort in the worker and
the worker may be unable to deal with the client "as he really is."

In working with Third World clients, it may be important to
note that the feelings of guilt and remorse may develop in a worker because the worker may feel that he/she is somehow directly or
indirectly responsible for the societal conditions impeding the
client. Many workers may feel responsible because they are a
member of the privileged group in the society and fear that they
may be benefiting at the expense of those who are less fortunate.
On the other hand, the client's experiences may be too closely
reflective of the worker's experiences given the commonality and
experiences of racial, ethnic and cultural groups. At the same
time, the client's experiences may be too painful for worker to
comprehend and empathize. If the worker has not resolved difficulties around his/her racial identities then the task of therapy
may present major problems. Above all, workers of all races may
be victims of the "self-fulfilling prophesy" of perceiving only that
which they have been socialized through the greater Western society to see. Therefore, the worker may not be able to appropriately

assess the strengths/weaknesses, positive/negative, construc-
tive/destructive and congenial and uncongenial qualities of the
Third World client.

Most of all, social caseworkers and the social work profession seem to utilize the standards and values of European middle
class norms as the basis for determining the behavior which require acceptance and/or nonacceptance. The way of life of the
ethnic and racial minority group is usually ignored or minimized in
the principle of acceptance. Most workers, Black and non-Black
alike find it difficult to apply the principle of *acceptance* to behavior which differs from their own culture. This is more particularly
the case when the worker may be aspiring to middle class values
or when a worker is uncomfortable with the middle class status in
which he/she belongs.

In addition to the above, social caseworkers of all ethnic and
racial origins must do away with the "liberal" premise of "freedom from racial and ethnic prejudices." This premise mitigates
the principle of *acceptance* in the worker/client relationship in
that the worker may be possessed with "proving" and "justifying"
his/her liberalism to the point that it hampers an effective therapeutic relationship. This notion of "proving acceptance" is not the
proper use of the principle of acceptance. The mere action of
trying to prove acceptance or to "prove" that one is not prejudiced
is a tacit indication of the opposite. The "liberalism" in social
work literature and social work profession which propose such
views as "the commonality of human beings transcends racial and
ethnic differences" and "identification with the client's ego is to
identify on a human level which supersedes race and ethnicity"
prohibits genuine acceptance. Such "liberal" disposition prohibits
the opportunity for the worker to develop self-awareness, self
insight and growth as well as prohibits the opportunity for workers to address the inherent negative myths, stereotypes and assumptions which may interfere with the worker looking at the
client "as he really is."

Firstly, social caseworkers must be comfortable with acceptance of self in relationship to Third World individuals as well as
the racial or ethnic group in which the worker belongs. This is an
area which presents a lot of difficulties for many social casework
practitioners. For example, in the presence of minority individuals
or groups, the white social caseworker adopts the view that "I just

happen to be white," "I just happen to be a member of the majority race" or "I am human first and white second" as an apology for
the atrocities that the white society may have perpetrated against
such minority groups. In this instance, the white individual is saying that he could have been "Black" or a member of any other
minority group and he has provided an escape for having any
association with what the white race may have done to Third
World groups. Most of all, the white worker may be saying that
he/she identifies with the oppression and connection with humanity existing among Blacks in spite of the racial identity.

On the other hand, there are Blacks and other Third World
individuals who cry "I happen to be Mexican or Black," "I am
human first and Black second" or "I am a social worker first and
Black second" as a means of de-emphasizing their racial/ethnic
identity as a measure of who they are. In the same way that whites
may de-emphasize their race to identify on a common level with
minorities, there are minority individuals who de-emphasize their
race to identify with values attached to being white.

First of all, it is not accidental, coincidental or circumstantial
that an individual is born into a particular race, minority group or
ethnic group. Such action is determined without request or permission of the person involved. Yet, it appears to be an attempt on
the part of many Third World caseworkers to assign uncongenial,
negative and destructive myths to their race thereby disassociat-
ing themselves from their racial identity by saying "I happen to be
Black." In order for a worker to be effective in a therapeutic
relationship with a client of the same or different racial/ethnic
group, the worker must liberate self from all the negative assumptions and inferior qualities assigned to him/her due to ra-
cial/ethnic identity. At the same time the worker must proceed in
destroying the assimilated negative myths, stereotypes and assumptions existing in the client so as to psychologically liberate
the client. Often times, the negative assumptions and stereotypes
existing in clients regarding their own racial/ethnic identity interferes with the treatment process.

The above is not to suggest that the worker should acquiesce
to his social status in the society, or to the client as a person.
Instead, there must be a reinforcement or the notion that improvement in "role" and "status" in the society should not be associated
with "better" or "superior" but viewed as being merely different in

the same way that cultures are merely different from one another and not "superior or inferior."

ROLE OF THE WORKER

It is important now to look at the role of the social caseworker with Third World clients as related to the principles of acceptance. They may be as follows:

Look at culture/ethnicity and race as merely being different and not superior or inferior to one another.

Recognize, acknowledge and identify the cultural, racial and ethnic biases and prejudice which may exist in self and debilitating to the principles of acceptance.

Recognize and accept the fact that "total freedom" from ethnic, racial and cultural biases is impossible but identify the area of conflict where you are apt to coerce your views in making the client what "you want him to be."

Assess, recognize and confront your feelings on accepting a member of a different and/or the same race bases on racism, elitism, and prejudices.

Development of self awareness and self insight in relation to race, ethnic and culture.

NON-JUDGMENTAL ATTITUDE

According to the principle of non-judgmental attitude:

Conviction that the casework function excludes, assign guilt or innocence, or degrees of client's responsibility for causation of the problem or needs, but does include making evaluated judgments about the attitude, standards or action of the attitude which involves both thought and feeling element, is transmitted to the client.[5]

In the practice of social work, the assignments of "good" or "bad" and "guilt" or "innocence" to the behavior and attitudes of

a client are completely contradictory to social work values. The
development of prejudices and judgments is a natural part of the
socialization process for individuals, however blatant or subtle. In
the context of social casework with Third World clients, the socialization and negative ingrained values within the Western society regarding Blacks, Puerto-Ricans and others are so well rooted
into the Western World until it is impossible for any worker to
have escaped the effects. Oftentime, Third World individuals strat-
ify themselves on the social ladder based on their closeness, association and physical identity with those of the Western World.

Subtle indications of the manifestation of stereotypes as they
affect Third World clients can be seen in many examples of the
socialization process in America. It is the "good guys" who wear
the *white* hats and the "bad guys" who wear the *black* hats. In an
old television commercial, there was a duel between a white
knight and a black knight and invariably the white knight always
won. In the grocery stores in the American society, one will find
that there is the white ("angel food") and black ("devil food").
These factors, looked at in a vacuum or separately from the components of culture would appear to be of little significance. Nonetheless, as we closely analyze the relationship between culture,
language and white supremacy, we will find that these examples
are merely indicators and reflectors of the culture. The relevance
of this thesis is applicable to all Third World minorities in America
because they are all people of color.

It is a challenge for the social casework profession to implement the non-judgmental attitude given the negative definitions
and assumptions regarding color. If one picks up any dictionary in
the Western World, one will find Black defined as:

> The word blackness has synonyms, 60 of which are distinctly
> unfavorable, and none of them even mildly positive. Among the
> offending 60 were such words as blot, smut, smudge, sullied, be-
> grime, soot, becloud, obsure, dingy, murky, low-toned, threatening,
> frowning, foreboding, forbidding, sinister, baneful, dismal, thund-
> ery, wicked, malignant, deadly, unclean, dirty, unwashed, foul, etc.
> In addition, and this is what really hurts, 20 of those words—and I
> exclude the villainous 60 above—are related directly to race, such
> as Negro, Negress, nigger, darkey, blackamoor, etc.[6]

All Third World individuals are people of color and there is an
accompanying negative definition of their culture by the Western

World. For a more definitive description and understanding of the relationship between the definitions, language, culture, Third World and non-judgmental attitudes, we must understand the correlation between these variables. First of all, there appears to be a causal relation whereby language influences culture, culture influences language and thought, and thought and culture influence language. Language is seen by many as a transmitter of culture thereby substantiating the fact that the definitions above are not in isolation or in a vacuum from the culture. Therefore, the definition and description of Third World people cannot be viewed as separate components of the society and a judgmental attitude is implicit given the cultural definitions of Third World people.

In view of the above factors, it is impossible for any caseworker, despite ethnicity and race, to be completely free from the contaminations of the negative judgments depicting Third World people. Therefore, these negative variables interfere with the worker/client relationship of all clients and workers. The tasks faced by social caseworkers are to determine if their judgmental attitude is of such a nature that it may prohibit effective casework with clients. Secondly, the caseworkers must be cognizant of the judgmental attitudes they possess and attempt to keep control of those attitudes manifesting themselves in the casework relationship. Since the feelings and attitudes of the worker are "transmitted to the client," the social caseworker's willingness to expose and confront his/her insecurities and inadequacies regarding ethnicity and race in the casework relationship is a major step of progress for mitigating a nonjudgmental attitude. It is impossible for a worker to be totally free of prejudices and judgments regarding race and ethnicity. Therefore the possession of prejudices is permissible, but when a worker acts on these prejudices and stereotypes, it is destructive in the relationship. In reference to a worker being selective about the ethnic or racial group he/she chooses to work, it is accepted that some caseworkers are unable to work with particular clients for various reasons. Traditionally, individual social workers have not been penalized for their priorities, choices and preferences in working with the handicapped, blind, aged and others. This practice is crucial to the principle of nonjudgmental attitude because "the attitude (of the worker) which involves both thought and feelings is transmitted to the client."

In social casework practice with Third World clients and the implementation of non-judgmental attitude, the worker is not to assume that his/her cultural mode of operation is such that the client must imitate the worker in seeking a resolution to the problem presented. Therefore, there is no room for the assignment of guilt or innocence or good or bad to the client's behavior. Such behavior and actions on the part of the worker interfere with the non-judgmental attitude, principle and process in that the client will begin to devalue his/her innate strengths and self worth. It is impossible for non-judgmental attitudes to take place if the worker adopts the superior attitude that "I have the answers to your problems", and you must adopt my values if you are to conquer these difficulties. The above phenomena is particularly prevalent in the cases where the Third World worker and client are of the same ethnic and racial group.

Non-judgmental attitude is not in opposition to making evaluative judgments about the attitudes, standards or actions of the client. However, these evaluative judgments must be used as reflective discussions in helping the client to reach the goals they are setting for themselves. Most important of all, these "evaluative judgments" must not be reflective of the moral and philosophical values of "right" and "wrong" in the worker's culture.

Social casework practitioners must begin to look at social behavior as functional and dysfunctional rather than "good" or "bad" or "right" and "wrong." In other words, all behavior of clients are functional/nonfunctional and must be viewed in objective behavioral terms rather than normal/abnormal, deviant/nondeviant, good/bad, righteous/evil, sinful/nonsinful. Such concepts as "good" and "bad" are heavy-laden with subjective value judgments rather than focusing on the specific actions of the client in behavioral terms. Each individual must be viewed as striving to obtain self-fulfillment and self-actualization with some individuals having less difficulty achieving this status than others. It is the responsibility of the caseworker to make an "evaluative judgment" on the factors inherent in the client's life as well as the client's environment which may prohibit him/her from achieving the goals of self-actualization. This view of identifying behaviors, expressions, attitudes and actions in objective terminology will link the relationship between behavior and its cause. The notion of "good" and "bad" and "right" and "wrong" are attitudinal in nature and cannot be measured in behavioral terms but are reflective of subjective thought.

ROLE OF THE WORKER

The role of the caseworker in actualizing the non-judgmental attitudes with Third World minorities should be kept in the following perspectives:

> Viewing behavior as functional and dysfunctional with the role of the worker being to assist the client in modifying his/her environment or psychological status to obtain self-fulfillment and self-actualization.

> Recognize that the movement toward nonjudgmental attitude is deeply related to the acceptance of the premise that any negative feelings, however, conscious or unconscious may be communicated to the client tacitly and overtly.

> Caseworkers with Third World clients must attempt to establish early in the relationship the feelings and attitudes about the client having a worker as a member of his/her race, ethnicity or a different race/ethnicity.

> Social caseworkers must adopt the view that all human beings are "treatable" in a therapeutic relationship.

> The differences in the Third World culture and the Western culture are real issues but not the basis on which to determine behavior.

CLIENT SELF-DETERMINATION

Client self-determination is an all encompassing principle which governs every aspect of the casework relationship. According to Biestek, Client Self-Determination is:

> The practical recognition of the right and need of clients to freedom in making their own choices and decisions in the casework process. Caseworkers have a corresponding duty to respect

that right, recognize that need, stimulate and help to activate that potential for self-direction by keeping the client to see and use the available and appropriate resources of the community and of his own personality. The client's right to self-determination, however, is limited by the client's capacity for positive and constructive decision-making by the framework of civil and moral law and by the function of the agency.[7]

In the principle of self-determination, the worker must recognize and accept the unequivocal right of the human being to make decisions for self and accept the consequences of those decisions. Secondly, the worker must recognize the basic right of a human being to fail, if he/she so chooses, without the intervention of forces by the worker to prevent him/her from failure. As stated in the definition of self-determination, the only limitation placed on the right of self-determination is when the client's right interferes with moral and civil law. The failure of a client to succeed must be viewed as a non-negotiable right. Failure must be viewed as a "stepping stone to success."

Social caseworkers must abolish the attitude of "joy in victory" and "agony in defeat" when working with clients. This is not a "win" or "lose" situation. In research and practice with Third World clients, the above factors become paramount oftentime with a loss of perspective for individual self-determination. The purposefulness of behavior necessitates that workers should look at all actions and behaviors on the part of the client as a "learning experience" for the client. As far as the worker is concerned, the old medical adage that "you can have a successful operation but the patient died" applies. On the other hand, this assumption should not rule out genuine empathy, concern and sincerity for the client. Simultaneously, there is no "wrong" or "right" decision on the part of an individual client in determining his/her future.

All decisions are made on the basis of options and possible consequences and the client's knowledge of what those consequences might be. Man is never aware of all the options nor does he have control over all of them. Yet, there are specific difficulties pertaining to the social casework practice and self-determination of Third World clients which must be addressed and they are as follows:

Caseworker's view of the client's failures as reflection of the worker's effectiveness and ability to relate to Third World clients.

Subtle view of the profession that a worker's lack of success with Third World clients is an indication of insecurities, inadequacies and adjustment problems of the worker.

Glorified professional praise for social caseworkers demonstrating an effectiveness with clients of different racial and ethnic groups.

The prevailing assumption in the Western World that Third World clients are incapable of making effective decisions regarding their lives.

ROLE OF THE WORKER

Self-determination is easily realized by the social casework practitioner who has trust in humanity and humans to think and make choices for themselves under the philosophical foundation that people learn best by their own trials and errors in search of knowledge and wisdom to resolve their problems. Wisdom is gained through experience and is not transferable through advice. In working with Third World clients, the practitioner will not stimulate self-determination if the understanding of human behavior from a cultural perspective is either overlooked or misunderstood. It is the responsibility of the worker in the process of stimulating self-determination to utilize the systematic approach of deductive reasoning and reflective discussion to assist the client in reaching his/her decision for it is the client who must ultimately implement the action. There are many untold stories involving clients who have attempted to follow the advice of practitioners but failed. Therefore, the role of the social caseworker with Third World clients may be as follows in regard to self-determination.

Recognize and accept the fact that self-determination is a God-given right and self-determination must be viewed from a cultural context.

Caseworkers must recognize "Where their right to self-determination begins and ends" and where the self-determination of the client's "begins and ends." They must also be cognitive of the specific cultural lifestyles of the Third World minorities and

*utilize the unique cultural variables to implement solutions to
the presenting problem.*

In many cases, it may be difficult for a social caseworker to
utilize the cultural dimension and variables of a particular minority group culture in stimulating self-determination because the
values of social work may be antithetical to the very foundation of
the Third World's culture. Consequently, such actions may appear
to undermine the essence of social work knowledge and threatens
the "authority" and vested interest of the social work profession.

Some of the roles of the social casework practitioner and self-
determination with Third World clients include the following:

Must have a genuine internalized belief and trust in the rights
of individual freedom.

Must empathize with the experiences of Third World clients
through an understanding of their culture as solutions are
sought to the problems.

Do away with the need to "standardize" and generalize options in behavior as being acceptable only if it falls within
norms of the majority culture.

Must not view the freedom of choices and options chosen by
a client's behavior as a rejection of the practitioner.

Recognize that the foundation and epitome of effective casework practice is to assist the client in reaching decisions
based on alternatives rather than providing advice from the
worker's prospective and cultural view.

PURPOSEFUL EXPRESSION OF FEELINGS

According to Biestek, Purposeful Expression of Feelings is:

The recognition of the client's need to express his feelings
especially his negative feelings. The caseworker listens pur-
posefully, neither discouraging nor condemning the expression of
these feelings, sometimes even actively stimulating them when they
are therapeutically useful as part of the casework service.[8]

The major ingredients of purposeful expression of feelings are (1) freedom of expressing, (2) expression of negative feelings, (3) purposeful listening of the worker, (4) neither condemning nor discouraging negative feelings, and (5) actively stimulating negative feelings when they are therapeutically useful. In social casework with Third World clients, the worker must particularly stimulate and encourage negative expressions and feelings without condemnation nor discouragement as it pertains to the client's view of the worker in addition to the client's view of his environment or self. Therefore, a key and significant aspect of purposeful expression of feelings in regard to social casework with Third World clients is the encouragement of those negative feelings as they are directed toward the worker's race and ethnicity. It may be easy for the caseworker during the therapeutic relationship to encourage negative feelings as long as they are directed away from the worker. The degree of emotional anxiety, insecurity and self exposure is heightened on the part of the worker when those negative feelings are directed toward him/her. The dynamics are the same even in the relationship between minority worker and client of the same or different minority group.

Given the nature and dynamics of the inter-relationships between worker and clients of different and similar racial and ethnic groups, the question regarding the client's feeling about having a worker of a particular ethnic or racial group should be raised as early in the relationship as possible. This is not to suggest that all the problems of a particular client may relate to specific concerns of race or ethnicity. However, in cases where there are racial concerns it is accepted that the worker will never be able to get to the more subtle problems that a client may bring to the relationship until the racial and ethnic concerns are addressed. The rationale for addressing the question of race is for the worker to build a bridge for frank and honest dialogue at the present which may prevent other problems as the case progresses. It is much easier for the worker to address this concern earlier in the relationship than to attempt to address the issue once the relationship becomes solidified.

Another aspect of social casework related to purposeful expression of feelings and Third World clients is the inability of worker from a different cultural group to interpret the experiences of Third World clients and reply or listen purposively. Often-

Third World clients cannot accept the authentic feelings and behaviors of workers from the Western World.

This issue is of particular importance when there is a relationship between worker and client of different racial and ethnic groups. The worker may have difficulty in addressing certain aspects of the therapeutic relationship for fear that the client cannot accept the authentic observation and analyses of the worker. This posture of dramatized through condensation of the client is damaging to the concept of controlled emotional involvement and the therapeutic relationship.

CONFIDENTIALITY

Biestek defines confidentiality as:

> The preservation of secret information concerning the client which is disclosed in the professional relationship. Confidentiality is based upon a basic right of the client; it is an ethical obligation of the caseworker and is necessary for effective casework services. The client's right, however, is not absolute. Moreover, the client's secret is often shared with other professional persons within the agency and in other agencies . . . the obligation then binds all.[10]

Confidentiality is another one of those all encompassing principles in the casework relationship in that it underlies each and every principle stipulated. Given the systematic and historical destruction of privacy and confidentiality among Third World societies by members of the Western World, Third World clients are most suspicious and reluctant to reveal material of a confidential nature.

It is important, then, to look at confidentiality with Third World clients as being more than a "preservation of secret information" although this variable is important. The attitudinal dimension of trust and confidence must be intertwined with confidentiality for without the client's trust and confidence in the caseworker the "preservation of secret information" is futile. The successful internalizing and implementation of the principles of individualization, acceptance, purposeful expression of feelings, nonjudgmental attitude, controlled emotional involvement and self-determination are the stimuli for the development of trust and confidence which will lead to the dynamic relationship for gathering confidential information for therapeutic use.

Implicit in the principle of confidentiality is the element of the worker's respect for the individuality and personal well-being of the client's as well as respect for the information given. It is essential that the worker engage in discussions early in the stages of the relationship with client about the purpose, goals, parameters, boundaries and limitations of confidentiality. Secondly, the attitude of confidentiality rests with the comfort and security of the worker in asking pertinent questions of the Third World client. For many reasons, workers from the Western society may feel hesitant to ask or uncover certain materials because the data may be different from the experiences they know. This hesitancy, ambivalence and insecurity may be transmitted to the client and misinterpreted to denote incompetence in the worker's skills.

Finally, the over-eagerness on the worker's part to gain information may interfere with gaining confidential information from a Third World client. For many social workers, the first opportunity to experience an intensive relationship with someone of another cultural, ethnic or racial group is in the worker/client relationship. Therefore, the eagerness to penetrate for information may handicap communications. Once this is detected by the client, confidentiality and trust are questioned and destroyed in the relationship.

ROLE OF THE WORKER

The behavioral manifestation of confidentiality is relatively easy to perform by the worker but the attitudinal aspect of confidentiality and trust is more difficult. Therefore, the role of the worker in confidentiality may be as follows:

Preserve confidentiality (information).

Early discussion and explanation of confidentiality in the casework relationship.

Innate respect for individual dignity and personal worth of Third World individuals.

Awareness of Third World minorities' sensitivity to confidentiality.

Belief in the intrinsic and non-negotiable right of confidentiality.

Breach of confidentiality is usually irreparable in a therapeutic relationship.

Confidentiality enhances trust, confidence and communication between worker and client.

CONCLUSION

The importance and role of negative and positive assumptions which the worker may hold cannot be overemphasized nor overstressed in regard to the worker/client relationship of Third World clients. It is natural that humans operate out of certain assumptions regarding every action they may take. Sometimes those assumptions are conscious while other times the assumptions may be unconscious. An example of an unconscious assumption is going into an office building freely and uninhibitingly without concern or recognition of one's physical safety, yet having made an unconscious determination that the building is safe.

On the other hand, if one sees a building which appears by its structure to be unsafe, the conscious reaction would be different. In each case, an assumption has been made with one being conscious and the other being unconscious. It is necessary, then, for the worker to make and internalize positive assumptions rather than negative ones.

In conclusion, it is the responsibility of schools of social work and social work agencies to encourage caseworkers to make positive assumptions rather than negative assumptions for it is the negative assumptions which are destructive to the effective implementation of the principles of the casework relationship. Listed below are a few of the positive assumptions which social casework practitioners should internalize in their work with Third World minority clients.

"I may be part of the problem."

Minorities have a heritage and culture of which they are proud.

Be the first to confront the difference and conflicts in the worker/client relationship.

Third World minority individuals desire to be independent and self-sufficient.

Expression of pro-ingroup ethnic and racial consciousness/pride is not necessarily anti-white.

Race/ethnicity is an important variable in worker/client relationship.

Minorities can handle the authentic feelings and behavior of workers from other ethnic/racial groups.

References

1. Ignacio Aquilar. "Initial contacts with Mexican American", *Social Work*, May, 1972, page 66.
2. Felix Biestek. *The Casework Relationship*, University Books, London: 1967, page 25.
3. Esther Fibush."The White Worker and the Negro Client", *Social Casework*, Vol. XVI, (May, 1964), page 274.
4. Felix Biestek, *Casework Relationship*, page 25.
5. Ibid. page 90.
6. Ossie Davis, "The English Language is my Enemy", in Arthur C. Smith, *Language, Communication and Rhetoric in Black America*, Harper & Row, New York, 1972, page 74.
7. Felix Biestek, page 103.
8. Ibid. page 35.
9. Ibid. page 50.
10. Ibid. page 121.

IV. RELATIONSHIP IN THERAPY

The purpose of this section is to examine and analyze the dimensions of sensitivity, self-insight and self-awareness in the delivery of human services to minorities. There will be specific case illustrations of the worker/client relationship highlighting the relevance of increased self-insight, self-awareness, and sensitivity in the conceptual framework of social work with minorities.

The acquisition of human relation skills in the area of self insight, self-awareness and sensitivity to others are essential in the social work and counseling profession. When the variables of race and ethnicity enter the social intervention process, the worker's sensitivity to culture difference must become intensified. Yet, the cognitive understanding of cultural, racial and ethnic diversities are just as important as the cultural sensitivity and self-awareness. This reader provides an integration of the cognitive and cultural sensitivity awareness.

After (1) the development of adequate interviewing skills, (2) observation and understanding of the cultural dimension, and (3) an understanding of the inherent difficulties in the interaction and relationship between worker and client of different racial and ethnic groups, then there is the question of effective therapeutic skills to apply in the relationship. That is, the worker must know the techniques and strategies which are applicable to both People of Color and European ethnics. It seems obvious that the treatment skills necessary for middle class white America may not be totally applicable in another culture. Some techniques, however, may be generic enough to cut across ethnic and racial boundaries while others may need to be discarded when working with People of Color. By the same token, other strategies and techniques may need to be created. Many of these issues are raised in the literature made available.

The significance of culture in determining treatment strategies, techniques and goals cannot be underestimated. The Native

Americans' view of the universe, their environment and relationship to other people is quite different from that of Puerto
Ricans, Koreans, or Black Americans—although there may be
similarities between white middle-class culture with other ethnic
and racial groups.

The essence of this section is to acquaint educators, practitioners, and students with a perspective and provide a frame of
reference for developing and refining the tools utilized in the therapeutic relationship. The authors in this section give us the benefit
of their thinking, knowledge, and experience in this area. All of the
material is pertinent to the issues and concerns we must address
in the therapeutic relationship with members of minority cultures.

SOCIAL WORK PRACTICE WITH WEST INDIAN IMMIGRANTS*

Beverly Sewell-Coker, Joyce Hamilton-Collins, and Edith Fein

Immigrant groups challenge social service agencies that have a responsibility to serve vulnerable populations. One such group is the increasing West Indian population. There are over 26,000 West Indians in Hartford, Connecticut; they constitute the second largest West Indian population, after New York City, in the United States,[1] and Jamaicans are the largest subgroup. Like most immigrants, West Indians come to the United States and other developed countries, such as Canada and England, to seek job and educational opportunities and a better way of life. They leave areas of high unemployment and little opportunity for education or training.

BACKGROUND

The islands of the West Indies extend from the coast of Florida in the north to Venezuela in the south. They were so named because Christopher Columbus thought he had arrived in the Indies of Southeast Asia, via a new route. The West Indian islands, which include Barbados, Jamaica, Trinidad and Tobago, and others, differ widely, topographically and culturally, and each islander is

*Reprinted by permission of the authors and *Social Casework: The Journal of Contemporary Social Work* 66:9 (November 1985) 563–568; copyright © 1985 Family Service America.

proud of his or her heritage and does not want to be incorrectly identified.

West Indians are of African, Indian, and Spanish and other European descent. The West Indian family structure has both nuclear and extended family elements. Such West Indian immigrants often have difficulty adjusting to their new lives, which reflects, in part, their pattern of immigration. A parent usually comes first, unaccompanied by children, who are often left in the care of a relative, frequently the maternal grandmother, or a friend. This reinforces the strong role of the grandmother in a society in which females already have a dominant role in child rearing. The move is supported by the entire family and is seen as an opportunity for advancement. The parent stays with a relative until he or she is able to find employment, establish residence, and ensure financial stability and independence.

During this time, close contact is maintained with family members back home through frequent correspondence, occasional telephone calls, and periodic visits. For some West Indians, it may be several years before they see their children or family. Money, clothing, and food are often sent to the children and extended family members, and this continues even after the children have been sent for.

Culture Shock and the Transitional Period

The difficulties of transition do not end when the parents and children are reunited. The newly arrived members of the family must adjust to a different society and culture, but, in addition, parents and children who have long been separated may find themselves strangers. The children may also be bonded to the island grandmother and may view the mother as the "lady" in America who sends money and clothing. The parents may also have missed their children's formative years, but when the children arrive, the parents must undertake their parental roles. This often results in conflict, around family relationships, communication, and the discipline of children, especially where they clash with the new culture. Emotionally, the family is vulnerable to the stresses of the urbanized technological society that does not provide the supports they were accustomed to at home.

The West Indians who come to the United States are highly

motivated and wish to achieve not only for themselves, but also for their relatives and friends on the islands. Proud, hard-working people, they regard work and education as the means of obtaining the things they value, including social status and prestige. The average West Indian parent has high hopes for his or her children and is willing to spend time and energy to create opportunities for them.

West Indians, regardless of class, value property, since in the West Indies, it is associated with economic security, freedom, and high status. Thus, they often work at more than one job in order to acquire property.

Problems with Assimilation

Some West Indians in North America try to hold onto every aspect of their culture and thus make little attempt to assimilate. This causes conflict with other groups who resent such strong cultural ties. It can also create difficulties for the children who find that their parents are overprotective and impose many restrictions to keep them close and under strict control. Adolescence is a time of particular difficulty, but the stress of a new culture, combined with the parents' desire to keep their children from making the same mistakes they may have made, create special problems. One study of Jamaicans shows that even island parent-child relationships are characterized by conflicts, usually springing from the young person's desire for independence.[2] But in the United States, teenage youths especially yearn for freedom of action and the right to make their own decisions and to choose their own friends.

The Double Standard

West Indians follow a double standard in the rearing of boys and girls, and this standard is continued in the United States. Boys are allowed more freedom, whereas parents are more concerned with their daughter "getting in trouble." As a result, it is usual to find that teenage boys are not clients of social service agencies because their behavior tends to be more acceptable to their parents, except when they rebel by joining the Rastafarian Movement.

Girls are trained to be passive, obedient, and domestic, to become
good wives and mothers.[3] They are referred as clients when they
rebel,[4] in an attempt to gain freedom and to be like their American
friends.

School and Peer Group Pressure

West Indian children have their own adjustment problems. Education in the islands, to a large extent, is based on the British system,
although it is changing. Jamaica, in particular, is revising its curriculum to conform more to the U.S. system. The children who come
to the United States must become familiar with a different school
system and different levels of educational exposure. As a result,
some children excel and others require remedial help to meet
their grade requirements. In addition, it may be difficult for youngsters to make themselves understood because of their accent or
the expressions they use. Self-consciousness about speech can
inhibit children who are not yet familiar with a new culture, and
they may appear shy and withdrawn. West Indian children also
tend to be physically smaller than American children and thus
may be viewed by their teachers as immature.

This period of transition may also cause difficulties within the
family. The parents, who may appear strict in comparison to
American parents, often have difficulty adjusting their values in a
society that allows children a great deal of freedom. Strictness
may also accompany high expectations for academic accomplishment, which may not be based on the child's true abilities. Rules
regarding the child's behavior and performance of household
tasks may be rigidly enforced by corporal punishment, the traditional discipline on the islands. This may result in the child acting
out by running away from home, stealing, or joining the
Rastafarian Movement. Such behavior baffles the parents who
believe that children should be mannerly, obedient, and respectful
of adults.

USE OF SERVICES

The parents' feelings of frustration and helplessness in their
efforts to control their children lead many of them to public or

private social service agencies in a desperate attempt to find help. Many have reacted in ways most familiar to them in response to their problems, and although discipline and physical punishment are administered with what the parents perceive as love and a concern for the child, they can be harsh and even severe. When discipline is labeled child abuse and reported to Protective Services, West Indian parents become angry and defensive, as they feel that the law should not interfere in family matters.

Therapy is a relatively new phenomenon in the West Indies. Social workers there have more concrete roles, such as teaching arts and crafts and organizing programs. Only within recent years has formal social work counseling been recognized. In the United States, as the idea of counseling is introduced to West Indians, many parents become defensive and resist it because it is unfamiliar and they are more comfortable sharing family problems with their family or pastor. They are often self-referred, but only after having been involved with school personnel or Protective Services.

The therapist, in an effort to establish a relationship, must explain why certain questions are being asked and describe the therapeutic process exactly, since many clients may have the idea that therapy will be for only one session and that only the child will be involved. Many parents attempt to discipline their children by threatening to send them back to the West Indies, failing to realize that they might be angrily reacting to the long parent-child separation. This, too, requires careful understanding and explanation. West Indians tend to do best in short-term treatment contracts in which there is a clear focus on goals; personal experience has shown that they terminate prematurely in long-term therapy when personality issues are involved.

West Indians, a conservative people, do not readily express emotion. They tend to show feelings by doing and giving, but say little. This is nonadaptive in U.S. culture, and therapy may help them be more verbally expressive. Many West Indians do not maintain direct eye contact, not because of any clinical pathology or lack of trust, but rather because they were raised to respect people, older people, in particular, and a sign of respect is not looking someone directly in the eye. Americans, however, are socialized not to trust people who do not maintain eye contact. West Indians, also, are more formal; for example, they address adults by their last names. In therapy, therefore, it is important that thera-pists show the same respect that is being shown them by clients.

To sensitize staff working with this vulnerable group, Child and Family Services, a large multiservice child welfare and mental health agency in Hartford, developed a variety of responses. One was in-service training for staff on cultural issues: a series of workshops for the entire staff—led by the Hispanic, Black, and West Indian staff—that focused on the background and needs of each ethnic group. In addition, West Indian culture seminars were held for the sixteen agency psychology and social work interns.

Direct services are offered in individual and family counsel-ing by professionals of the same ethnic group. Further, a curricu-lum was developed through the family life enrichment program geared toward the West Indian population. This program serves groups of people who meet weekly for six sessions in which a common theme, problem, or developmental task is discussed. In-structions are didactic, and discussions are led by a social worker within a well-structured framework. Topics covered in the group include

1. The differences between growing up in the West Indies and growing up in the United States;
2. The impact of the Rastafarian Movement;
3. Legal and school-related problems (guest speakers);
4. Communication-listening skills;
5. Building self-confidence;
6. Communicating love.

The West Indian groups are led by one of two West Indian social workers. The use of professionals of the same ethnic group helps motivate people to begin in groups and to continue to attend them. This is also true for individual and family counseling.

The credibility of the agency and the legitimacy of its mental health services are further enhanced as West Indian staff are en-couraged to lecture and lead seminars for West Indian community groups and to consult with school personnel. As the school system includes more West Indian children, consultation on the heritage, culture, and needs of these children becomes an important service component.

Case Examples

The following vignettes illustrate the problems and solutions typical of the West Indian immigrant experience.

The G's. Mrs. G was referred by the probation department of the courts because her fourteen-year-old daughter, Pauline, had stolen a watch. Pauline had become rebellious, staying out late at night without her mother's permission, and was becoming interested in boys. As Mrs. G imposed more restrictions, fearing that Pauline would become pregnant and not complete her education, Pauline's acting-out increased. During the course of treatment, Pauline received a beating, severe enough to leave scars on her body, for staying out late. The worker filed a report with the state Protective Services, which made Mrs. G angry at the worker and at Protective Services for interfering. This was the first time the worker, a West Indian, had ever made such a report. It was difficult for her to do, she felt guilty about the report, and her guilt was reinforced by the client's anger. The report became an issue in therapy, but as it was discussed and resolved, the relationship between Mrs. G and the therapist became closer.

Mrs. G's child management practices changed as a result of individual counseling and attendance at the family life enrichment group, where she saw other West Indian parents changing. She began allowing her daughter more reasonable hours; Pauline, in turn, was more responsible, and their relationship improved. Pregnancy and contraception were discussed with Pauline, and she went for birth control assistance. She was able to complete high school and planned to go to college.

The T's. Mrs. T came to the United States when she was eighteen years old, leaving her seven-month-old daughter, Monica, in the care of her own mother. Some seven years later, Mrs. T sent for Monica. By then Mrs. T had married and had two other children, one a three-week-old daughter. From the outset, Mrs. T and Monica had great difficulty relating to each other. Mrs. T found that Monica, shy, mannerly, compliant, and quiet, did not seek affection and attention as her sisters did. She also had difficulty getting along with her sisters and was having trouble in school. Mrs. T felt that Monica's best friend was a bad influence, telling Monica she was being used too much to baby-sit and encouraging her to defy her parents. Referral to the agency was made by Protective Services after the police caught Monica stealing candy in a department store.

Mrs. T was angry and at first resisted therapy. She was helped to understand counseling and how it could be useful to her family, and subsequently she and Monica were seen, individually, once a week. Mrs. T expressed concern about not being able to show affection to her children. With the worker's help, she began to learn how to communicate love and to develop a relationship with Monica through positive feelings. As she became aware of cultural issues, she was less critical of Monica. These tasks were difficult for her, but her relationship with the West Indian worker helped her to be more open and to participate in the worker's family life enrichment group. She gained support from other group members and was able to apply her new insights to new behaviors. Monica was helped to adjust to the United States and to find her place in the family, and the mother and daughter relationship improved. The relationship with the worker was maintained with occasional phone calls after therapy ended, which gave the worker confidence that any further difficulties would be caught early.

QUESTIONS AND IMPLICATIONS

The agency response to the West Indian clients can be summarized as follows:

1. Deliberate efforts to acquaint group members with counseling, a foreign concept to them, and to make them feel comfortable in counseling;
2. An attempt to deliver services by professionals of the same ethnic group;
3. Efforts to offer a variety of services to serve a variety of needs. Services included lectures, seminars, and school consultations; inservice training for agency staff on cultural issues; and individual and family counseling;
4. Establishment of a family life enrichment program, with a special curriculum for West Indian groups.

These efforts attracted a large number of West Indian clients, but they also raise questions about practice implications as the agency seeks to extend them to other vulnerable groups. One such question is as follows: What are the advantages and disadvantages of service by professionals of the same heritage (for example, West Indian therapists and West Indian clients), by professionals of the same racial group, but of a different heritage (for example, black American therapists and West Indian clients), or, by majority group professionals sensitized to the minority group heritage (for example, white American therapists and West Indian clients)?

Research findings were mixed in evaluations of patient-therapist racial matching. In some studies, minority group members felt that higher quality services are delivered by majority group professionals,[4] but others found minority group matching more comfortable. Many writers feel that common background is less important than is claimed and that special training and sensitivity can compensate for differences between worker and client.[5,6] This raises two questions: What are the characteristics of the minority group and their expectations for therapy that would lead them to accept or to reject majority group professionals? What training is needed when minority professionals are not available?

This leads to another question: How can an agency demonstrate its commitment by extra outreach efforts?

The perception of elitism in established agencies can bar service use by many minorities, but outreach in the community can be used to contact groups not apt to come to agencies on their own. Outreach, however, is also the extra effort in therapy to engage clients who may have difficulties with forms and procedures. This may be the result of resistance, unfamiliar concepts, or the therapist's rigidity. The therapist, however, must be creative in dealing with such problems, and the agency must support innovative approaches that will effect such outreach.

Accessibility of service is always a problem. Are there changes in service delivery patterns that make services more accessible, such as flexibility in scheduling, new programs, and a demonstrated tolerance for cultural differences?

Office visits by clients are only one mode of service delivery. For the West Indians, for example, who revere education, the best point of entry may be the school system. Perhaps socialization groups for new immigrant children will generate parental referrals when conflicts become unmanageable. With other vulnerable groups, the workplace, social club, or even the street may be the most productive contact. Agencies can respond with evening or weekend hours to be more flexible in service delivery, and appointments can be shifted each week to accommodate the client's time off.

A last question regards encouraging clients to use other agency services: Can family life enrichment groups be so used?

All family life enrichment curricula can be modified to meet the needs of a particular minority group. Divorce, bereavement, alcoholism, child management—these are universal issues. A curriculum geared to the cultural heritage of the clients creates a feeling of understanding and trust in which communication can occur; allows groups not familiar with mental health services to be introduced to them in an emotionally neutral, supportive climate; permits sharing of problems as clients gain relief and realize that others are in the same situation; and provides an introduction to agency services, after which other, more intensive services may be implemented.

Such responses to the needs of the West Indian population in Hartford can be readily adapted to other vulnerable groups. It is important that social work practice be based on the background, heritage, and needs of each group. It is especially important for agencies to demonstrate, with their institutional support, an understanding of the groups' vulnerabilities and the workers' efforts to turn them into strengths.

This article was adapted from a paper presented at the National Association of Social Workers' Annual Meeting, Washington, D.C. November 1983.

Notes

1. "West Indians in Hartford," *The Hartford Courant*, 31 July 1983.
2. A. S. Phillips, *Adolescence in Jamaica* (Kingston, Jamaica: Jamaica Publishing House, Ltd., 1974).
3. Janet Brice, "West Indian Families," in *Ethnicity and Family Therapy*, ed. Monica McGoldrick, John K. Pearce, and Joseph Giordano (New York: The Guilford Press, 1982).

4. Shirley Cooper, "A Look at the Effect of Racism on Clinical Work," in *Social Casework: Introductory Readings*, ed. Anthony Maluccio and Wendy Winters (West Hartford, CT: University of Connecticut School of Social Work, 1978).
5. Evelyn Robinson, "Reflections on the Cross-Cultural Racial Relationship," in *Training for Service Delivery to Minority Clients*, ed. Emelicia Mizio and Anita J. Delaney (New York: Family Service Association of America, 1981).
6. Emelicia Mizio, "White Worker—Minority Client," *Social Work* 17 (May 1972): 82–87.

A THEORETICAL MODEL FOR THE PRACTICE OF PSYCHOTHERAPY WITH BLACK POPULATIONS*

Anna Mitchell Jackson

Traditional clinical intervention strategies have been used with Black clients with varying degrees of effectiveness (Adams, 1970; Banks, 1972; Branch, 1977; Di-Angi, 1976; Griffith, 1977; Jackson, A. M., 1973; and Wilson, 1974). Indeed, clinical practices as they pertain to Black populations have been based primarily on European and American constructs (Baldwin, 1976; Nobles, 1972; Jackson, G., 1977; Offer & Sabashin, 1966). Black culture, if cited at all, often is evaluated as a variant of European culture.

Increasingly, Black theoreticians have questioned the application of traditional treatment approaches to Black populations, citing as evidence the lack of congruence of these practices with the Black experience, life style, and culture (Akbar, 1977; Allen, W., 1978; Amini, 1972; Buck, 1977; Leonard & Jones, 1980; Jackson, G., 1976). In addition to race and culture, systematic and systemic practices of racism also have been noted as important in researching inequities in client diagnosis, disposition, and treatment involvement (Griffith, 1976; Jackson, Berkowitz, & Farley, 1974; Thomas & Sillen, 1972; Warren, Jackson, Nugaris, & Farley, 1973).

Models of personality and treatment based on African and African-American frames of reference have been proposed as corrective mechanisms by certain theoreticians (Baldwin, in press;

*Reprinted by permission of the author and *The Journal of Black Psychology* 10:1 (August 1983) 19–27; copyright © 1983 The Association of Black Psychologists.

Jones, 1980; Toldson & Pasteur, 1975). The stated goals of these theories by and large is the incorporation of particular aspects of Black culture thought to be germane to the adaptive functioning of Black individuals. A treatment model proposed in this paper is based on similar referents. The purpose of the model is to clarify basic underlying values and behaviors believed to be essential to the understanding of behavioral dynamics and to potential positive treatment outcomes.

CULTURAL THEORIES

Psychological theories provide a mechanism for understanding human behavior and for developing treatment models. However, theoretical formulations are germane only to the extent that the importance of culture is recognized and relevant cultural values incorporated (Hall, 1977). In this section, selected Black cultural theories will be examined and their potential relevance to treatment of Black individuals explored. These theories collectively emphasize the importance of African values and language structure in understanding Black behavior either as maintained intact or as modified by encounters with racial discrimination (Akbar, 1977; Baldwin, in press; Jackson, 1979; Jones, 1980; Toldson & Pasteur, 1975; Turner, 1969; Vaas, 1979).

Cultural theories in Black psychology are characterized generally by an emphasis on "wellness" or normality instead of psychopathology. The focus on normality in turn is based on an African value system. These theories are quite discrepant with existing psychological formulations about human behavior in general and Black behavior in particular (Baldwin, 1976; Chimezie, 1973; Nobles, 1972).

Prominent among the cultural values advocated by Black psychologists are those of group centered behavior, strong kinship bonds, inherent feelings of cooperation and sharing, enhanced sensitivity to interpersonal issues, and an over-arching religious orientation that provides structure, direction, a philosophy of the interrelatedness of all things and a comprehensive way of interpreting the universe and life (Mibiti, 1971; Nobles, 1972). Behaviors that deviate from these norms are perceived largely as erosions of Black identity or cultural values. The prescribed task when erosions of this nature occur is one of resocialization. Notably absent in reconstructive prescriptions are concepts of disordered development and a reliance on individual recompensation except as individual efforts are influenced by group goals or extended self-identity (Baldwin, 1976; Jackson, 1982; Mibiti, 1971; Nobles, 1976). In illustration of the type of synthesis and philosophy described above, the theoretical formulation of several Black psychologists will be reviewed.

A noted Black theoretician, Na'im Akbar (1977), has creatively combined religious and cultural beliefs with insightful observations of Black behavior. He has stressed the absence of competitive attitudes in his writings and a pervasive sense of caring and concern as core behavioral traits that characterize Black people. A "feeling" or affective orientation is also stressed by him. These core traits are perceived as instrumental in the adaptive functioning of Black individuals; traits that have permitted Black people to deal effectively and innovatively with the malignant form of racism experienced during and following slavery. The heightened sense of caring and empathy, in his opinion, also carries with it an obligation to help establish a more stress free and equitable environment. Cooperative efforts and respect for others are cardinal tenets in his theory. Based on his writings, his perception of human motivation appears to be that basic intentions and drives are benevolent in nature and that people are propelled largely by their desires to help others. Human potential seems to be conceptualized in terms of mastery. In keeping with a strong religious orientation, Akbar has also stressed the role of naturalness in human behavior, spirituality, and the holistic organization of man and the universe in theoretical presentations (1976, 1977).

In his theoretical formulations regarding the structure of Black personality, Joseph Baldwin (in press) has emphasized the biogenetic origins of Black character traits. Since Black personality traits are conceptualized as innate, culture specific, and unique, changes in basic characteristics can only occur through dilution of the African genetic structure itself. However, confusion regarding African values and Black identity can occur through the incorporation of beliefs discrepant with those previously held. When this occurs, "misorientation" results and a progressive loss of Blackness occurs. As the underlying structure for Blackness is genetically based in this theoretical system, "misorientation" can be readily reversed by resocialization. In this model, then, deviation from the norm is described as a maladjustment that can be conceptualized in terms of loss of contact with cultural roots. Although maladjustment can reach levels of moderate severity in this system, adjustment problems can be addressed effectively by the reestablishment of cultural linkage and by cognitive restructuring. No assumption is made about underlying or unconscious mechanisms in the development of maladjusted behavior.

The importance of biological and cultural underpinnings for Black behavior is underscored by Gerald Jackson (1976, 1977). He is also of the opinion that social and political influences shape behavioral responses. The influences of social and political forces are strongly alluded to in the prior theoretical systems discussed as well. Jackson conceptualizes the uniqueness of Black behavior along several dimensions. He describes socialization experiences that help in the solidification of group-centered behavior and parenting styles that help cultivate respect for age, cooperation, and role flexibility. Motivation is described as group-centered in his system. Cognition and problem solving are described as inductive in nature, a view that is supported by other Black psychologists. He emphasizes a need for increased political sophistication and influence.

The type of socialization experiences and cultural training that Jackson described results in unique cognitive and perceptual styles. Thomas (1980) reported a vigorous evaluation and screening component in her analysis of self-esteem and perception that insures a Black referent. This active process relies heavily on group consensual validation and facilitates reculturation. In keeping with this perspective the author (Jackson, 1979) described divergent thinking (inductive reasoning) as a pervasive problem-solving technique in Black adolescents. This cognitive style was thought to be characteristic of Black people in general.

The salient value of Black culture and life style in treatment approaches have been addressed increasingly by Black psychologists (Jackson, 1982; Jones, 1980; Toldson & Pasteur, 1975) and varying assessments of the effects of racism and the impact of these experiences and cultural beliefs on behavior (Jones, 1980).

from widely different backgrounds. It is envisioned that inclusion of Black professionals from diverse backgrounds will be a systematic means of effecting change across a broad spectrum of behavior and systems and will permit a reinstitution of "groupness" that has been eroded by time, history, and social and political circumstances.

Race, Black identity, and Black culture are cornerstones of the model. These factors have spanned time, history, and circumstance to perpetuate a sense of uniqueness as a people and as an individual member of the racial group. Synchrony among all of these factions, then, may be viewed as optimal adjustment or optimal mental health. Effective operational behavior within systems, networks, and environments is seen as enhancing optimal adjustment.

Within the framework of the Black clinical practice model, the Black helping professional becomes an integral part of the network and family resources of the individual. To enhance therapeutic effectiveness, concepts of individual, group, family, and multiple impact therapies may be utilized within the confines of overlapping community, cultural, and political network systems.

Despite the seemingly logical nature of the model and consistency with described Black cultural values, numerous barriers to implementation exist. Some major barriers are discussed below.

BARRIERS TO IMPLEMENTATION OF THE CLINICAL PRACTICE MODEL

Theoretically the proposed Black clinical practice model is consistent with existing concepts of Black culture and psychotherapeutic approaches. However, notwithstanding the logical nature of the model itself, the final proof must be practical implementation.

Implementation of the Black clinical practice model would entail open-ended involvement on the part of helping Black professionals, requiring creative funding mechanisms and supportive networks. These could prove to be sizable deterrents to implementation. Considerable risk-taking behaviors would be involved on the part of helping professionals as well as the abandonment of acquired personal economic and political advantages.

In addition to the factors mentioned below, another sizable barrier to the development of the Black clinical practice model is the vast variability of Black people. Black people differ in perspectives, perceptions, and personality even though basic cultural values and behavioral styles are postulated (and observed). Because this is likely, the Black helping professional must make assessments of the client on many different dimensions. Assessment might involve actual participant observation for a period of time in the social and family environs of the client.

Credibility poses still another barrier to implementation. Skepticism about motivation and competency may impede client involvement and therapist effectiveness. Although this is a traditional barrier to treatment involvement, distrust of Black helping professionals takes on special significance. In certain instances Black professionals may be seen as extensions of white institutions and as indistinguishable from white professionals. This could be because of inferred similarities in employment settings and educational and clinical experience. Also, internalization of pervasive opinions about the competency of Black people may negatively influence the formation of trusting relationships.

Societal, political, and individual factors in the implementation process are potentially the largest barriers of all. In societal structures where power is determined by race, there are always problems of influence and control over crucial life experiences for both therapist and client. Social and political structures set real limits on goals.

Yet certain aspects of the Black clinical practice model can be implemented. Emphasis can be placed, for example, on family and group procedures. Psychotherapy with Black clients can include family members and other significant persons on a routine basis. Also the range of Black consultants can be expanded to include anthropologists, sociologists, economists, urban planners, and lawyers. Community development and education can be consistently emphasized as well.

Nevertheless, actual implementation of the treatment model in all of its aspects will require extensive deliberation and study. Although formidable, this appears to be a goal worthy of pursuit.

Without alternative clinical practice procedures, traditional approaches will continue to be used. Given the continuation of traditional approaches as central clinical practices, past difficulties in treatment, in involvement, and outcome are predictable.

CONCLUSION

The need to develop treatment models and personality theories consistent with the cultural values and life experiences of Black people has been advocated by Black theoreticians. Activities in this area have increased in recent years. The theoretical Black clinical practice model proposed in this article is an attempt to embellish this line of discourse and to spur creative efforts at refinement and implementation.

Presented in fuller version under the title, "The Practice of Psychology: A Black Perspective" at the Association of Black Psychology Convention, Cherry Hill, N.J. August 16, 1980.

Notes and References

Adams, P. L. Dealing with racism in bi-racial psychiatry. *Journal of the American Academy of Child Psychiatry*, 1970, *9*, 33–43.

Akbar, N. *The community of self*. Chicago: Nation of Islam Office of Human Development, 1976.

Akbar, N. *Natural psychology and human transformation*. Chicago: World Community of Islam, 1977.

Allen, W. The search for applicable theories of Black family life. *Journal of Marriage and the Family*, 1978, *40*(1), 117–129.

Allen, S. The African Heritage. *Black World*, 1971, *20*(3), 14–18.

Amini, J. M. *An African frame of reference*. Chicago: Institute of Positive Education, 1972.

Baldwin, J. Black psychology and Black personality: Some issues for consideration. *Black Books Bulletin*, 1976, *4*(3), 6–11, 65.

Baldwin, J. *Afrikan (Black) personality: From an Afrocentric framework*. Chicago: Third World Press, in press.

Banks, H. C. The differential effects of race and social class in helping. *Journal of Clinical Psychology*, 1972, *28*, 90–92.

Branch, T. S. Race and therapist status and variables in the therapeutic process (Doctoral dissertation, University of Washington, 1976). *Dissertation Abstracts International*, 1977, *37*(7-B), 3597.

Buck, M. Peer counseling from a Black perspective. *Journal of Black Psychology*, 1977, *3*(2), 107–113.

Chimezie, A. Theorizing on Black behavior: The role of the Black psychologist. *Journal of Black Studies*, 1973, *4*(1), 15–28.

Di-Angi, P. Barriers to the Black and White therapeutic relationship. *Perspectives in Psychiatric Care*, 1976, *14*(4), 180–183.

Griffith, M. S. Effects of race and sex of client on duration of outpatient psychotherapy (Doctoral dissertation, University of Colorado, 1975). *Dissertation Abstracts International*, 1976, *36*(8-B), 4157.

Griffith, M. S. The influence of race on the psychotherapeutic relationship. *Psychiatry*, 1977, *40*(1), 27–40.

Hall, E. T. *Beyond culture*. New York: Anchor, 1977.

Jackson, A. M. Psychotherapy: Factors associated with the race of the therapist. *Psychotherapy: Theory, Research and Practice*, 1973, *10*, 273–277.

Jackson, A. M. Performance on convergent tasks by Black adolescents. In W. D. Smith, A. K. Burlew, M. H. Moseley, and W. M. Whitney (Eds.), *Reflections on Black psychology*. University Press of America, 1979.

Jackson, A. M. Psychosocial aspects of the therapeutic process. In S. M. Turner and R. T. Jones (Eds.), *Behavior therapy and Black populations: Psychosocial issues and empirical findings*. New York: Plenum Publishing Corporation, 1982.

Jackson, A. M., Berkowitz, H., & Farley, G. K. Race as a variable in the treatment involvement of children. *Journal of American Academy of Child Psychiatry*, 1974, *13*(1), 20–31.

Jackson, G. The African genesis of the Black perspective in helping. *Professional Psychology*, 1976, *7*(3), 363–367.

Jackson, G. The emergence of a Black perspective in counseling. *Journal of Negro Education*, 1977, *46*(3), 230–253.

Jackson, G. The origin and development of Black psychology: Implications for Black studies and human behavior. *Studia Africana*, 1979, *13*, 271–293.

Jones, A. C. A conceptual model for treatment of Black patients. Personal correspondence, 1980.

Leonard, P., & Jones, A. C. Theoretical considerations for psychotherapy with Black clients. In R. C. Jones (Ed.), *Black Psychology* (2nd ed.). New York: Harper and Row, 1980.

Mibiti, J. *African religions and philosophy*. New York: Anchor Books, 1971.

Nobles, W. W. African philosophy: Foundations of Black Psychology. In R. L. Jones (Ed.), *Black Psychology*. New York: Harper and Row, 1972.

Nobles, W. W. Extended self: Rethinking the so-called Negro self-concept. *Journal of Black Psychology*, 1976, *2*(2), 15–24.

Offer, D., & Sabshin, M. *Normality: Theoretical and clinical concepts of mental health*. New York: Basic Books, 1966.

Thomas, A. *A reinterpretation of the development of Black self-esteem*. Dissertation Proposal, 1980.

Thomas, A., & Sillen, S. *Racism and psychiatry.* New York: Brunner Mazel, 1972.

Toldson, I. C., & Pasteur, A. B. Developmental stages of Black self-discovery: Implications for using Black art forms in group interaction. *Journal of Negro Education,* 1975, *44*(2), 130–138.

Turner, L. D. *Africanisms in the Gullah dialect.* New York: Arnold Press, 1969.

Vass, W. K. *The Bantu-speaking heritage of the United States.* Los Angeles: Center for Afro-American Studies, University of California, 1979.

SOCIAL WORK WITH THIRD-WORLD PEOPLE*

Armando Morales

The most recent issue of the *Encyclopedia of Social Work* lists the following groups under the term "minorities": American Indians, Asian Americans, Blacks, Chicanos, Puerto Ricans, and white ethnics.[1] The term "white ethnics" is frequently used to refer to the descendants of eastern and southern European immigrants such as Jewish, Greek, Hungarian, Lithuanian, Italian, Irish, and Scandinavian Americans who came to the United States between 1880 and 1920. They number approximately fifty million persons and are sometimes called "middle Americans."[2] They generally do not share the same socioeconomic characteristics often found in other minority groups. For example, white ethnics have been successfully acculturated into American life, they earn more money than Anglo-American Protestants, and their educational mobility is greater than that of other Americans.[3]

Because white ethnics are less likely than other minorities to be welfare recipients and, therefore, social work clients, this article focuses on the remaining minority groups—Blacks, Hispanics, Asian Americans, and American Indians, who are frequently referred to as Third-World people.[4]

In 1975, the Third-World population of the United States consisted of 24,000,000 Blacks, approximately 11,200,000 Hispanics, 2,000,000 Asian Americans, and 1,000,000 American Indians.[5] These groups constitute 17 percent of the total U.S. population.

*Reprinted by permission of the author and *Social Work* 26:1 (January 1981) 45–50; copyright © 1981 National Association of Social Workers, Inc.

The internal segmentation of these groups reflects their diversity. For example, the black population comprises at least three subgroups: those who are born in the United States, those who are born in and emigrate from the West Indies, and those who are born in and emigrate from Africa. The Hispanic population consists of 6,690,000 persons of Mexican descent, 1,600,000 Puerto Ricans, 743,000 Cubans, 671,000 Central Americans, and 1,428,000 persons termed by the census as "other Spanish." All these Hispanic subgroups include persons who are born in or immigrate to the United States. With the exception of the Brazilians who speak Portuguese, these subgroups share a common language—Spanish. However, they are not homogeneous and they have different needs. Asian Americans consist of the following subgroups: Chinese, Japanese, Filipinos, Koreans, Samoans, Guamanians, and Indo-Chinese. In addition to language differences, each of these subgroups has a distinct culture. The American Indian and Alaska Native population is most diverse, consisting of 481 identified tribal groups. Half of all Indians belong to nine tribes; the largest tribal group is the Navajo, with a population of 140,000.

Street has maintained that the increasing racial, ethnic, and political consciousness of these groups binds them together under the term "Third World" and enhances their appreciation of themselves and their relationship with each other.[6] This emerging consciousness has led Third-World groups to coin such catchwords as "black power," "brown power," "yellow power," and "red power," all of which reflect their ideologies, programs, and strategies to achieve power. Their ideologies and strategies, however, differ from and threaten those of white society.

Prager has described an ideology of whiteness that enables whites to protect white privilege.[7] He has found several components that constitute the white ideology, one of which is the rejection of ethnic or racial consciousness expressed through such terms as "Third World," "Chicano," and "Native American." Such ethnic consciousness is viewed as a challenge to what whites perceive as an ideal nonracial, integrated society. Within this ideological context, separatism, language differences, and cultural enhancement are thought to be improper responses for building a society for all. Thus, the ideology of whiteness provides a framework for evading and denying Third-World realities. According to Street, this ideology partly reflects the social science theories on race relations, which affect the planning and implementation of human service programs. Often, these theories constitute barriers to the delivery of services to Third-World people.[8]

INDICATORS OF WELL-BEING

Discrimination and prejudice result in the economic, social, and psychological deprivation of Third-World groups. The economic position of these groups is far inferior to whites.[9] For example, in 1972, the median family income for blacks had declined to 59 percent of that for whites. Over the last twenty years, unemployment rates for blacks were more than twice as high as those for whites. The economic situation for American Indians is even worse. Their current income averages between one-fourth and one-third of the national per capita average. And over the last twenty years, the unemployment rates for Indians were even higher than those for blacks. In some years during this period, Navajo unemployment reached 60 percent. It is a myth that Asian Americans are comparatively better off than other Third-World groups. In 1969, the median income for Chinese men living in urban areas was among the lowest recorded for all groups. The median income for Filipino men was lower than that of the white, black, or Spanish-speaking male for all urban areas except New York and Chicago.

Furthermore, the economic and emotional stability of Third-World families is threatened by arrests, and Third-World people are more likely to be arrested than are whites. In California, for example, the imprisonment of blacks increased 28 percent between 1950 and 1970, although the general black population increased only 2 percent during this period. Among persons institutionalized in California during 1970, blacks had a three-to-one chance of going to prison, and whites had a three-to-one chance of going to a mental institution.[10] Street asserted that

> arrest rates are higher in those towns where the police take a defensive or offensive stance toward Third-World people, where they try to protect "whitetown" from "blacktown."[11]

The author compared the number of arrests made for drunkenness and drunken driving in a white community and a Mexican

American community in Los Angeles. The two communities had comparable general populations, identical ratios of alcoholism, and identical major crime ratios. The author found that Mexican Americans had a nine-to-one greater chance (9,676 to 1,552) of being arrested for their drinking behavior than had whites because of the large number of police assigned to the Mexican American community. Altogether, 375 officers, averaging 13.5 officers per square mile, were assigned to the Mexican American community, as compared to 151 officers assigned to the white community, averaging 3.5 officers per square mile.[12]

Health statistics also reveal that the conditions of life for Third-World people are worse than they are for whites. For example, the rate of infant mortality for all American Indians is 32 per 1,000, compared to 15 for whites, and the rate on the Navajo Reservation is more than twice the national average.[13] Moreover, conditions of life for American Indians are literally the poorest in the nation.

In analyzing national data on the institutionalized population, Gruber found inequality in the social services. He demonstrated how race and class are used by organizations to assign diagnostic categories and award services. The outcome is the propelling of minority and poor persons into institutions in which failure becomes a way of life.[14]

In the areas of health, education, work, and housing in relation to Third-World people, the structure of inequality is glaring. Third-World groups recognize the inequality they face and commit themselves to equalize attainment in these areas. The goal of many of these groups is to improve their life situations by gaining control of self and community. Given the needs of Third-World people and given class discrimination and institutional racism as the causes of inequality, how should the social work profession respond? In addressing this question, the author focuses on an ecosystems model for practice with Third-World people.

ECOSYSTEMS MODEL

Social work practice focuses on the interaction between the person and the environment. The term "person" may refer to an individual or may represent people in the context of a family, large or small group, organization, community, or even larger structures of society. Social work intervention might be directed at the person, the environment, or both. In each case, the social worker seeks to enhance and restore the social functioning of people or to change social conditions that impede the mutually beneficial interaction between people and their environment.

The interaction between Third-World people and their environment involves multiple factors—social, economic, racial, political, and the like—all of which have adverse effects on the life situations of this population. In providing services, the social worker should seek to understand the attitudes of Third-World people about such factors and the impact of these factors on them. This orientation would aid the practitioner in identifying the unique needs of Third-World people and in achieving social work goals—"to enhance and restore social functioning and to improve social conditions."

A major problem in achieving these goals, however, is related to the conceptual constraints imposed by social work methods. In other words, social workers, as Nelsen points out, perceive phenomena exclusively and narrowly through the lenses of the methods in which they have been trained.[15] Meyer believes that

> the use of any methodological model as an anchoring or conceptual point of reference is like viewing something through the wrong end of the telescope—the view is too restricted and narrow to account for the breadth of the phenomena to be captured.[16]

Meyer adds that for years social work has been offering its well-honed methods to those who could use them instead of first finding out what was needed and then selecting the method from its interventive repertoire or inventing new methods. She believes that the methods framework has been functional in maintaining social work's denial of what had to be done with regard to broader social problems. Meyer proposes the use of an ecosystems orientation to practice. This orientation involves the application of ecology and general systems theory to professional tasks. In explaining the ecosystems perspective, Meyer points out that it

> allows social workers to look at psychological phenomena, account for complex variables, assess the dynamic interplay of these variables, draw conceptual boundaries around the unit of attention or

the case, and then generate ideas for interventions. At this point methodology enters in; for in any particular case—meaning a particular individual, family, group, institutional unit, or geographical area—any number of practice interventions might be needed.[17]

This model of practice would promote social workers' understanding of the (1) psychosocial problems experienced by Third-World people, (2) crippling effects of institutional racism, and (3) oppressive neocolonial environments in which Third-World people struggle to survive.

Assuming that social work abandons its constricted methods framework and adopts the ecosystems perspective, this question must be asked: What new objectives should social work seek to fulfill to help Third-World people meet their psychosocial needs more effectively? Social workers should pursue at least three basic objectives. These objectives focus on manpower issues in the profession, the use of Third-World human services agencies, and the development of proactive intervention strategies.

MANPOWER ISSUES

In analyzing the manpower needs of social work, it becomes apparent that bilingual, bicultural practitioners are badly needed. The use of translators interferes with the accuracy of the diagnosis and represents second-class treatment. Furthermore, although one can perceive depression as a universal feeling, its manifestations and course may vary from culture to culture and be further complicated by a person's level of acculturation. In short, the clinical needs of Third-World people require bilingual, bicultural social workers who are familiar with the language and culture of the persons whom they attempt to help. English-speaking social workers can assist the more acculturated English-speaking Third-World persons. A major goal of schools of social work, therefore, must be the active recruitment of students who have a bilingual and bicultural capability.

A related manpower issue concerns education and training. Meyer asserts that graduate schools of social work educate students in accordance with the idiosyncratic interests of their faculties and that students learn one model of practice, especially the clinical model, and not others.[18] Given the emphasis that schools of social work place on the clinical orientation, one must ask whether the theory and practice of clinical social work with Third-World people is being taught by bilingual, bicultural faculty members who have had experience in treating Third-World clients. Furthermore, practitioners with experience in poor communities—labeled "underground social workers" or "weekend activists" by Dean—should become an important part of social work faculties.[19] They should train students to provide services effectively in Third-World communities and teach new and existing theory and practice techniques for handling social problems in those communities. Without this preparation, Dean concludes that the social work profession as a whole will have little to contribute to helping its most troubled clients.

Sanction, the authority and permission for social workers to practice, is another manpower issue that is directly related to the benefits—or lack of benefits—received by Third-World populations. Because a disproportionate number of Third-World people are among those in poverty and in the criminal justice system, it is more likely that they will be involuntary clients than will whites. They will probably encounter social workers who are carrying out a function of social control for the state. Research findings suggest that when social workers practice within a framework of social control with involuntary clients, their interventive efforts may not be as effective as when they work with voluntary clients who are actively seeking their help with a specific problem.[20] In one instance, the state and its sanctioned representatives (the social workers) define the problem and the goals for involuntary clients, and in the other the sanctioning voluntary clients define the problems and goals. Imposing treatment on involuntary clients, which has been known to cause deterioration, raises ethical questions for the profession and its relationship to Third-World people who are involuntary clients. In this respect Third-World people have a right to refuse treatment.

Social workers may find themselves in a dilemma in treating involuntary, Third-World clients because they are given legal sanction to carry out a function of social control that is inconsistent with the value social workers place on self-determination. Preferably, imposed treatment intervention as an act of social control should be used only in serious cases, such as those involving child abuse. Social workers have a role in advocating a person's right to refuse treatment, but this poses still another dilemma for those social workers who have historically asserted their professionalism through the status and authority of their agencies, especially those agencies chiefly concerned with a function of social control. On one hand, such advocacy may threaten the employment status of social workers, and on the other, it may also offer them a new challenge and an opportunity to shift the basis of their relationship with involuntary Third-World clients from that of a social control agent for the state to one of independent employment by clients. An increasing number of people are having their human services paid for by third parties—Medicare, Medicaid, and private insurance.[21] Third-party insurance coverage for licensed social workers became effective in California in January 1977 under vendorship legislation introduced by Assemblyman Art Torres.

The California law, however, limits licensed social work activities to "psychotherapy of a nonmedical nature."[22] This limitation reintroduces the old issue of clinical treatment versus social action. The Third-World community needs both levels of intervention. The New York law, which has preferable legal sanctions, defines the purpose of licensed social work practice as "helping individuals, groups, and communities to prevent or resolve problems caused by social or emotional stress."[23] This licensing language might be the ideal, since it permits licensed social workers to use a wide range of interventive strategies. The profession, therefore, should seek to make sure that vendorship laws sanction not only clinical intervention but also intervention in larger community systems. Social workers could then use third-party reimbursement in Third-World communities to provide help, upon request, in alleviating and preventing social problems. They would thus derive sanction from Third-World clients. If social workers continue to be licensed and reimbursed for clinical activities only, the profession might be compromising its humanistic values and neglecting some of the social needs of Third-World people.

THIRD-WORLD AGENCY

To help Third-World people meet their psychosocial needs more effectively, bilingual, bicultural social workers should be employed and deployed in traditional human services agencies when-ever their skills are indicated. Too often, these agencies lack em-pathy with Third-World people whose cultural patterns and clinical and social needs differ from established norms. They view ethnicity as a descriptive variable, often with "problem" implica-tions, rather than as a critical ingredient in determining the con-tent of service delivery. According to Jenkins, innovative ethnic agencies, in which ethnic clients and ethnic personnel predomi-nate, incorporate such ethnic factors as culture and con-sciousness "as positive components of service delivery," not as "problems."[24] Social work should therefore endorse the concept of the Third-World human services agency. However, the profes-sion views the growth of such agencies primarily as a political response to movements for minority rights.

Jenkins, in a systematic study of fifty-four Third-World human services agencies in several states, concluded that these agencies remedied serious deficits in traditional methods of ser-vice delivery. She also noted the following:

> As we examine "what worked" in the ethnic agencies, it is apparent that many of the examples related to primary-group functions. The ethnic agency stressed family supports, encouraging parents to ac-cept responsibility for their own children, maintenance of own lan-guages, career advancement for own clients, accommodations of traditional myths to meet service needs, and recruitment of minor-ity adoptive and foster parents.[25]

Social workers who oppose the use of Third-World human services agencies might argue that an endorsement of this concept might further polarize Third-World people and whites as well as create a duplication of services, resulting in increased admin-istrative costs. Proponents might argue that Third-World staff members should have decision-making power, that they under-stand the needs of Third-World people, and that the Third-World agency promotes group survival. The first argument is weak be-cause Third-World people are frequently denied services, directly and indirectly, at traditional human services agencies directed by whites to meet the needs of a white population. Because of their various levels of acculturation and life-style, perhaps Third-World people need access to both traditional human services and ethnic agencies.

INTERVENTION STRATEGIES

Proactive intervention strategies are initiated in anticipation of social problems. Three examples of such strategies are cited in this section to demonstrate their impact on the individual, group, Third-World community, and the larger society. The examples include the concepts of advocacy, empowerment, and "class action social work."

According to Briar, the social worker as advocate is

> his client's supporter, his advisor, his champion, and, if need be, his representative in his dealings with the court, the police, the social agency and other organizations that [affect] his well-being.[26]

Briar's definition describes the advocate as one who pleads the cause of an individual. Brager, however, takes another view. His definition describes the advocate as one who represents the interests of an aggrieved class of people:

> The worker as advocate identifies with the plight of the disadvantaged. He sees as his primary responsibility the tough-minded and partisan representation of their interests, and this supersedes his fealty to others. This role inevitably requires that the practitioner function as a political tactician.[27]

Third-World communities need both types of advocacy—in behalf of client and class. Although expressing a commitment to advocacy, the NASW Ad Hoc Committee on Advocacy perceived a dilemma concerning the choice between direct intercession by the social worker and mobilization of clients in their own behalf.[28] Some members of the profession might argue that it is a disservice to clients when social workers advocate in their behalf—that advocacy emasculates clients and makes them more dependent. It is difficult to determine whether this argument would be based on solid quantitative data or whether it would represent an intellectual rationalization for remaining uninvolved. Advocacy in behalf of some powerless special populations, such as dependent children or mentally ill jail inmates, might, however, be appropriate. When advocacy is deemed inappropriate, social workers could help clients help themselves through the application of empowerment.

A recent trend evolving in social work relates to the concept of client empowerment, which is defined by Solomon as

> a process whereby persons who belong to a stigmatized social category throughout their lives can be assisted to develop and increase skills in the exercise of interpersonal influence and the performance of valued social roles. Power is an interpersonal phenomenon; if it is not interpersonal it probably should be defined as "strength." However, the two concepts—power and strength—are so tightly interrelated that they are often used interchangeably.[29]

According to Solomon, empowerment enables the client to perceive his or her intrinsic and extrinsic worth. It motivates the client to use every personal resource and skill, as well as those of any other person that can be commanded, in the effort to achieve self-determined goals. The social worker attempts to develop in the client a conviction that there are many pathways to goal attainment. Solomon suggests three roles for the practitioner that hold promise for reducing a client's sense of powerlessness and lead to empowerment: the resource consultant role, the sensitizer role, and the teacher-trainer role.

Empowerment as a concept also holds promise in clinical social work. At a recent invitational forum on clinical social work held in Denver in 1979, the author presented a paper in which he demonstrated how the concept of power could be used effectively in clinical social work with persons who find themselves in a powerless or subordinate role to the practitioner in authority.[30] Often these persons are involuntary clients. The act of providing clients with the power to determine whether they wish to participate in treatment is seen as improving the treatment outcome if *they* choose to participate.

The purpose of social work is "to enhance the quality of life for all persons." Social work's impact on social problems, such as poverty and racism, is often limited by the clinical model or inappropriate interventive strategies. A referred client with a "problem" may not really have a problem. The problem may be *in* the referring system. For example, a school may refer a problem student to the social worker to help the student adjust to the requirements of the school system. The school system, however, may have major defects, which are the primary cause of the student's problems. The goal of the social worker should then be to help the school system meet the educational needs of the student. Rather than attempting to work individually with each student to document the deficiencies in the school system, the social worker could deal with one student who represents other students with similar problems. A class action in behalf of the student could then be undertaken to improve conditions in the school. Class action is a legal concept that has promising implications for social work. Closer working relationships will have to be cultivated with the legal profession to enable lawyers to conceptualize broad social work concerns and to translate these concerns into legal class action suits. Such an approach could be called "class action social work." Victories in the courts could provide relief for thousands of poor people.

Collaborative, interdisciplinary efforts involving social workers and lawyers usually have a clinical focus; these professionals serve clients in such areas as premarital or cohabitation counseling, divorce and custody proceedings, and estate planning for the elderly.[31] In some states, social workers have made pioneering efforts to enter the legal arena in behalf of the poor on a broader social scale, which could also be called class action social work. In California, for example, the Greater California Chapter of the National Association of Social Workers presented an award to John Serrano, a social worker, for his actions in the widely publicized *Serrano* v. *Priest* case, which argued that the quality of a child's education should not be dependent on the wealth of a school district.[32] In this case action suit filed by the Western Center on Law and Poverty, which had a social worker as president of the corporation, the California Supreme Court ruled that the California public educational financing scheme, which relied heavily on local property taxes, violated the equal protection clause of the Fourteenth Amendment to the U.S. Constitution. In other words, wealthier school districts were favored to the detriment of poorer districts. The significance of *Serrano* transcends California's boundaries because all states, except Hawaii, use similar discriminatory educational financing systems.

Considering the *Serrano* precedent, might not the areas of welfare, health, and mental health services also represent a set of circumstances as unique and compelling as education? A right to public education may not be maximally enjoyed if the child is

poorly housed, impoverished, malnourished, and in need of physical and mental health care. *Serrano* may ultimately lead the way
for further challenges in a wide range of governmental services,
including those in which social workers already have knowledge
and experience. The opportunity for class action collaboration
between law and social work in behalf of the Third-World community and the oppressed poor is on social work's doorstep and can
become a significant tool of social work intervention.

SUMMARY

The recently televised 1980 Democratic and Republican presiden-
tial conventions revealed few Third-World participants. On the
basis of what was seen on television, it would not be surprising if a
foreign visitor refused to believe that there were thirty-eight million Third-World people residing in the United States. Unlike most
segments of white society, the social work profession cannot continue to evade and deny the existence of the Third-World population. The profession must understand and accept that the term
"Third World" refers to an aggrieved class of people who share a
common experience of political and economic exploitation. These
people, however, often do not share a common culture or language, and they have different needs. Such an understanding
would aid social workers in defining the needs of this population
and in achieving social work goals.

   This article points out that social work's methods framework
is too constricted to account for the breadth of the phenomena to
be captured in Third-World communities. Rather, it proposes the
use of Meyer's ecosystems model, which allows for a comprehensive psychosocial assessment. Following this assessment, methods can then be applied, for in any particular case any number of
practice interventions might be needed.

   To help Third-World people meet their psychosocial needs
more effectively, social work should pursue several related objectives concerning manpower, human services resources, and proactive intervention strategies. Schools of social work must demonstrate a greater commitment to the recruitment of bilingual,
bicultural Third-World students. Students should be trained not

only to provide clinical services in the Third-World community but also to deal with broader social issues. To do this, Third-World faculty members must also be recruited.

It is suggested that a social control framework may diminish the therapeutic effectiveness of social work intervention. Involuntary clients have a right to refuse treatment, and social workers have a role in advocating such a right. The potential options in licensing might provide the challenge and opportunity for social workers to shift the basis of their relationship with involuntary clients from acting as social control agents for the state to being independently employed by clients. The New York licensing law permits a wide range of social work practice activities that would be consistent with Third-World needs.

In delivering services to Third-World people, white English-speaking agencies use traditional methods that have serious deficits. Jenkins, in a study of innovative ethnic agencies, concluded that Third-World agencies remedied these deficits. Social work should therefore endorse the development and use of Third-World human services agencies by Third-World clients. Because of their various levels of acculturation and life-style, however, Third-World people need access to both the traditional white agency and the Third-World agency.

Proactive intervention strategies, which include the concepts of advocacy, empowerment, and class action social work, also address the needs of the Third-World community. Advocacy is most often indicated when it pertains to some special powerless population such as dependent children. Client empowerment—helping clients reduce their sense of powerlessness—has been found to be particularly helpful with persons living in oppressed communities. This concept also holds promise in clinical social work when the involuntary client is given the power to determine whether he or she wishes to participate in treatment. Class action social work allows lawyers and social workers to translate broad social concerns into legal class action suits. Favorable court decisions, such as *Serrano*, could provide relief to thousands of poor people. This concept has potential for becoming a significant tool of social work intervention.

At the first meeting on Conceptual Frameworks in 1976, a participant said that the goal of social work was to "find out what people need and want and help them get it."[33] This article represents an effort to outline some of the objectives for the profession in meeting the needs of Third-World people. It is now the profession's responsibility to take the next steps and help the Third-World community obtain what it needs.

Notes and References

1. Lloyd Street, "Minorities," in John B. Turner, ed., *Encyclopedia of Social Work*, Vol. 2 (17th issue; Washington, D.C.: National Association of Social Workers, 1977), pp. 931–984.
2. Special Populations Subpanel on Mental Health of Americans of European Ethnic Origin, *The President's Commission on Mental Health*, Vol. 3, (Washington, D.C.: U.S. Government Printing Office, 1978), p. 879.
3. Andrew M. Greeley, "Minorities: White Ethnics," in Turner, *Encyclopedia of Social Work*, Vol. 1, *op. cit.*, pp. 983–984.
4. The author has used the following sources as background for this article: Joel Fischer, "Is Casework Effective? A Review," *Social Work*, 18 (January 1973), pp. 6–20; Louis L. Knowles and Kenneth Prewitt, eds., *Institutional Racism in America* (Englewood Cliffs, N.J.: Prentice-Hall, 1969); Carol H. Meyer, "What Directions for Direct Practice?" *Social Work*, 24 (July 1979), pp. 267–272; Armando Morales, "The Collective Preconscious and Racism," *Social Casework*, 52 (May 1971), pp. 285–293; Morales, "Beyond Traditional Conceptual Frameworks," *Social Work*, 22 (September 1977), pp. 387–393; Morales and Bradford W. Sheafor, *Social Work: A Profession of Many Faces* (2d ed.; Boston: Allyn & Bacon, 1980); Lloyd Street, "Minorities," *op. cit.*, pp. 931–946; and Bo Thiemann and Mark Battle, *Specialization in Social Work Profession* (Washington, D.C.: National Association of Social Workers, 1974).
5. U.S. Bureau of the Census, *Current Population Reports*, Series P-20, No. 292 (Washington, D.C.: U.S. Department of Commerce, March 1976).
6. Street, *op. cit.*, p. 932.
7. Jeffrey Prager, "The Minds of White Folk: An Analysis of Racism in America," pp. 42–48. Unpublished manuscript, University of California, Berkeley, 1970.
8. See *New York Times*, November 29, 1975, p. 30; and *A Study of Selected Socio-Economic Characteristics of Ethnic Minorities Based on the 1970 Census*, Vol. 2, *Asian Americans* (Washington, D.C.: U.S. Government Printing Office, 1974).
9. See Street, *op. cit.*, p. 941.

10. Betty Ogleton, Stephanie Crittendon, and Cozetta Seda, "An Examination of Institutional Racism: Black People in California's Criminal Justice and Mental Health Systems," Monograph No. 2, Faculty Development—Minority Content in Mental Health (Boulder, Colo.: Western Interstate Commission for Higher Education, 1974), pp. 6–7.
11. Street, *op. cit.*, p. 943.
12. Armando Morales, "Institutional Racism in Mental Health and Criminal Justice," *Social Casework,* 59 (July 1978), p. 391.
13. See Edgar S. Cahn, *Our Brother's Keeper: The Indian in White America* (New York: World Publishing Co., 1969); and Federal Commission on Civil Rights, "The Navajo Nation: An American Colony" (Washington, D.C.: U.S. Department of Health, Education & Welfare, 1975).
14. Murray L. Gruber, "Inequality in the Social Services," *Social Service Review,* 54 (March 1980), pp. 59–75.
15. Judith C. Nelsen, "Social Work's Fields of Practice, Methods, and Models: The Choice to Act," *Social Service Review,* 49 (June 1975), pp. 264–270.
16. Meyer, *op. cit.*, p. 269.
17. *Ibid.*, p. 271.
18. *Ibid.*, p. 268.
19. Walter R. Dean, Jr., "Back to Activism," *Social Work,* 22 (September 1977), p. 373.
20. Fischer, *op. cit.*
21. George Mace Summers, "Public Sanction and the Professionalization of Social Work," *Clinical Social Work Journal,* 4 (Spring 1976), p. 53.
22. Morales and Sheafor, *op. cit.*, p. 337.
23. *Ibid.*
24. Shirley Jenkins, "The Ethnic Agency Defined," *Social Service Review,* 54 (June 1980), p. 250. Jenkins's definition of the term "ethnics" included blacks, Puerto Ricans, American Indians, Japanese, Chinese, and Mexican Americans.
25. *Ibid.*, p. 260.
26. Scott Briar, "The Current Crisis in Social Casework," *Social Work Practice, 1967* (New York: Columbia University Press, 1967), p. 28. *See also* Briar, "The Casework Predicament," *Social Work,* 13 (January 1968), pp. 5–11.
27. George A. Brager, "Advocacy and Political Behavior," *Social Work,* 13 (April 1968), p. 6.
28. The Ad Hoc Committee on Advocacy, "The Social Worker as Advocate: Champion of Social Victims," *Social Work,* 14 (April 1969), pp. 6–22.
29. Barbara Bryant Solomon, *Black Empowerment: Social Work in Oppressed Communities* (New York: Columbia University Press, 1976), p. 6.
30. Armando Morales, "Clinical Social Work with Special Populations," in Patricia L. Ewalt, ed., *Toward a Definition of Clinical Social Work* (Washington, D.C.: National Association of Social Workers, 1980), pp. 66–74.

31. Barton E. Bernstein, "Lawyer and Social Worker as an Interdisciplinary Team," *Social Casework*, 61 (September 1980), pp. 416–422.
32. Morales and Sheafor, *op. cit.*
33. "Excerpts from the Discussion," in Special Issue on Conceptual Frameworks, *Social Work*, 22 (September 1977), p. 382.

SELF-VALUATION AMONG BLACKS*

Madison Foster and Lorraine R. Perry

The prevailing view of blacks over the years has been that they suffer from negative self-esteem manifested in feelings of self-hate and a lack of self-actualizing behavior. Oppressive social and economic conditions confronting blacks, caused by racism and discrimination, as well as black people's attempts to identify with the values of the dominant white society, have been the major factors believed to contribute to this negative self-valuation. Public policies have been formulated and implemented based on a deficiency theory of blacks' behavior that stems from such assumptions. Proponents of this theory assume that blacks lack internal psychological resources—namely, positive self-valuations—and that this lack not only explains the behavior of blacks but also indicates the need for programs aimed at restoring the deficiency. Examples of such programs can be found in the areas of education, human development, and social welfare.

Although it cannot be denied that racism and discrimination abound and take their toll on blacks, the assumption that there is a direct relationship between the effects of racism and negative self-esteem among blacks, independent of other intervening forces, is questionable. In fact, one of the findings of a six-month survey of the quality of life of residents in metropolitan Detroit was that, despite their dissatisfaction with some of the social and economic conditions of their lives, blacks reported higher levels of self-valuation than did whites.[1] Specifically, 75 percent of the blacks in

*Reprinted by permission of the authors and *Social Work* 27:1 (January 1982) 60–66; copyright © 1982 National Association of Social Workers, Inc.

the study, compared with 61 percent of the whites, were completely or highly satisfied with themselves.

This finding calls into question many of the underlying assumptions in the conceptual literature on black self-esteem. This doubt is further compounded by the ambiguity surrounding the concept of self-esteem, its determinants, and its consequences. Moreover, general studies on self-esteem have been focused primarily on white Americans. Finally, only limited attention has been directed to assessing the determinants and consequences of self-valuation or to validating the existence of negative self-esteem among blacks in general or for particular subgroups of blacks.

This article examines in more depth the findings from the Detroit study. Its aim is to determine whether blacks' valuation of themselves and of life as a whole vary among different subgroups. The major research question addressed is whether levels of self-valuation vary among blacks based on demographic characteristics or satisfaction with internal and external factors in their lives.

LITERATURE ON SELF-ESTEEM

James suggested some time ago that the notion of "self" should be an integrating concept including such constituent parts as physical traits, family, work, and the like.[2] Consequently, any analysis of the concept of self-valuation is inevitably complex. Although the possible correlates of self-valuation selected for study by the authors do not encompass all possible components that could be considered, they do include some of the major conceptual components that have been cited in the literature on self-esteem.

Notwithstanding the ambiguity in its conceptualizations, self-esteem is believed not only to be central to the process by which people evaluate themselves, but also to influence people's behavior, self-actualization, and adjustment to the external world. A variety of studies have been conducted to understand and clarify the determinants and consequences of self-valuation, most of them from the perspective of developmental psychology.

Various writers have attempted to develop sociological theories of self-esteem, its correlates, and its consequences. Gurin, Veroff, and Feld, for example, showed that people's views about their adjustment to life tend to be conditioned by their sex, age, education, and income.[3] Of major importance was their finding that feelings of self-worth do not imply satisfaction with one's surroundings or environmental conditions.

The work of Rosenberg focused more on economic determinants of self-esteem.[4] One of the major findings from his examination of the dynamic development of self-valuation in the behavior of different groups of adolescents was that social class was only weakly related to self-esteem. He concluded from this that, contrary to popular belief, the broader social context does not play as important a role in influencing one's evaluation of self as had previously been assumed. Similar findings about social class were also reported by Coopersmith.[5] Contrary to Gurin, Veroff, and Feld, he found that, in general, self-esteem was not closely related to material assets. However, people with irregular patterns of employment had more negative views of themselves.

The evidence of these studies concerning the determinants of self-valuation is inconclusive, particularly in regard to the variables of income and education. Unfortunately, as already noted, there is a dearth of material on the social and economic correlates of self-esteem in the general population and in regard to blacks in particular.

Many discussions imply or state that blacks make more negative assessments of themselves than do whites. In a society where racial awareness begins during childhood, blacks are thought to assimilate the prevailing judgment that black is bad. Social science analysis and popular commentary have stressed blacks' own negative self-concepts and admissions of inferiority. For example, many developmental studies testify that black and white children alike prefer a white doll over a black one.[6]

The view of the self-hating black is often maintained by black as well as by white scholars. For example, the black therapists Grier and Cobbs have contributed to the literature denying the existence of positive self-esteem among blacks.[7] Clark adds to this view the idea that "it is still the white man's society that governs the Negro's image of himself.[8] Nor does Poussaint, a black psychiatrist and popular writer on what he termed the Negro psyche, deny that many blacks have feelings of self-hatred, but he sees nonassertiveness and suppressed rage as contributing to their low self-esteem.[9]

Much of this writing on blacks' self-valuation is based on small samples, laboratory experiments, or anecdotal evidence that is less than adequate to explain the complex behavior of black people in America. According to one black psychologist, most of this work is conceptual rather than explanatory.[10] Moreover, findings of more recent studies in the social sciences indicate that empirical evidence does not support the earlier view of negative black self-valuation. For example, Guterman concludes that the studies he reviewed comparing blacks and whites on measures of self-esteem ". . . suggest either that the level of self-esteem among blacks does not differ significantly from that of whites or that it is actually higher than that of whites."[11]

Although the concept of self-valuation has not been clearly defined in the social science literature, people who are happy and feel good about themselves are generally thought to have positive self-esteem. It is assumed that people evincing positive self-valuation are free of guilt, shame, or low self-esteem, including such feelings that might result from membership in a racially subjugated group. However, a positive valuation of oneself should not be equated with personal and social complacency—that is, feelings of self-worth do not necessarily imply satisfaction with surrounding social, economic, and political conditions. These generally held assumptions were the assumptions of the authors' study.

METHODOLOGY

This article attempts to specify further the correlates of self-esteem and those of blacks' self-valuation in particular. Specifically, it examines associations between individuals' levels of self-valuation and (1) selected demographic characteristics, including age, sex, education, marital status, income, occupational status, and family size, (2) certain personal factors, including happiness, confidence in one's ability to implement plans, and skin color, (3) external socioenvironmental factors, including satisfaction with family life, with job, and with income and perception of control over life plans, and (4) satisfaction with life as a whole.

The data in the Detroit study were collected through personal interviews using a structured interview schedule, with blacks interviewing blacks and whites interviewing whites. The population of the study was a random sample of 1,194 people in metropolitan Detroit. However, this article focuses only on the study's subsample of 286 blacks.

A 7-point scale was used in the original study to assess the respondent's level of self-valuation. The response categories ranged from "completely satisfied" to "completely dissatisfied" with self. For the analysis and presentation of the findings reported in this article, the 7-point scale was collapsed into three categories—high, medium, and low. Because the data were skewed toward the high end of the scale, the measures of all the external variables except income (satisfaction with family life, job satisfaction, and control over life plans) were as follows: A rating of 1 on the scale was considered high; 2 and 3, medium; and 4, 5, 6, and 7, low. For satisfaction with income, the high, medium, and low categories were based on ratings of 1 and 2; 3, 4, and 5; and 6 and 7, respectively.

A 3-point scale was used by the authors to measure happiness. Respondents rated themselves as to whether they generally felt "very happy," "pretty happy," or "not too happy." Interviewers in the original study classified respondents on skin color in categories ranging from "very dark" to "very light." In analyzing employment status, two separate classifications were used. One was for individuals in the job market—that is, for those employed or unemployed. The other was for those outside the job market and included housewives, students, retired people, and the disabled. The data were analyzed using percentage differences and gamma statistics to indicate the strength of associations.[12]

Several limitations of this methodology should be noted. Although valuation of oneself is usually viewed as attitude enduring over time, such appraisals can include both attitudinal and behavioral components. However, the Detroit study, using survey techniques, was limited to dealing with the subjective attitudes reported by respondents at one point in time. Behavioral aspects of self-valuation were not included, nor were sources of self-valuation investigated. Also, in regard to the classification of skin color, only the interviewer's subjective judgments were available. This posed another limitation because, with the possible exception of people who are extremely light or dark, little agreement exists concerning gradation of skin color. Finally, the study's findings are based on global appraisals of self-valuation. Therefore, definitions and meanings will have varied from respondent to respondent. As a result of these limitations, the insights provided by the study will require further validation. It should also be noted that the authors have tabulated only those data that showed an association as reflected by gamma.

DEMOGRAPHIC CHARACTERISTICS

The findings presented in Table 1 show that all the original associations between self-valuation and demographic characteristics were small or moderate. However, several conditional associations emerged when a third variable was controlled for. Age and education were the demographic characteristics most closely associated with self-valuation. Because young people have generally been strong advocates of black pride, it might be expected that they would express the highest levels of self-valuation, but this proved not to be the case. In fact, older blacks tended to appraise themselves more positively than younger blacks did. When sex was held constant, not only did older blacks have a higher valuation of themselves, but black males indicated higher levels of self-valuation than females.

Blacks with less education generally had a higher self-valuation than those with more education. An interesting finding was that those with only a grade school education had the highest valuation of self. This group, along with blacks who had received a college degree, had the fewest respondents expressing low self-valuation. On further examination, however, this association was found to exist only among females. There was no relationship between self-valuation and education for male respondents.

Among blacks in the job market, there was only a slight difference in levels of self-valuation between those who were employed and those who were unemployed, but those employed tended to have more positive views of themselves. Although there was little difference among groups of blacks who were not in the job market, students and the disabled had lower levels of self-valuation than housewives and retirees.

Examination of the remaining demographic characteristics—

Table 1
Levels of Self-valuation and Selected Demographic Characteristics

Demographic Characteristic	Level of Self-valuation							
	High		Medium		Low		Total	
	Number	Percentage	Number	Percentage	Number	Percentage	Number	Percentage[a]
Age[b]								
Under 30	10	16.7	25	41.7	25	41.7	60	100.1
31–45	27	32.1	25	29.8	32	38.1	84	100.0
46–56	24	34.3	27	38.6	19	27.1	70	100.0
51 and over	41	56.9	18	25.0	13	18.1	72	100.0
Education[c]								
Grade school	44	69.8	11	17.5	8	12.7	63	100.0
High school	81	50.6	46	28.8	33	20.6	160	100.0
College	29	46.0	24	38.1	10	15.9	63	100.0
Employment Status[d]								
Employed	68	48.2	52	36.9	21	14.9	141	100.0
Unemployed	11	45.8	6	25.0	7	29.2	24	100.0

[a]Percentages may not total to 100 because of rounding.
[b]Gamma = 0.3299.
[c]Gamma = 0.2033.
[d]Gamma = 0.1466. Figures for this category relate only to respondents in the labor force.

sex, marital status, income, and family size—indicated slight trends toward more positive self-valuation among males, married people, and those in smaller family units. With reference to income levels, those in the highest bracket had the highest levels of self-valuation, followed by those in the lowest income group.

In sum, except in regard to age, little evidence was provided to show that self-valuation among blacks is related to demographic characteristics. Such findings, therefore, are more consistent with the conclusions of Rosenberg and Coopersmith, noted earlier, than with those of Gurin, Veroff, and Feld. The one exception was the finding that older people have higher levels of self-valuation. Older people, who have dealt with the vicissitudes of life and who have overcome barriers and survived, may have greater feelings of self-valuation as a result. It is also possible that support systems in the black community, such as the church, fraternal organizations, and extended family systems, may have been more prominent in the lives of older people and thus contributed to the positive self-valuation among individuals in this group.

The tendency for women with less education to have greater self-valuation than other women was unexpected. Perhaps people with more education strive for increased upward mobility in society and consequently experience more frustration. It is also possible that black women who attain higher levels of education are confronted with relatively poor social opportunities in their lives.

To the extent that employment and marriage can be viewed as providing fulfilling central roles in life, people who are satisfied in these roles may be more satisfied with themselves. However, the findings in this study indicate only a slight tendency for employed and married blacks to express higher self-valuation than unemployed and single people.

That lower income does not necessarily produce a lower level of self-valuation may well be attributed to the presence of support systems in the black community. For example, after three years of participant-observation and interviews of garbagemen and other laborers in Ann Arbor, Detroit, and Minneapolis, Walsh found that these workers showed "a sense of superiority vis-à-vis the other more protected workers."[13] Furthermore, low income and "dirty work" did not preclude a sense of high self-esteem among these black laborers. Social accomplishments, survival, and support sys-

Table 2
Levels of Self-valuation and Personal Factors

				Level of Self-valuation					
	High		Medium		Low		Total		
Personal Factor	Number	Percentage	Number	Percentage	Number	Percentage	Number[a]	Percentage
Happiness[b]								
Very happy	47	83.9	8	14.3	1	1.8	56	100.0
Pretty happy	82	50.6	59	36.4	21	13.0	162	100.0
Not too happy	25	36.8	14	20.6	29	42.6	68	100.0
Confidence in ability to implement plans[c]								
Confident	88	57.5	49	32.0	16	10.5	153	100.0
Not confident	64	50.4	30	23.6	33	26.0	127	100.0
Skin color[d]								
Dark	27	46.6	17	29.3	14	24.1	58	100.0
Medium dark	70	54.7	41	32.0	17	13.3	128	100.0
Medium light	48	58.5	19	23.2	15	18.3	82	100.0
Light	7	50.0	3	21.4	4	28.6	14	100.0

[a]Totals differ from the total sample because all respondents did not answer all questions.
[b]Gamma = 0.5484.
[c]Gamma = 0.2136.
[d]Gamma = −0.0920.

tems in the black community may have bolstered the self-pride of the low-wage workers in the current study who reported high self-valuation. On the other hand, significant pecuniary attainment may account for the positive self-valuation of those in the highest income bracket.

PERSONAL FACTORS

The next set of findings concerns associations between levels of self-valuation and personal factors such as the respondents' assessment of the extent to which they were happy, the confidence they had in their ability to carry out their plans, and their skin color. (See Table 2.) One can assume that people with more positive appraisals of themselves are happier. This was true of the blacks in the current study. There was a strong positive relationship between level of self-valuation and degree of happiness. This association did not change when a third variable was controlled for, except in regard to education. The association between happiness and self-valuation was especially pronounced for people with a college education.

Only a small association was found between self-valuation and the perception of the ability to implement one's plans. Although blacks who had higher self-valuation tended to have more confidence in their ability to implement their plans, the differences were not great. However, people with only a grade school education had less confidence in their ability than those with more education.

Skin color historically has been thought to affect whites' views of black people and blacks' views of themselves. Conventional views of blacks' negative self-valuation have made particular reference to the effects on blacks' self-concept of social stratification based on skin color. In a review of the literature, Ransford found that problems of identity and confidence are often alleged to be associated with darker skin and that dark-skinned blacks are said to feel more powerless and worthless than light-skinned blacks. However, he himself presented evidence that feelings of worth and confidence are unrelated to skin color and are associated more with income and occupational status.[14] In addition,

Walsh has noted the positive influence of community institutions in providing support, group identification, and positive self-esteem, especially for dark-skinned, working-class blacks.[15]

In this study, there was generally no association between self-valuation and skin color. However, blacks who were either very dark or very light tended to have slightly lower levels of self-valuation than other respondents. The only exception was among people with college training. In this case, darker-skinned blacks had higher valuations of themselves than other blacks.

EXTERNAL FACTORS

The final analysis was devoted to an examination of the associations between self-valuation and external factors, including the perception of control over life plans and levels of satisfaction with family life, job, and income. (See Table 3.) In addition, general satisfaction with life as a whole was examined.

A high level of self-valuation was strongly associated with satisfaction with family life. This was particularly true for women. Moderate associations were found between self-valuation and satisfaction with one's job and income. When controlling for age, the association between self-valuation and job satisfaction was especially strong for people in their 30s and mid-40s. There was a tendency for people with high self-valuation to feel that they had more control over life plans. This was true for all respondents, except for those with only a grade school education and those between the ages of 45 and 55. For these two groups the reverse was the case. The final assessment of the study indicated that people who had higher self-valuation were more satisfied with their lives as a whole. (See Table 4.)

In general, levels of self-valuation were more strongly related to external factors and views of life as a whole than to the other groups of factors examined. Feelings of self-valuation are in particular closely tied to feelings about life as a whole. The strong association between positive self-valuation and satisfaction with family life further strengthened the notion referred to earlier that the family plays an important role in shaping blacks' attitudes about themselves. For blacks, the family has been one of the primary sources of support and protection that help them survive.

It also appears that the family has been the major reference group for generating and boosting self-pride in spite of heavy odds.

Of particular interest was a tendency for blacks with less education and high levels of self-valuation to have less confidence in their ability to implement their plans and to perceive that they had less control over external forces. Perhaps as a result of their limited education, this group of blacks encountered difficulties in implementing their plans and in controlling life events. However, other sources of encouragement, such as the family, neighborhood gatherings, and community institutions, may have provided the type of support that enabled them to maintain positive views of themselves. In fact, in addressing cognitive styles of adaptation, Horney discusses ways of warding off self-demeaning feelings and suggests that an individual can define and justify negative external consequences in such a way that it does not detract from his or her own sense of worthiness.[16]

IMPLICATIONS

In summary, the findings of the authors' analysis reveal that levels of self-valuation among blacks were related primarily to feelings of satisfaction with life as a whole and with family life, as well as with feelings of personal happiness. Secondary factors were age and satisfaction with job and income. Thus, blacks who had higher valuations of themselves were happier and more satisfied with their family life, job, and income and with life as a whole. Older blacks, particularly males, also reported more positive self-valuation. These insights provide some evidence that many blacks have positive concepts of themselves, irrespective of most demographic characteristics and in spite of oppressive social, environmental, and economic conditions.

During the past two decades, blacks across the nation have expressed solidarity and cohesion in their organizations and social interactions that have served to bolster self-pride, identification with blackness, and appreciation of black culture and life. As a result, "black pride" has often been viewed as a relatively recent phenomenon. However, from a historical vantage point, black self-esteem and expressions of ethnic superiority would not be seen as originating in the 1960s. There is, in fact, much historical support

Table 3
Levels of Self-valuation and External Factors

| | Level of Self-valuation | | | | | | |
| | High | | Medium | | Low | | Total | |
External Factor	Number	Percentage	Number	Percentage	Number	Percentage	Number[a]	Percentage[b]
Satisfaction with family life[c]								
High	111	77.6	22	15.4	10	7.0	143	100.0
Medium	29	27.9	49	47.1	26	25.0	104	100.0
Low	12	36.4	7	21.2	14	42.4	33	100.0
Satisfaction with job[d]								
High	49	71.0	16	23.2	4	5.8	69	100.0
Medium	13	33.3	19	48.7	7	17.9	39	99.9
Low	18	35.3	20	39.2	13	25.5	51	100.0
Satisfaction with income[e]								
High	69	68.3	28	27.7	4	4.0	101	100.0
Medium	49	49.0	30	30.0	21	21.0	100	100.0
Low	36	42.3	23	27.1	26	30.6	85	100.0
Control over life plans[f]								
Can control	118	56.2	62	29.5	30	14.3	210	100.0
Cannot control	33	47.1	17	24.3	20	28.6	70	100.0

[a]Totals differ from the total sample because all respondents did not answer all questions.
[b]Percentages may not total to 100 because of rounding.
[c]Gamma = 0.6257.
[d]Gamma = 0.4749. Figures for this category relate only to respondents in the labor force.
[e]Gamma = 0.3692.
[f]Gamma = 0.2251.

Table 4
Levels of Self-valuation and Satisfaction with Life

Degree of Satisfaction with One's Life[a]	Level of Self-valuation							
	High		Medium		Low		Total	
	Number	Percentage	Number	Percentage	Number	Percentage	Number[b]	Percentage
High	92	92.0	3	3.0	5	5.0	100	100.0
Medium	35	37.2	50	53.2	9	9.6	94	100.0
Low	25	28.1	28	31.5	36	40.4	89	100.0

[a]Gamma = 0.7128.
[b]Total differs from the total sample because all respondents did not answer all questions.

for the existence of positive expressions of black self-valuation and group cohesiveness during the 1790s and 1820s, during the late 1840s and 1850s, and during the high period of black nationalism that occurred from 1880 until 1920 with the end of Garvey's "back to Africa" movement and the Great Depression.[17] Broderick and Meier document black group identification of nationalist expression as a developing response to negative socioeconomic conditions prior to the so-called black power period of the 1960s.[18] Further, an examination of black writings and poetry from a historical perspective makes clear "that the literature as a whole damns as a falsehood the concepts of inferiority."[19] Black literature does not support the concept of negative self-valuation or the thesis that black pride is new.[20]

In addition, as has been suggested earlier, the positive impact of various support systems in the black community on blacks' valuation of themselves should not be overlooked. Black consciousness and positive self-valuation may be bolstered by both formal institutions and organizations, such as the family, church, and fraternal groups, and by informal associations, including friendships and social relationships that develop in settings such as neighborhood bars, barber and beauty shops, and social clubs.[21]

Several theoretical and practical implications can be drawn from the results of the authors' study, as they call into question the empirical and historical validity of the orthodox view of blacks as self-hating and deficient in self-esteem. Theoretical formulations are major sources of the information that is disseminated in educational institutions, and they frequently serve as guidelines for research on the formulation and implementation of public policy. Therefore, it is of great importance that these theoretical formulations be valid, and they must be reassessed from time to time. The social science and anthropological literature provides insufficient evidence to support the traditional negative view of blacks' self-valuation. In addition, the dynamic interaction over the past two decades of a host of social, political, economic, and cultural forces has not been adequately incorporated into previous conceptualizations of blacks' self-valuation. For example, these conceptualizations ignore the different manifestations of black identity and their meaning. Consequently, the meaning of self-concept as it relates to blacks must be reexamined and reconceptualized. Such a reexamination would not only serve to enhance understanding of how blacks perceive themselves but would also shed light on possibly faulty assumptions about blacks.

Of particular importance in such a process would be a reexamination of the assumption that blacks were or are deficient in resources that serve to maintain a positive self-valuation. More attention might be focused on a systematic assessment of the role of the family and other community support systems in fostering blacks' valuation of themselves as well as on the consequences of unemployment. Based on the findings reported in this article, less emphasis should be placed on differences in demographic characteristics, satisfaction with environmental conditions, or the effects of skin color as determinants of self-valuation.

A better understanding of positive self-valuation among blacks and the factors contributing to these attitudes might help practitioners in fields like education, mental health, and social welfare to incorporate such information in the design and implementation of programs. For instance, practitioners aware of the strengths of the black family as a major support system could draw on it as an additional resource to be integrated into the planning and structuring of social welfare programs. Family and other support systems might be integrated into educational activities through more extensive use of the community school system.

In addition, consciousness-raising needs to take place among staff working in public social service programs related to welfare, human development, and community mental health. Programs of this kind usually serve people with little education, and staff members often assume that such people are irresponsible and apathetic and lack internal resources. These workers must recognize that positive self-appraisals may not be directly related to the individual's environmental situation. Practitioners also need to devote more effort to reinforcing strengths instead of stressing weaknesses in their work with black individuals, families, and groups. Special attention needs to be given to planning and developing counseling services for black females, especially those with more education, because this group in particular seems to have a negative view of itself.

The findings reported in this article are limited to a subsample of blacks in the city of Detroit and may not be representative

of blacks across the nation. Nevertheless, the findings indicate
that attention needs to be given to the traditional assumptions of
negative self-valuation among blacks.

*The authors wish to express their sincere appreciation to
Robert Marans and Willard Rodgers, principal investigators of
the original study, for their assistance in obtaining the data and
to Orian Worden, Donald Roberts, and Lorenzo Freeman for
their assistance and support in the development and preparation
of this article. An earlier version of this article was presented at
the Center for Afro-American and African Studies Lecture Series, University of Michigan, Ann Arbor, December 1977.*

Notes and References

1. *A Study of the Quality of Life: Metropolitan Detroit* (Ann Arbor:
Institute for Social Research, University of Michigan, 1975).
2. William James, *The Principles of Psychology* (New York: Smith, 1890).
3. Gerald Gurin, Joseph Veroff, and Sheila Feld, *Americans View Their
Mental Health* (New York: Basic Books, 1960).
4. Morris Rosenberg, *Society and the Adolescent Self-Image* (Princeton,
N.J.: Princeton University Press, 1965).
5. Stanley Coopersmith, *The Antecedents of Self-Esteem* (San Francisco:
W. H. Freeman & Co., 1967).
6. Kenneth B. Clark and Mamie P. Clark, "Skin Color as a Factor in
Racial Identification of Negro Pre-School Children," *Journal of Social
Psychology*, 2 (1940), pp. 154–167; M. J. Radke and H. C. Trager,
"Children's Perceptions of the Social Roles of Negroes and Whites,"
Journal of Psychology, 29 (1950), pp. 3–33; Abram Kardiner and
Lionel Ovesey, *The Mark of Oppression: Explorations in the Person-
ality of the American Negro* (New York: Morton, 1951); M. E. Good-
man, *Race Awareness in Young Children* (Reading, Mass.: Addison-
Wesley Press, 1952); C. Landreth and B. C. Johnson, "Young Children's
Responses to a Picture and Inset Test Designed to Reveal Reactions to
Persons of Different Skin Colors," *Child Development*, 24 (1953), pp.
63–74; H. W. Stevenson and E. C. Steward, "A Developmental Study of
Race Awareness in Young Children," *Child Development*, 29 (1958),
pp. 339–410; Robert Coles, "It's the Same But It's Different,"
Daedalus, 94 (1965), pp. 1107–1132; and J. K. Morland, "Racial Accep-
tance and Preference of Nursery School Children in a Southern City,"
Merrill-Palmer Quarterly, 8 (1950), pp. 271–280.
7. William H. Grier and Price M. Cobbs, *Black Rage* (New York: Basic
Books, 1968).
8. Kenneth B. Clark, *Dark Ghetto* (New York: Harper & Row, 1965), p. 64.

9. Alvin F. Poussaint, "A Negro Psychiatrist Explains the Negro Psyche," *New York Times Magazine*, August 20, 1967, p. 52.
10. William A. Hayes, "Radical Black Behaviorism," in Reginald L. Jones, ed., *Black Psychology* (New York: Harper & Row, 1972), p. 51.
11. Stanley S. Guterman, ed., *Black Psyche: Modal Personality Patterns of Black Americans* (Berkeley, Calif.: Glendessary Press, 1972), p. 87.
12. The following gamma coefficients indicate the strength of the associations:

Little or none	0.00–0.10
Small	0.11–0.30
Moderate	0.31–0.50
Strong	0.51–0.80
Almost complete to complete	0.81–1.00

13. Edward J. Walsh, *Dirty Work, Race and Self-Esteem* (Ann Arbor: Institute of Labor and Industrial Relations, University of Michigan-Wayne State University, 1975), p. 210.
14. H. Edward Ransford, "Skin Color, Life Chances, and Anti-White Attitudes," *Social Problems*, 18 (1970), pp. 164–179.
15. Walsh, *op. cit.*
16. Karen Horney, *Our Inner Conflicts* and *Neurosis and Human Growth* (New York: W. W. Norton & Co., 1945 and 1950, respectively).
17. See John H. Bracey, Jr. et al., eds., *Black Nationalism in America*, (Indianapolis, Ind.: Bobbs-Merrill Co., 1970).
18. Francis L. Broderick and August Meier, eds., *Negro Protest Thought in the Twentieth Century* (Indianapolis, Ind.: Bobbs-Merrill Co., 1965).
19. Herbert Aptheker, "Afro-American Superiority: A Neglected Theme in the Literature," in Rhoda L. Goldstein, ed., *Black Life and Culture in the United States* (New York: Thomas Y. Crowell Co., 1971), p. 167.
20. See *ibid;* and Bracey et al., *op. cit.*
21. See Walsh, *op. cit.*

V.
TRANSFERENCE/COUNTERTRANSFERENCE

The most significant element of the therapeutic process is the matter of transference and countertransference. In any worker/client relationship, transference is necessary if an effective therapeutic relationship is going to take place. An effective therapeutic relationship is considered functional when the client transfers both his or her negative/positive feelings and emotions from the significant others in their life to the worker. The treatment process is considered at its apex when this occurs. By the same token, however, the worker often transfers negative/positive feelings and emotions to the client based on significant others in his/her life. This is countertransference and it is considered counter-productive in the therapeutic process because the worker loses all objectivity. On the other hand, countertransference in a limited sense is a natural phenomenon and it is the responsibility of the worker to control the degree to which countertransference affects the therapeutic relationship. Consequently, it is the purpose of this section to look at transference and countertransference dynamics in relationship to the various worker/client interactions. There is, in addition, a particular focus of Native American non-interference which has implications for transference and countertransference.

It goes without saying that one of the major taboos in transference is to "over identify" with the client. This has far-reaching implications for the worker/client relationship particularly when the worker and client are of the same ethnic and racial grouping. When workers over-identify, usually effective therapeutic skills cannot function. This is of particular concern at a time when racial and ethnic identity is heightened by group solidarity and identity consciousness. Even though the worker and the client may somehow share the same views due to the similarities in their cultural experiences, it is the responsibility of the worker to assist the client in looking at her or his personal experiences/observation and identify solutions to the problems presented.

The same is true when the worker and client are both members of the same European ethnic groups and share similar experiences due to culture. For example, when a white worker observes racial and ethnic prejudices in a white client, it is the responsibility of the worker to assist the client in looking at that problem even though the worker may share similar views. This is no different from any other personal problem that a client may present which is similar in nature to a problem the worker may be experiencing. The responsible options are to remove one's self from the case or prevent one's personal views from entering the interaction and relationship.

Finally, when the worker and client are of different racial and ethnic groups, a new set of problems may develop in relation to transference. Since many of those factors have been discussed previously in the section on interviewing, relationship in therapy, and interracial/interethnic/intervention, they will not be repeated here. Nonetheless, the literature in this section addresses those issues and concerns in a way that provides for both theoretical orientation and a frame of reference for further study and development.

The ultimate implications for the knowledge, skills and sensitivity gained in social work counseling education is to enhance practice techniques. The role of counseling and social work practice is to assist individuals and groups in a society to modify their behavior in order that they can function adequately in the environment in which they live.

In this section, scholars will analyze, explore and evaluate the practice phenomenal of transference, countertransference, rapport and communications as they relate to therapeutic techniques and skills with minorities. The question of the relevance of race, ethnicity and culture to transference and countertransference will be analyzed with case illustrations. In addition, specific counseling strategies are analyzed in relation to specific minority cultures.

The techniques and skills described in this literature will provide the practitioner and potential practitioners with a conceptual framework for employing effective intervention strategies with minorities. Above all, the approaches and dynamics utilized by expert practitioners in case illustrations may serve as a frame of reference for current practitioners. The primary rationale for social theory and the establishment of social agencies is to benefit individuals, groups, and communities by effective services. The further acquisition of knowledge, theory and skills regarding People of Color should enhance the profession by making it more relevant. Most of all, effective and successful intervention strategies will benefit the client, the community and society.

RACIAL FACTORS IN THE COUNTERTRANSFERENCE: THE BLACK THERAPIST AND THE BLACK CLIENT*

Maynard Calnek

Currently, and perhaps for many years to come, Afro-Americans are and will be torturously struggling to achieve self-identity and self-determination. Amidst this struggle, barriers are being surmounted, doors are being opened, and an increasing number of black professionals are entering the mental health field. This paper is addressed to those professionals, especially to those who work with other blacks in a therapeutic relationship.

The literature does contain some discussion of the problems of the black therapist with the white client and the general problem of being a black in America. (6, 7, 10, 11, 15, 19) Several of these articles will be referred to here, but on the whole more emphasis will be placed upon the relationship of black professionals to members of their own race. Other studies, though an insufficient number, have centered on the problems of the self-image and racial and social-class identification of blacks, and their handling of anger towards whites. (8, 11, 15, 19) The notable fact, however, is the reluctance of therapists and the professional literature to discuss racial factors. My premises are that the importance of these themes has not been emphasized enough and that they *must* be acknowledged, brought up, and, if of any conse-

*Reprinted by permission of the author and publisher from the *American Journal of Orthopsychiatry*, 40:1 (January 1970) 39–46; copyright © 1970 by the American Orthopsychiatric Association, Inc.

quence, dealt with in the psychotherapy of the black client, no matter whether the therapist is black or white.

Though many blacks feel that they have not suffered personal discrimination, nevertheless their self-image is subject to daily assault by the way in which blacks are portrayed in the mass media and by the visibility of the low status of blacks in American society. Failure to note such heavy influence on personality is tantamount to not helping the client.

Black therapists who work with black clients have an unusual burden, for they have to deal with both their own feelings and the feelings of their clients about being black. Black therapists have to look at the ways in which they have been interacting with other blacks for years. Part of our problem is not only the possible projection of our own self-image onto other blacks, but also the adoption of white stereotypes of how blacks think, act, and feel. In an experiment studying the personality traits of blacks and whites as viewed by black subjects, it was seen that black college students characterize other blacks as having less productivity and less energy and vitality than whites and as being less serious-minded, more happy-go-lucky, and as having less restraint. For every characteristic, "the means for whites were in the direction of presenting better personality adjustment. This might result from the combined tendencies to idealize the aggressor and to incorporate his negative views toward the minority group."(3) The need for black therapists to control the countertransference is obviously a serious problem, but it is not an insuperable one.

Countertransference is used here in the sense of those subjective and irrational feelings, needs, and impulses aroused in the therapist in reaction to the client's feelings and actions. Countertransference, if left unresolved between client and therapist, may impede the course of therapy. Black therapists, of course, do not necessarily have to have any of the countertransference problems which I will discuss, but the probability exists that a few will crop up for every black therapist in this white-oriented American culture.

One primary problem is that few whites know much about Afro-American culture, much less about the black psyche. Therefore, white supervisors are not too much help when blacks work with blacks. In fact, they may provide an added impediment because of (1) their frequent misinterpretations of characteristic black folkways and caste-motivated behavior as psychopathology, (2) their lack of conceptualization of that which is psychopathological and that which is normal in Afro-America and in the day-to-day relationship of blacks with whites, (3) their traditional inability to point up positives and strengths within the context of Afro-American life styles, (4) their inability to conceptualize the problems encountered and the hopes for progress in a close relationship between a black worker and a black client, and (5) their dismissal of the black community's definitions of "coping with" and "adapting to" a pathological ghetto environment. It is the very rare white professional who is aware of these various aspects of life among blacks and who can thus be very effective in helping black therapists who work with blacks.

On the other hand, too many black workers in order to attract the continued approval of white co-workers or in a general pursuit of white middle-class values have ignored their unique knowledge of their ethnic background and have aped traditional white-oriented perceptions of the behavior of blacks. Thus the problem is heightened by the paucity of knowledgeable black supervisors and consultants to help correct countertransference involving racial and cultural elements.

This is not to say that black therapists should not work with black clients. On the contrary, it would seem more appropriate in this period of history for blacks to work with blacks. In fact, black rather than white workers may have greater success with black clients. Between them exist the communality of race and, even more important, the similar experience of being black in predominantly white America, both of which make for a better understanding and closer relationship between worker and client. Even some research points in this direction. (2, 12–14)

Analysis of common problems involved in the worker-client relationship will be presented here in relation to a few specific themes: denial of identification, overidentification, self-image, and class differences and similarities between therapist and client. This is not to say that when the black therapist and black client work together everyone of these factors will always appear, but there is a likelihood, due to the psycho-social pressures of the wider white society, that they will occur.

DENIAL OF IDENTIFICATION

Many black therapists assigned to a black client seek to avoid acknowledging that the client is black. This dodging of the inescapable fact that both are black may reveal the therapist's fear of loss of his emotional control and dissolution of his "professional image." Being black in America, if not in most corners of the world, means being a member of a despised group. Taking stock of and discussion of this reality tends to bring out the anger and the hurt which rarely escape a black person in America. The black therapist must control these feelings lest they interfere in the therapeutic process.

Many times one way to forestall the possibility of loss of emotional control is to avoid the entire matter of race. But this avoidance may not so much cover up the racial problems in the relationship as ignore the client's own problems involving race. An example of such avoidance:

> Mr. T., an Afro-American, has been in therapy for several weeks with a black therapist at a mental health center. Among his many problems is his increasing difficulty in communicating with his wife.
>
> Therapist: I have noted the hesitancy with which you discuss some aspects of your difficulties. You seem to be unsure about bringing up some things with me. You haven't mentioned the racial issue directly and so I was wondering if your being black had anything to do with any of the problems that you and your wife are having.
>
> Mr. T.: Oh no! Race has nothing to do with it. I could be white and still have the same problem that I have with my wife.
>
> Therapist: Yes. That's true. I was just wondering if race entered into it. Apparently it doesn't. So, let's get back to. . . .

Here we have an example of a worker who actually broached the subject of race yet in the end kept his distance from further exploration of the area. Only when the racial issue is dealt with forthrightly in psychotherapy can there be an opportunity to deal with the manner in which it affects the client's life and how it affects the therapeutic relationship.

There are also those therapists who refuse to mention racial issues for therapeutic reasons. They feel that the immediate thera-

peutic situation takes precedence over the existing black thera-
pist/black client relationship. This seemingly honest attempt to
control countertransference actually covers up the therapist's almost unconscious pretense that he and his client are white and
that racial problems are of little consequence.

A variation on this theme of denial occurs when identification
is made on a racial level but avoided on a therapeutic level. This
tendency can be seen in the underestimation of a client's difficulties unrelated to race and the attributing of most-to-all of his
problems to external societal derivation. Of course, the other extreme is also a form of denial of identification—the therapist who
attributes most-to-all of his client's problems to the client's responsibility rather than to racial discrimination. This latter case is
well stated by Grier and Cobbs. They say that blacks in psychotherapy "may insist that white oppression has never exerted any
influence on their lives, even in the face of such realities as police
brutality, job and housing discrimination, and a denial of educational opportunities. It is a powerful national trait, this willful
blindness to the abuse of blacks in America. It is a blindness that
includes the victim as well as the crime."(15)

OVERIDENTIFICATION

In a study of the attitudes of black staff members toward black
children in a residential treatment center, it was found that these
attitudes ranged from denial of identification to overidentification.(5) Overidentification is defined here as a felt bond with another black person who is seen as an extension of oneself because
of a common racial experience. The tie is used primarily to
achieve personal satisfaction.

Overidentification is, understandably, perhaps the chief problem of most blacks who work with other blacks in any sort of
professional setting. In the therapeutic situation, the worker might
desire to change the professional context of interviews, implicitly
state that "we are all sufferers," and encourage joint worker and
client griping sessions. A similar blindspot in the worker might
cause him to give subtle or overt encouragement to the client to
gripe about racial problems without giving the client much help
with his nonracially-linked problems. Another instance would be

that of the aggression-inhibited therapist's encouragement of acting-out behavior on the part of the client. Therapists who act in
these ways are really working out their own difficulties rather
than those of their clients.

A major difficulty that often arises is the widely discussed but
rarely studied situation in which blacks displace their anger
against whites onto less feared targets: other blacks. Black therapists must learn how to deal adequately with both the reality of
their blackness and with their own anger in order to help their
black clients even minimally.

One theme that draws scanty references in the literature
about the Afro-American, yet is of immense significance, is the
relationship between black males and black females. Briefly, in
many sectors of the black community the female is often resented
by the male because, as in many white households, she holds the
dominant decision-making position, because of her overprotec-
tion of the children (in order to help them survive in the white
world), and because of her tendency to act superior to the male
and to devalue his abilities, (4, 11) a tendency seeming to stem
from historical depreciation of the role of black men in America
and the greater acceptability of black females by whites. Black
therapists must carefully examine the ways in which they relate to
black clients of the opposite sex.

CLIENTS, PASSIVE AND ASSERTIVE

In this day of rapid social change, blacks are increasingly asserting
themselves rather than remaining passive in order to survive. Today, though passive behavior is still required in many quarters,
blacks are more and more being permitted and permitting themselves some aggressive behavior toward whites. Out of this development have emerged two distinctly different types of black therapists: First, there are those who are conservative and traditional,
tending to prefer black clients who are passive and nonassertive.
Such clients appeal to them because this is the traditional behavior pattern in the black community. Second are those black workers who ally themselves with the Black Consciousness movement
and who are often quite intolerant of such docile clients.(15) The
client who is assertive and far from passive may very well threaten

the values of the traditional therapist, whereas a therapist who readily accepts assertive behavior in a black client may be quite content with such a client. All four situations have potential for negative countertransference reactions.

One issue that must be resolved is the kind of behavior that should be encouraged in black clients. This is actually a problem for white as well as black therapists, as is pointed out by Gochros.(9) It would seem at this point of the Black Revolution that the tendency toward docile behavior in blacks can be regarded only as self-degrading and incompatible with the changing self-image of blacks.

There are also other major therapeutic decisions that have to be made in light of the changing nature of the racial struggle. Dr. Chester Pierce has pointed out in his paper "Problems of the Negro Adolescent in the Next Decade"(17) that black adolescents have to be prepared for a society which is increasingly offering better education, employment, and other opportunities to black youth. The problem, it seems to me, applies to all-age blacks. Many black clients have to be made aware of this new situation without diminishing the truth about the concomitant white-created obstacles and hardships that have to be endured or fought. For instance, a black person employed in a business firm may be obliged to join a new coterie of solely white friends in order to retain his job. The black student who is admitted to an Ivy League school and given a full scholarship may then be expected to perform academically superior to the white students. Of course, it is not only the black client who must be prepared to face these changes; the black therapist is affected as well.

CLASS DIFFERENCES AND SIMILARITIES

The importance of class among blacks is not to be underestimated. In most discussions of blacks and their problems, much less of black clients, there is little distinction made between lower-class and middle-class blacks. However, the values of middle-class and lower-class blacks differ as do those of their white counterparts. And there are important differences in terms of cultural life styles and historical experience.(11)

Frazier(8) talks of how the middle-class blacks play at being middle-class whites. Though somewhat dated in parts, Frazier's work still holds true for the most part. He contended that with a rise in status position, blacks tend to distance themselves from and relinquish links with those of their own racial community. This theory has been upheld by the research of Parker and Kleiner.(16) We may therefore find the middle-class black therapist, in line with his own upward class strivings, overtly or covertly discouraging the undesirable behavior style of the lower-class black client in order that the client "act white," i.e., pretend that one is white and adopt the middle-class life style. The discouragement of this life style may betray the therapist's desire to avoid remembrance of his grueling struggle from the lower class to the middle class.

Many typical characteristics of the relationships of middle-class blacks with other lower-class and other middle-class blacks need not be discussed here. Attitudes such as "I made it. Why can't they?" and the jealousy and resentment against dealing with persons of similar class and educational background are not necessary for discussion because they are already dealt with in the literature on status-striving behavior among both blacks and whites in America.

STATUS-STRIVING

Therapeutic work with blacks is invariably low status work because of the almost universal negative images and myths associated with blacks.(6) A white as well as a black worker may unconsciously act malevolently toward the black client because work with this client is of low status. The anger resulting from this frustrating knowledge may then be displaced unto the client in an unconscious effort to drive him away.

The black therapist, who from the start has low status because he is black, sometimes tends to see himself as having even lower status by having a black rather than a white client. His anger may be projected upon the client who is then seen as "the bad nigger."(11) Furthermore, he may attempt to, in effect, reject this client with a host of labels, e.g., "untreatable," "poor prognosis," "unreachable." Such a course of events is even more likely if the client conveniently supplies the therapist with symptoms of rage or acting out. If those clients who embarrass the therapist are not "cooled out" by traditional cooling out procedures, (1) then they are subject to diluted or irrelevant treatment.

The worker who adopts white prejudices and sees his client as "the dumb nigger" (the inarticulate and usually passive black who is seemingly of low intelligence) would tend to resort to the use of the aforementioned methods also. However, the worker may be ignoring the possibility that the client is using the protective device of "playing dumb" to survive in the white man's world. Again, the focus is on white-based concepts of the behavior of blacks rather than on a black community orientation.

Sometimes the black therapist is particularly "hard" on the black client if and when the latter "acts white" because of fear on the therapist's part of his own tendencies in that direction. Thus, in this and other situations the therapist cues the client as to the type of behavior required of him. Those clients who fail to get the message or who reject it are themselves rejected. Above all, the client is frequently expected to act in such a way that the therapist can retain professional prestige, i.e., continuing favorable comments from white co-workers and supervisors.(15)

CONCLUSION

It has been a major contention of this paper that racial factors must be acknowledged and dealt with by the therapist. In a recent clinical article, Waite (20) warns against any great interest on the part of the therapist in the cultural values of the patient's ethnic group. Waite sees this emphasis as part of countertransference resistance, among other potential problems. These problems are very much akin to my discussion here in the sections on Denial of Identification and Overidentification. Waite also implies that belief in the uniqueness of the individual precludes the generalization of cultural attributes to most members of a minority group. I would argue with this thesis in terms of the experience of Afro-Americans. There are few black Americans who would deny the deep hurt, grief, sorrow, and anger that Grier and Cobbs (11) and Poussaint (18) denote as the black community's lot. Those who would deny these feelings are merely kidding themselves. Since these feelings are the experience of black Americans, they necessarily affect the work a black therapist performs with a black client. Therefore, a major prerequisite for the black psychotherapist working with a black client is the thorough examination of one's own feelings on being black and one's way of coping with his own anger.

I have attempted to state that because of the American racial situation there are some difficulties involved but not necessarily total roadblocks to working successfully with black clients. One of my major points is that the black family and the black community, not the white family and the white community, should be the reference points for diagnosis and therapy with any black person. I have also tried to point to the need for the black therapist to identify with the black community and to be committed to and responsive to the total needs of the black client instead of treating him as essentially an alien.

In addition, it must be stressed that there are several areas which must be investigated more rigorously than they have been in the past: specifically, the black male/black female relationship; the use of aggression by blacks toward other blacks and toward whites; the cultural styles of Afro-American; normal and psychopathological behavior amongst blacks; and white racism not only in the United States but throughout the world.

Finally, because most of the mentioned racial pitfalls involve the inculcation of white prejudices in the minds of blacks through the years, many white therapists will be able to profit from this discussion by relating these same prejudices to their own work with blacks.

References

1. Adams, P., and McDonald, N. 1968. Clinical cooling out of poor people. *Amer. J. Orthopsychiat.* 38:457–463.
2. Baratz, S. 1967. Effect of race of experimenter, instructions, and comparison population upon level of reported anxiety in Negro subjects. *J. Personality and Soc. Psychol.* 7:194–196.
3. Bayton, J., et al. 1965. Negro perception of Negro and white personality traits. *J. Personality and Soc. Psychol.* 1:253.
4. Billingsley, A. 1968. *Black Families in White America.* Prentice-Hall, Englewood Cliffs, N.J.
5. Chethik, M. 1967. A quest for identity: treatment of disturbed Negro

children in a predominantly white treatment center. *Amer. J. Orthopsychiat.* 37:71–77.

6. Curry, A. 1964. Myth, transference, and the black psychotherapist. *Psychoanal. Rev.* 51:7–14.

7. Curry, A. 1964. The Negro worker and the white client. *Soc. Casework.* 45:131–136.

8. Frazier, E. 1957. *Black Bourgeoisie.* Free Press, New York.

9. Gochros, J. 1966. Recognition and use of anger in Negro clients. *Soc. Work* 11:33.

10. Grier, W. 1967. When the therapist is Negro: some effects on the treatment process. *Amer. J. Psychiat.* 123:1587–1591.

11. Grier, W., and Cobbs, P. 1968. *Black Rage.* Basic Books, New York.

12. Katz, I., et al. 1965. Effects of task difficulty, race of administrator, and instructions on digit symbol performance of Negroes. *J. Personality and Soc. Psychol.* 5:53–59.

13. Katz, I., et al. 1968. Effects of race of tester, approval-disapproval and need on Negro children's learning. *J. Personality and Soc. Psychol.* 8:38–42.

14. Katz, I., and Greenbaum, C. 1963. Effects of anxiety, threat, and racial environment on task performance of Negro college students. *J. Abnorm. and Soc. Psychol.* 63:562–567.

15. Lindsay, I. 1947. Race as a factor in establishing a casework relationship. *Soc. Casework.* 28:101–107.

16. Parker, S., and Kleiner, R. 1964. Status position, mobility and ethnic identification of the Negro. *J. Soc. Issues.* 30:85–102.

17. Pierce, C. 1968. Problems of the Negro adolescent in the next decade. In *Minority Group Adolescents in the United States.* Williams and Wilkins, Baltimore.

18. Poussaint, A. 1967. A Negro psychiatrist explains the Negro psyche. *New York Times Magazine,* August 20, 1967:52–53+.

19. Silberman, C. 1964. *Crisis in Black and White.* Random House, New York.

20. Waite, R. 1968. The Negro patient and clinical theory. *J. Consult. and Clin. Psychol.* 32:427–433.

TRANSFERENCE AND COUNTERTRANSFERENCE IN INTERRACIAL ANALYSES*

Judith S. Schachter and Hugh F. Butts

This paper will deal with some of the features and vicissitudes of transference and countertransference as well as other reactions of the analyst, in analyses in which analyst and patient are of different races. Emphasis in the literature is on the drawbacks of disparities of culture and status. Clinical examples from two analyses will be cited to highlight the following generalizations:

(i) Racial differences may have little or no effect on the course of the analysis. (ii) Racial differences may have a catalytic effect upon the analytic process, and lead to a more rapid unfolding of core problems. (iii) Stereotypes of race and color occasionally induce both analyst and patient to delay the analytic process, either by obscuring reality or by overestimating its importance. (iv) Subculturally acceptable pathology or acting out may evoke overreactions in the analyst, while material fitting racial stereotypes may be ignored. (v) Countertransference may coincide with stereotypes and delay the analytic process.

Although the focus of this paper is on the analytic relationship, we are necessarily cognizant of the current social revolution. Many patients are involved in the interracial tensions which permeate our society. The major efforts being made to upset the structured patterns of discrimination are an important factor in

*Reprinted by permission of the authors and publisher from the *Journal of the American Psychoanalytic Association*, 16:4 (October 1968) 792–808; copyright © 1968 by The American Psychoanalytic Association.

the patient's awareness of choice and increase the possibilities of interracial analysis. We do not discuss, although we recognize, that on the conscious level, Negro-white relationships are directly related to the values, ethics, group norms, and sociopolitical philosophy of the participants, and this fact plays a part in the material both patient and analyst choose to work with as well as in the nonverbal cues the patient receives. The Negro analyst may be closer to understanding the value system of his white patient than the white analyst is to his Negro analysand's, particularly if the latter is from a very different social or economic status. Values which are compatible with healthy adjustment are, of course, respected by all analysts, but here the analyst's concept of "health" influences the ego ideal he sets before the patient. Specifically, this is true in choice of a marriage partner and marriage ideal which has special significance in American life and is of great importance in the analyses reported.

Oberndorf, in 1954, stated that interracial therapy could not be effective because of the divergence of psychological biases in such treatment situations. He felt that a positive transference could be most easily established and analyzed if the psychological biases held by the doctor and patient did not differ too widely. Further, "integration of the mentally disturbed individual can best be achieved if he is treated by one of those who understand his motivations, rather than by one considered expert in a particular form of mental illness" (5).

Abraham Kardiner and Lionel Ovesey (3) describe the effect of social and economic discrimination upon the personality integration of Negroes. They regard suspicion and distrust among Negroes as a "normal" consequence of the continuous frustrations which, during childhood, are mediated by families that bear the "mark of oppression."

Janet Kennedy (4) has also emphasized that many Negro patients enter treatment with fear, suspicion, and distrust of the white therapist based upon specific life experiences. She highlights the necessity for enabling a Negro patient to acquire a realistically attainable ego ideal not predicated on skin color. The removal of stereotypes held by Negro patients, both of themselves and of their therapist, is a necessary precursor in meaningful reconstructive therapy.

Viola Bernard (1) insists that in interracial analyses the clinician must expand his personal awareness and control his own conscious and unconscious racial attitudes and reactions, since both he and his patients are participating members of a society with intergroup tensions and cultural prejudices. She emphasizes certain countertransference problems in white analysts which create difficulties in treating Negro analysands: "One of the most disastrous results of too much race consciousness on the part of the analyst, for whom his patient's skin color obscures his view of the whole man, is his proneness to interpret too much in terms of racial conflicts and thereby deprive the patient of thoroughly reaching and working through whatever his basic difficulties may be. On the other hand, the analyst's blinding himself to the racial factor may also play into the patient's resistances as well as deny some of the social realities of his current existence." Stereotypy on the part of the analyst can lead the patient to feel that interest lies solely in his being a Negro, rather than a person. This leads either to feelings of painful personal rejection or to unhealthy narcissistic satisfaction in being special, with reinforcement of the patient's own proneness to stereotyped racial responses.

White analysts have elucidated some of the specific unconscious meaning of dark skin color to their white patients. Sterba (7) has concluded that rejection of Negroes based on repressed sibling rivalry equates the Negro with the unwanted younger siblings. Hate and aggression against Negro men unconsciously represents repressed hostility toward the father. Like the Devil, who is also dark, the Negro man is a substitute for the father insofar as he is hated and feared. Terry Rodgers (6) has described the evolution during analysis, of an active anti-Negro racist and has further developed Sterba's analysis of the meaning of this darkness to the white man. Unconsciously, the Negro man represents the hated father, particularly the father at night.

Andrew Curry (2) also refers to the myths in which Satan, Lucifer, and Judas represent darkness, death, and evil. Transference to the Negro therapist is set by the utilization of these myths and symbols. Curry distinguishes between true transference to the Negro therapist and certain other responses by white patients which are "archaic, mythological responses which will have crucial effects upon the eventual manifestation of the transference, which occurs later in time." He also describes the dynamic-economic forces operative when reference to the therapist's race constitutes a source of resistance.

CASE PRESENTATIONS

1. A White Man Analyzed by a Negro Male Analyst

A thirty-five-year-old white professional man of Jewish extraction was referred by his cousin, a former patient of the analyst. He sought analysis because of his inability to get married. During each of two engagements he had become progressively depressed and anxious and in each instance had broken off the relationship. A second complaint, premature ejaculation, had begun a year before the patient sought help. Vocationally, he was insecure despite the fact that he worked in an executive capacity. He was ingratiating with fellow employees and fearful that he might not be able to control his anger in work situations.

His most vivid memories of early childhood dated back to age six, with recollections of visits to his white Jewish aunt and grandmother in Harlem. He took pride in making the subway trips alone, but recalled mixed feelings of anxiety and excitement. The Harlem community of that period was racially integrated. His anxiety was predicated upon his fear of physical attack, and his excitement seemed rooted in sexual fantasies which utilized racial stereotypes and myths.

An intense fear of losing his parents pervaded his childhood. He was a good student and active in athletics, but frequently needed his mother's intervention on his behalf during altercations with other children. At home, his mother was a severely critical, domineering, anxious woman who subjugated her husband and chided him for being weak, inadequate, and a poor provider. She lamented her difficult lot in life and confided the intimacies of her marital dissatisfaction to the patient. The father was physically and emotionally inaccessible.

Castration anxiety increased at age fourteen when his parents' concern about the size of his penis led them to consult a physician. He was embarrassed to shower with schoolmates for fear that they would discover that his penis was small. Adolescence brought sexual interest and exploration; he dated, but was always inhibited and anxious. During this period he shared his sister's bedroom, but recalls only one instance of embarrassment, when she giggled when overhearing him masturbate.

Concern about the size of his penis persisted into adulthood. After completion of Army service and college, he worked in an executive position, continuing to live with his parents. He perceived phallic women as castrators, and used prematurity and impotence to defend against castration. With men, he was "the nice guy," obsequious, ingratiating, and controlling his rage. His nonassertiveness socially, sexually, and vocationally was a derivative of his need to control his rage.

Early dreams gave form to the negative transference of the first six months and highlighted one of the patient's key problems: the Negro man was presented as physically assaultive, drunk, and debased, and the patient feared his analyst's aggression and sexual exploitation.

In his associations he dwelt on the theme of the menacing Negro, juxtaposing his sexual inadequacy, fear of women, and his perception of women as castrating, humiliating creatures. Soon after beginning the analysis he moved from his parents' home, magically utilizing the therapist's strength as a buffer against his mother. The move was accompanied by a great deal of anxiety, represented in dreams as a fear of starving to death. He began to date and to attempt sex, expressing his lack of assertiveness and his dependency orientation in dreams such as the following:

> In my apartment with C. We were necking. I had her breasts in my hand. There were many women around. They were exposing their breasts. I was completely fascinated and felt pleasure.

The therapist challenged his fragmented view of women and its emotional counterpart, his affective isolation and his wish to present himself as dead emotionally. His dreams and associations were replete with his wish to be regarded as a helpless infant, which was interpreted, at that time, as a defensive retreat to a position of dependent safety designed to avoid castration. The patient was then able to associate this with his difficulty in separating from his mother to attend kindergarten.

Ten months after the beginning of analysis he triumphantly

reported that he was able to penetrate a woman sexually despite intense anxiety and fear of impregnating her. He plied the analyst with questions about contraception, in actuality seeking plaudits for his sexual accomplishments. The analyst's mild disbelief in the therapeutic significance of the patient's achievement in part reinforced the patient's stereotyped perception of the Negro as a virtual sexual superman, thus widening the gulf between analyst and analysand. Another source of difficulty during this period was the analyst's need to disclaim his therapeutic power to achieve such a great effect with the patient. This problem was rooted in the analyst's insecurity about his effectiveness which was combined, however, with a need to assert his greater power over the patient.

With continued attempts at intercourse, a pseudohomosexual theme emerged in a dream:

> I was in bed with S. She got on top of me. We were having intercourse. But it was not S.'s face. It was a man's face. I was frightened.

He discussed the anxiety in the dream, adding, "I'm afraid of women so a man is safer. But why am I afraid of women? My mother is a woman."

The second year of analysis was concerned with his efforts to separate emotionally from his parents, to improve his sexual adaptation, and to deal with his chronic anxiety. During this period he maintained a relationship with one woman, advanced vocationally, and began to see himself as having an existence separate from that of his parents, with lessening anxiety about their death. References to the therapist's race were minimal, although when the patient's fear of the therapist mounted, the menacing Negro would reappear in his dream life:

> A Negro trooper strikes a white policeman in the stomach. The white man beats him up.

Increased separation from his family brought mounting anxiety about his relationship with the analyst, and he reconsidered his childhood visits to his aunt's home in Harlem, which were marked by a mixture of pleasurable excitement and fear. The omission of his father's role in the family, previously justified by his father's absence at work during the patient's childhood, became a therapeutic focus, particularly since any information about father had been transmitted by mother. During the latter part of the second year of analysis, material emerged indicating that his father had protected him against the mother and against destructive women in general. His dreams became less frighteningly destructive and he dreamed of father and therapist in terms of helping figures. He was married in the third year of analysis and terminated six months later. His functioning had improved considerably in all areas.

2. A Negro Man Analyzed by a White Woman Analyst

An unmarried man of mixed Negro and Caucasian extraction entered analysis at the Columbia Psychoanalytic Clinic because of his inability to form a stable relationship with a woman, and increasing awareness of his inability to face marriage. He was also troubled by difficulties at work, particularly with a woman supervisor, which had contributed to his recent loss of a job. He was unable to express his feelings or to tolerate the expression of feelings by others, and appeared passive, isolated, and dependent upon his mother.

Early childhood was spent in a white commercial neighborhood in a northern city, living in the maternal grandfather's home with his light-skinned mother and father. During the Depression, the family moved to Harlem. Thus, at six, he believed that it was his dark color that necessitated the family's choice of home. At twelve to thirteen years, he was the successful vice-president of a gang because of his boxing skill, and two years later he was caught in his first serious delinquency, pilfering from the mail. After high school graduation he got a construction job and began passive homosexual activities in toilets, apparently after his mother arranged for his girlfriend's abortion. On the job he suffered a minor injury, and during the subsequent hospitalization he applied to and was accepted by a large Negro college out of town.

Once there, he lived with an older woman off campus and avoided both school contacts and fraternities, which were divided on color lines. He associated only with men who were appreciably darker than himself. After graduation, he returned to his mother and sporadic employment until he was encouraged by a super-

ferences. As he grappled to understand the nature of the sexual barrier between us, and between him and mother, he repeatedly came back to color. In a dream, the slow analytic train was held up by white barriers, which represented the analyst, who would cause the crash and hurt the driver. Further associations were to the analyst's open and free attitude toward color in comparison to his own feelings of prejudice against dark women. His angry self-justification was: "You've had a better life than I. . . . You can afford to be more liberal, freer of prejudice than I. . . . how can you understand what it is to be a Negro in America . . . a bitter thought . . . it's one thing to see something from the outside and another to live within it."

During the last year of treatment he re-examined why the analyst was not afraid of his impulses, or of him. "The only reason I can think of your being scared is because of color; it's the way I separated myself from my mother. I associate all my failures with color. My uncle drove a coal truck and was dirty and I identify him with color."

Setting his wedding date precipitated more anxiety, focused now on fears of having a dark child. He was forced again to face his prejudices and his feeling that his child would make him more identifiable, as did his fiancée, who was approximately his color and had a "pug" nose. At the same time, the realities of his life made him more aware of his opportunities. The pleasures ahead of him and guilt at leaving the analyst as well as his parents behind, became the final theme of the analysis.

Follow-up has shown that the patient has consolidated the gains made in analysis. The opening up of his ambitions, particularly in the beginning of the sixth year of analysis, has expanded to active and successful work. He sees himself as a leader in his profession and of his race. His marriage appears stable and successful. Although he was momentarily upset at the birth of a child lighter than either he or his wife, he recognized and coped with these feelings, identified the child as his own, and made plans for another.

DISCUSSION

Racial differences between analyst and patient involve issues of unconscious meaning at various levels analogous to differences in sex between analyst and patient. They must be recognized and utilized, but only rarely do they create an either unanalyzable barrier or a serious obstacle to treatment. The choice of analyst by our patients was predicated only in part upon racial stereotypes which facilitated the white patient's entrance into treatment and played an unconscious role in the expectations of the Negro analysand. The white patient's selection of the Negro analyst who had successfully treated his cousin was prompted in part by his utilization of magical dependency antedating the beginning of the analysis. He saw the analyst realistically as having greatly benefited his cousin. He equated "Negro" with the sexual potency and strength he hoped to attain. In fact, he concretized this wish by introducing himself to the analyst in the men's room of a banquet hall at the time of his cousin's wedding. The discomfort engendered in the analyst by this first encounter was handled by resorting to greater formality than is his wont during the subsequent treatment. He recognized that his unconscious reaction produced a distance between himself and the analysand. When the patient's early dreams made reference to men's rooms or toilets, the concrete image of the manifest content became the focus of interpretation and access to latent content was discouraged.

The Negro was realistically limited in his opportunities for treatment, and his choice of the analytic clinic, where his analyst would almost certainly be white, was not useful for an understanding of his rejection of Negroes and of his stereotypes associated with them. The analyst chose the patient because of both realistic and unconscious needs. The scarcity of male patients likely to remain in analysis made her feel that the geographically less mobile Negro might make a better long-term patient, while her involvement with civil rights and the underdog enabled him to serve as the object of an identification. Rescue fantasies focusing on a man rejected by other analytic students, his mother, and society were also operating.

The catalytic effect of the analyst's race upon the development of the transference occurs when the racial stereotypes are concerned with the same affects and conflicts as the transference. These stereotypes do not reflect a transferring of feelings from earlier significant figures onto the therapist. They provide the structure upon which a problem can be hung, and much of the transference can be worked out around the racial issues that are brought up early in treatment. If the stereotype and the developing

transference are both reflections of the analysand's personal difficulties, this confluence of transference and stereotype will facilitate the analysis. As an example, the white patient's racial stereotype of Negro men was that of sexual athletes. The developing
positive transference posited the analyst as an omniscient, benevolent superman who could magically infuse his strength into the
frail anemic patient. Both of these reactions facilitated the analysis of the patient's unconscious mechanisms of magical repair and
of his conviction of helplessness, upon which these reparative
methods were based.

The Negro man's stereotyped assumption that white women
were sexually cold and not easily seduced provided a degree of
protection at first, as did associations to the concept of fairness.
These stereotypes immediately catalyzed his feelings toward
mother and at the same time provided a lever for questioning their
appropriateness. The alternative to coldness was seductiveness,
and finally he could say, "You're just being you, like mother. I wish
you'd look bad." Protective feelings toward the analyst originally
aroused by his family's outspoken anti-Semitism similarly allowed
access to the deeper need to protect mother from exposure both
as a Negro and as a failure.

Analysis of resistance remained a major part of this analysis.
Three aspects can be the foci of generalization. First, the suspicious, even paranoid questioning of trust and acceptability
which continued for almost six years at deeper and deeper levels
was more intense than that expected in a white analytic patient.
For example, the change to private status at the end of a year and
a half of analysis revealed the fantasy that the analyst's private
office in an apartment building was a part of the clinic facilities; in
effect he had denied acceptance and equality with other private
patients. Early in his fifth year of analysis he recognized the selec-
tiveness of the Clinic when someone he knew was rejected. Although able to enjoy the idea that he had been accepted, he revealed the reservation that the analyst had had no choice; she was
simply doing her job. Fortunately, aspects of this resistance were
continuously accessible to analysis, and in this last instance, the
original childhood fantasy that he was not his father's child but
that the father had chosen to care for him provided a deeper
meaning.

A second aspect of the resistance is its use of race as the

vocabulary in terms of which to rationalize and thus to fend off anxiety about closeness. Interpretations were focused upon this aspect. Color issues came up to separate us and often provided justification for withholding material which he felt I could not understand. This was illustrated by a dream in which he walked hand in hand with the analyst through a crowded restaurant. He felt uncomfortable and pulled away, but the analyst said, "No, come on," so he put his hand back.

A third aspect, closer to that seen with the white patient, was less prominent, but still important. This patient's difficulty in openly criticizing, complaining, or demanding was evident in his life and in the analysis, but he was able to use the vehicle of the racial stereotype to express hostility when the analyst did not participate as much as he wished in the sessions, and as a control so that he could feel free to express love to her. Material which possibly might have been unverbalizable by a similarly obsessive white patient was made available through the language and analysis of the stereotypes.

Bernard (1) has pointed out a further ramification of interracial analysis: the parent-child power disparity either blends with or runs counter to the social power disparity involved as the background of the analysis, so that early feelings of familial rejection and exclusion become intertwined with social rejection and exclusion. Thus, the Negro patient, who had felt excluded and rejected by his cold light-skinned mother, frequently used the inequality in emotional involvement between the analyst and himself to bolster feelings of helplessness and to deny both his mother's and the analyst's concern for him. To the extent that color gave the analyst even more power in relation to him as a patient, his vulnerability was increased and regressive aspects were accentuated. Utilizing the other pole of this disparity, another of our patients felt that she was picking an "underdog" like herself in the Negro analyst, whom she could regard as a social reject. In a session early in treatment, she alluded to the "rough life" she imagined her therapist had had because of his race, comparing his lot to hers as a child.

Stereotypes may also delay analysis of character defenses, particularly when the analyst is white and the patient Negro, since the analyst may have difficulty distinguishing the pathological aspect of a characteristic that fits within his racial stereotype of the analysand. The double negatives, ain'ts, and Southern accent of the Negro patient, once questioned, were quickly revealed as an unconscious identification with mother, the presumably brighter and better educated parent who had retained these modes of expression despite her Northern upbringing. This understanding of aspects of his feminine identification had to wait until the beginning of his fifth year of analysis because of the analyst's inability to recognize the pattern as completely inappropriate. Tentativeness about the norms of Negro speech and the assumption that he was retaining a class or racial identification caused the delay which would not have occurred with a white patient.

Inability to place subculturally acceptable pathology in perspective may also lead to overreactions and prevent the analyst from understanding the patient's character problems. The opening phrase of the Negro patient's analysis was replete with instances in which he described aberrant behavior which was more common and acceptable in a part of his Negro subculture than in the white, such as drunkenness, exploitation of women, irresponsibility toward those emotionally dependent on him, and acceptance of stealing. Although this behavior was described in terms of his own culture, he was aware of the analyst's background and was motivated by his need to fend her off by a recital of irresponsible acting-out behavior. Another aspect of his character, bordering on the psychopathic, involved the concept of himself as a victim, without choice. Identification as a Negro solidified this insistence that he was not a deliberate participant and thus deserved special treatment because of his deprivation. The question of the patient's analyzability arose at one point and included a countertransference flight from the dangerous image he evoked, as well as difficulty in accurately appraising the pathology. Analysis proved that these defenses in this anxious, obsessive Negro man did not have the serious prognostic significance that they would have had in a white male graduate student. Despite the plethora of defenses and escape mechanisms used, the patient never showed signs of an integrative disorder and with a greater time latitude was able to accept identification with the white analyst despite his guilt at surpassing his parents on a socio-economic as well as emotional level. As returns from society increased, the support for his passivity diminished and he could accept the responsibility, for example, of paying off a loan and thus allowing himself wider choice of a job.

Because the Negro analyst encompasses the greater part of the white culture, only minor aspects of his patient's life may cause him to overreact. The white patient's insistence on dining at his parents' home with unerring regularity was, on the one hand, an index of his dependency upon them and, on the other, a sub-cultural institution with widespread acceptance, probably not warranting the concern evoked in the analyst. This patient's pride in his "freedom from prejudice," manifested in his sitting in the rear of the bus while stationed in Mississippi, elicited a warm reaction from his analyst, who had been stationed there himself. This reaction was useful in creating greater closeness between the analyst and patient, by accepting the analysand's identification with his analyst and thereby facilitating the treatment; it pre-vented, however, the analysis of the motivations underlying the statement.

The analyst's sexual countertransference mainly consisted of his unconscious denial of anxiety about the original meeting with his patient in the men's room. In addition, his disbelief in the therapeutic significance of the patient's sexual achievements was based both on his unconscious need to see himself as sexually more adequate than the analysand as well as the aforementioned inability to see himself as an effective analyst.

CONCLUSIONS

The evidence of these cases of interracial analysis indicates the difficulties to be anticipated, but suggests that these are appar-ently no greater than the obstacles encountered in analyses in which race is not an issue. The white patient with a Negro analyst used stereotypes mainly as a way of expressing his transference to him. The Negro patient did this to a lesser degree, and the focus was primarily on the resistance aspect.

Awareness and analysis of the resistances and stereotypes may facilitate progress beyond that anticipated and enrich the treatment. In these examples, the stereotypes did not prevent the patients from achieving good analytic results. Moreover, racial disparity served as a catalyst for the developing analytic process. The countertransference reactions were also influenced by racial stereotypes. With the white analysand, the Negro analyst's unconscious need to deny his anxiety about sexual competitiveness merged with the racial stereotype to impede the progress of the analysis. With the Negro analysand, the white analyst questioned his analyzability as a means of fleeing from the dangerous stereotyped images evoked by her patient. The confluence of countertransference and stereotypes serves to delay the analysis.

SUMMARY

Vicissitudes of transference and countertransference in analysis wherein analyst and patient differ racially permit these generalizations:

1. Obscuring or overestimating racial stereotypes by analyst or patient may induce a delay in the analysis.
2. Subculturally acceptable pathology may evoke overreactions, while racial stereotypes may be ignored.
3. Racial differences may catalyze analyses.

References

1. Bernard, V. W. Psychoanalysis and members of minority groups. *This Journal*, 1:256–267, 1953.
2. Curry, A. Myth, transference and the black psychotherapist. *Psychoanal. Rev.*, 51:7–14, 1964.
3. Kardiner, A. & Ovesey, L. *The Mark of Oppression.* Cleveland: World Publishing Co., 1951.
4. Kennedy, J. A. Problems posed in the analysis of Negro patients. *Psychiatry*, 15:313–327, 1952.
5. Oberndorf, C. P. Selectivity and option for psychotherapy. *Amer. J. Psychiat.*, 110:754–758, 1954.
6. Rodgers, T. C. The evolution of an active anti-Negro racist. *The Psychoanalytic Study of Society*, 1:237–247. New York: International Universities Press, 1960.
7. Sterba, R. Some psychological factors in Negro race hatred and in anti-Negro riots. *Psychoanalysis and the Social Sciences*, 1:411–427. New York: International Universities Press, 1947.

NATIVE AMERICAN NONINTERFERENCE*

Jimm G. Good Tracks

The standard techniques and theories of social work that bring positive results with many groups, including lower-class Anglo-Americans (Anglos), Negroes, and assimilated Mexicans, are not successful when applied to native Americans.[1] In fact, all the methods usually associated with the term "social work intervention" diminish in effectiveness *just to the extent that the subject has retained his native Indian culture.* The reason is that any kind of intervention is contrary to the Indian's strict adherence to the principle of self-determination. The less assimilated and acculturated the individual, the more important this principle is to him. Some time ago Wax and Thomas described this principle as noninterference.[2]

Many human relations unavoidably involve some influencing, meddling, and even coercion or force. Indians feel, however, that Anglos carry these elements to an extreme while professing an entirely different set of values. Anglos say they prize freedom, minding one's own business, and the right of each person to decide for himself, yet they also think it right to be their brother's keeper, to give advice and take action in their brother's best interest—as interpreted by the Anglo, in and by the Anglo social context.

In native Indian society, however, no interference or meddling of any kind is allowed or tolerated, even when it is to keep the other person from doing something foolish or dangerous. When an Anglo is moved to be his brother's keeper and that broth-

*Reprinted by permission from *Social Work*, 18:6 (November 1976) 30–34; copyright © 1976, National Association of Social Workers, Inc.

er is an Indian, therefore, almost everything he says or does seems rude, ill-mannered, or hostile. Perhaps it is the Anglo's arrogant righteousness that prevents him from grasping the nature of his conduct. But if the Indian told the Anglo that he was being intrusive, the Indian would himself be interfering with the Anglo's freedom to act as he sees fit.

COERCION AND SUGGESTION

Coercion appears to be a fundamental element in the peoples of Western Europe and their colonial descendants. All the governments and institutions of these societies use a variety of coercive methods to insure cooperative action. Traditional Indian societies, on the other hand, were organized on the principle of voluntary cooperation. They refrained from using force to coerce.

In recent times Euro-American societies have tended to rely less heavily on physical violence, but they have only replaced it with verbal forms of coercion and management. Anglo children appear to be taught by their elders, peer groups, and mass media to influence, use, and manipulate others to achieve their personal goals. They begin to try to manipulate others early in life while at play and in their relationships with adults. They continue to improve their manipulative skill throughout their lives as they study psychology and apply it to marriage counseling and psychotherapy. Their newspapers print "Dear Abby" letters from people who want someone else to tell them what to do or how to make others do as they wish. This ability is rightly called a tool essential for living and achieving success in Anglo society. Anglo economic development and exploitation could not otherwise exist. But even when verbal manipulation has superseded physical force, it still remains a form of coercion and constitutes interference. This does not disturb Anglos who feel there is a distinction.

Even a nondirective teacher utilizes some coercion when he wants his pupils to acquire a certain skill, express themselves with certain prepared materials, or participate in a group activity. It appears that the compulsion to interfere is so habitual among Anglos that even when they have no particular business to accomplish in a conversation, they will still tend to be coercive. For instance, one person may remark that he wishes to buy a new car. Someone will immediately tell him where he should buy one and perhaps what kind. In the most friendly manner Anglos are always telling each other and everyone else what they should do, buy, see, sell, read, study, or accomplish—all without any consideration of what the individual may want to do.

But whether it is a subtle suggestion or an outright command, it is considered improper behavior and an interference by Indian people. The Indian child is taught that complete noninterference in interaction with all people is the norm, and that he should react with amazement, irritation, mistrust, and anxiety to even the slightest indication of manipulation or coercion.

RESPECT AND CONSIDERATION

The following incident illustrates noninterference in the simplest of matters. I was visiting my cousins when one of them put on his coat and said he was going down town. He had no car, so one could assume he was going to walk. I restated his intention and volunteered to drive him. The cousin showed noninterference with my activities by not asking or even suggesting that I drive him, although that is certainly what he wanted. If he had asked directly and I had not cared to drive him, I would have been put on the spot. I would have been forced to refuse unobligingly or agree unwillingly. But by simply putting on his coat and announcing his intentions, he allowed me to accept or reject his desires without causing bad feelings for anyone. I could volunteer to take him or pay no attention to his actions.

A cross-cultural misunderstanding might occur in the following way. A non-Indian guest at my mother's home, having enjoyed a rice dinner, might pay my mother this compliment: "Your rice was so good! I should be happy to have your recipe, if I may. And do you want some of my rice recipes in exchange?" The offer of recipes might strengthen friendship among Anglos, but to an Indian it cancels the compliment. If my mother had wanted other recipes she would have suggested it to her guest. When the guest makes the offer on her own initiative, it implies she did not really care for my mother's rice and knows a better way to prepare it. If the guest had talked only about various ways of preparing rice, she would have given my mother the opportunity to ask about any that interested her.

An Indian will usually withdraw his attention from a person who interferes. If the ill-mannered person does not take the hint, the Indian will leave. In the event he is unable to leave, he will attempt to fade into the background and become unnoticed. In this way, he will avoid provoking the ill-mannered person to further outbursts and at the same time save the person embarrassment by not witnessing his improper behavior. This reaction also reprimands the one who interferes in a socially sanctioned manner. At such times, an Indian can only wonder at the person and wish he could leave. On occasion, however, when pushed beyond endurance, he may lose his self-control and drive the aggressor away with verbal or physical force.

Much delicacy and sensitivity are required for Indian good manners. If one is planning a gathering, for example, a feast to give a child his Indian name, one does not urge people to come. This would be interfering with their right to free choice. If people wish to come, they will come. Under most ordinary circumstances, an Indian does not even speak to another unless there is some indication that the other desires to turn his attention to him. If one wishes to speak with another, whether it is a friend, relative, or spouse, he will place himself in the person's line of vision. If the person's behavior does not indicate an acknowledgment of one's presence, one waits or goes away until later. Should one be talking with a friend and without forethought bring up a subject that may be sensitive or distressing to the listener, the latter will look away and pretend not to hear or suddenly change the subject.

The rules of etiquette are generally followed even by many assimilated Indians. They express a deep respect for the interests, responsibilities, and pursuits of other people. The same respect can be seen even in the behavior of young children. They play in the midst of adults who are having a conversation and yet never interrupt. A child may come and lean for a while against his parent or relative, but without a word or act of interference. Only in an emergency does a child try to attract an adult's attention, and then in a way that will not interrupt the adult's activity. A child who gets hurt playing, for example, might come in crying and then go lie down on a bed. The adult hears the crying and decides if he wishes to attend to the child. A bold child who wants something quietly comes up to his parent, stands there a while, and then whispers the request. It seems that even the youngest Indian children do not bother older people when they are preoccupied.

This behavior is taken for granted by Indian people as the proper way to behave. Learning it probably takes place on an unconscious level. Indian infants and those beginning to walk do not make loud attempts to attract their parents' attention as Anglo babies do. This suggests that demanding attention is actually taught the Anglo infant. Indian adults do not respond to interfering demands, so the child does not learn coercive methods of behavior. This does not imply that Indian children are never aggressive, but only that the culture does not reward aggression when it interferes with the activity of others. Indian children are taught to be considerate through the example of their elders, and the adult treats the child with the same respect and consideration that he expects for himself. It is generally against the child-rearing practices of Indian people to bother or interrupt their children when they are playing or to make them do something against their will, even when it is in their own best interest. Some Anglo educators show their ignorance of this principle by condemning Indian parents for not forcing their children to attend school.

IMPLICATIONS FOR PRACTICE

This principle explains much of the general failure of social workers to treat the social and psychological problems of Indian clients. There are other factors, of course, such as the Indian's perception of the worker as an authority figure representing a coercive institution and an alien, dominating, and undesirable culture. The physical appearance of the worker is another factor, and so is his ignorance of the manners of Indian people. The relationships that both client and worker have with the agency make for further complications, but an understanding of the principle of noninterference can still have an important effect on the worker's role. It can teach him what to expect in his social work relationships with Indian clients and thus enable him to be more effective in helping Indian people.

From an Indian client's viewpoint, the worker is expected to perform only the superficial and routine administrative functions of his office. Clients may request him to increase their aid grants, to draw upon some of their own funds from the agency Individual Indian Monies (IIM) accounts, to assist with a government form, or to submit a boarding-school application. These tasks involve no real social involvement, as involvement is understood both by Indians and non-Indians. The Indian client does not allow or desire the worker to have any insight into his inner thoughts. That would not be a proper part of work.

This expectation does not, of course, correspond to the professional social worker's own concept of his function. A worker could become quite frustrated just shuffling papers about and doing little actual social work when there might be plenty of social problems evident among his clientele. Nevertheless, the worker must not intervene unless the people request an intervention, and he is likely to wait a long time for such a request. The credentials of his profession, his position, status, knowledge, skills, achievements, and authority, though respected by the agency, are in most cases completely without merit among the Indians. Such things belong to Anglo culture and are not readily translatable into Indian culture. His standing in the Anglo community does not give him a license to practice intervention among Indian people.

The explanation for the social worker's initial uselessness is easily given. His professional function is generally performed from within the Indian culture, and no foreign interference is desired or contemplated. If a man's problems seem to be a result of his having been witched, for example, he will seek out the properly qualified person to help him alleviate the condition. He will have no need of any outside diagnoses or assistance. Should a personal or family problem be of another nature, it is addressed again to the proper individual, an uncle (mother's brother) or a grandfather— not to a foreigner such as the social worker. In every case, the people utilize the established, functional, culturally acceptable remedy within their own native system.

WORKER'S APPROACH

Can a worker ever convey his potential for helpfulness to Indian clients without breaking their norms? How can he do this while they adhere to the principle of noninterference?

Patience is the number-one virtue governing Indian relationships. A worker who has little or no patience should not seek
placements in Indian settings. Native temporal concepts are
strange to the non-Indian. Some non-Indians even believe these
concepts are unstructured and dysfunctional, and perhaps they
are—in the Anglo conceptual framework. But the social worker's
success may well be linked with his ability to learn "Indian time"
and adjust his relationships accordingly.

Native temporal concepts have no relation to the movements
of a clock. They deal in terms of natural phenomena—morning,
days, nights, months (from the native concept of "moon"), and
years (from the native concepts of "seasons" or "winters"). Ignorance of these concepts makes it impossible to understand the
long time it takes any alien to become established in the Indian
community. For although they are seemingly without interest, perhaps even indifferent to the new worker, the people will at length
carefully observe the manner in which he presents and carries
himself. It would be well for the worker to know how slow this
evaluation process is likely to seem, for he must not become
impatient. The evaluation will progress in accordance with native
temporal concepts. Perhaps in a year or so a majority of the people will have come to some conclusions about the worker's character. Basic acceptance comes only after there has been enough
observation to determine with reasonable assurance that the
worker will not inflict injury with his activities.

There is little or nothing the worker may do to expedite the
process; to push things along would be interfering with the process and the people. In the meantime, as he performs his superficial functions for the people, he may discreetly interject bits and
pieces of his potential for further assistance. But discretion is
needed to the utmost in order to avoid the slightest coercive suggestion. If the worker inflicts a coercive tone in conversation and
thus thwarts an individual's self-determination, it could be a major
setback and perhaps mean complete failure with that individual.

Only time can bring the fruition of the worker's occasional
hints. One day a person may decide to test the words of the
worker with a real problem. It would not be a preconceived act,
discussed beforehand in the community, but merely an impulse on
the part of one individual to find out the truth of the worker's
boasting. Nevertheless, there will be many among the people who
are likely to be aware of it.

A great deal may depend upon this trial case, perhaps the entire future relationship between the worker and his clientele. The worker should recognize the importance of this opportunity and be keenly aware of its possible ramifications. A positive solution to the test problem can be the best way to advertise the worker's potential usefulness. A success will travel quickly by word of mouth throughout the close-knit Indian community, and as the good word spreads the worker's worth to the community becomes recognized. Other clients will come forth.

It will never be necessary to perform "social work intervention" and interfere with an individual or the community norms. The people will incorporate the worker into their functional system. He will perform social work in agreement with the native system rather than try to intervene on the basis of a foreign system. Otherwise he would alienate the people.

An alien, it should be noted, is anyone who is not a member of the tribal group. Among Navajos, a Cheyenne would be as alien as an Anglo, though his acceptance may be more readily attainable.

WORKING WITHIN THE SYSTEM

Needless to say, this discussion has excluded numerous complications that are always present in reality, but an effective approach to the noninterference norm is basic to any social work with Indians. If the worker is ever mindful of this norm and how it conditions his role and acceptance, he should be able to deal with the other problems.

A continued adherence to engagement from within the preexisting native framework will assure the confidence and trust of Indian clients. In time they may use the worker to assist with personal problems pertaining to matters outside the native system and even with problems inside the native system that for one reason or another cannot be resolved by the regular native approaches. In the latter case, however, the problem would actually be resolved by a regular approach, inasmuch as the worker would have become a native approach by functioning within the native framework.

But even then it should be kept well in mind that the worker is still an alien. His degree of acceptance is based entirely on how well he is able to work within the preexisting native systems and norms. Perfect acceptance comes only with the loss of the worker's alien status, which cannot be achieved except through adoption by Indian people. To become one of the people is, of course, most unlikely, but not impossible.

References

1. The author's experience indicates that the statements made in this article apply to the Navajo and the tribes of the Northern and Southern Plains. Much that is said here might also be true of the Pueblo and other tribes.
2. Rosalie H. Wax and Robert K. Thomas, "Anglo Intervention vs. Native Noninterference," *Phylon*, 22 (Winter 1961), pp. 53–56.

TRANSFERENCE/COUNTERTRANSFERENCE IN INTER-RACIAL THERAPY*

David R. Burgest

In the early development of social casework and the social work profession, the theory of psychoanalysis had a profound effect on the clinical frame of reference for social casework intervention skills. Such clinical foundation is rooted in much of social casework practice today. Therefore, it is necessary for a basic understanding of those concepts as we approach transference and countertransference from an inter-racial and inter-ethnic perspective.

Sigmund Freud, the Father of Psychoanalysis and composer of the dynamics involved in transference and countertransference, defines transference as:

> ... New editions of facsimiles of the tendencies and fantasies which are aroused and made conscious during the progress of the analysis, but they have this peculiarity, which is characteristic of their species, that they replace some earlier persons by the person of the physician. To put it another way: a whole series of psychological experiences are revived, not as belonging to the past, but as applying to the physician at the present moment.[58]†

Greenson adds another dimension to the concept of transference when he states that transference is:

> ... a distinctive type of object relationship. The main characteristics are the experience of feeling toward a person which do not

*Reprinted by permission of the author and University Press of America, Inc. from the author's *Social Casework Intervention with People of Color* (Lanham, MD: University Press of America, 1985), 69–80.
†Note numbers appear here as in their original chapter sequence.

benefit that person, and which actually apply to another. Essentially, a person in the present is reacted to as though he were a person in the past.[59]

Since the popularization of transference and countertransference as a phenomena, there has developed a host of unresolved questions regarding these concepts. The controversy on transference in the worker/client relationship focuses on the following concerns:

> Whether transference is directly related to an unresolved Oedipal Complex in that the Oedipus Complex is the central problem area of each client prior to the onset of the neurosis.[60]

> Whether or not transference is regressive in nature, primitive in striving and infantile in nature.[61]

> Whether or not transference is strictly a conscious and/or unconscious phenomenon. That is, whether it is a conscious coping mechanism of the client in relationship to the therapist or whether it is an unconscious reaction to the therapist.[62]

> Whether or not transference is displacement or projection and whether it is the significant others in the person's life who may be transferred to the therapist or whether all persons in the client's life may be considered.[63]

> Whether or not transference is the result of anxiety provoked by the therapist, which leads to defense coping mechanism of the client.[64]

> Whether the nature of positive and negative transference interact in its implication for psychotherapy or whether all transference is absolutely negative or absolutely positive.[65]

> Whether there is any validity to the concept of transference or whether it is a defense reaction of the therapist who is unwilling to look objectively at the characteristics of his/her behavior in relationship to the client.[66]

Given all of the debates and controversy on transference, there appears to be consensus of the following:

> The client oftentimes irrationally views the therapist as persons of significant others in his/her past and reacts to the therapist accordingly.

> It is the role of the worker to utilize his/her relationship skills in assisting the client to overcome the transference and, thereby, resolve the underlying psychological difficulties.

Negative transference is the client's unrealistic transfer of negative characteristics onto the therapist from experiences with significant others in the past, and positive transference is the transfer of irrational positive characteristics onto the therapist from experiences with significant others in the past.

It is through the effective use of transference that the therapist is able to pinpoint many of the major difficulties inherent in the client's psychological problems.

The reality base of the client's response to the therapist's behavior is not transference but may provoke a countertransference reaction in the worker.

The therapist must be cognizant of his/her reactions to the client that may result into countertransference.

Countertransference is another significant phenomenon in the casework therapeutic process. According to Ruesch:

Countertransference is transference in reverse. The therapist's unresolved conflicts force him to invest the patient with certain properties which bear upon his own past experiences rather than to constitute reaction to the patient's actual behavior. All that was said about transference, therefore, also applies to countertransference, with the addition that it is the transference of the patient which triggers into existence the countertransference of the therapist.[67]

It is apparent from the definition above that therapists may have years of supervised experience and academic training but are still subject to countertransference reactions. Erwin Singer in his book, *Key Concepts in Psychotherapy*, states that:

Countertransference is understood as a development highly analogous to transference. It is assumed that its appearance is governed by essentially the same processes, drives and tendencies which authors posit in their respective explanation of the transference phenomenon.[68]

As the debate continues on the nature of transference in psychotherapy, there is a corresponding debate on the use and management of countertransference. Most authorities seem to agree that:

Countertransference exists.

Countertransference on the part of the therapist is usually provoked by the transference reaction of the client or produced by unresolved anxieties in the therapist.

The recognition of countertransference by the therapist may be utilized as a therapeutic component in the therapeutic relationship.

Remaining unchecked, countertransference reaction on the part of the therapist will cause further deterioration to the client.

Countertransference is the result of a lack of self-awareness on the part of the therapist or the therapist's reluctance to know and/or learn something about him/her self.

On the dynamics of transference and countertransference, the following questions must be asked. What is the relationship of the classical phenomena of transference and countertransference on inter/intra-racial and ethnic therapeutic relationships that must be confronted? Is there any relationship or significance of transference and countertransference that must be understood in relationship to race and culture? Is race and ethnicity a factor to be considered in transference and countertransference or should caseworkers deny race and ethnicity of worker and client as significant in transference and countertransference? Is the classical definition of transference and countertransference applicable to differences in race and ethnicity of therapist and client? These and other questions must be analyzed and addressed in order to understand the relevance and significance of differences in ethnicity and race of caseworker and client.

The relevance of transference and countertransference in inter-racial relations is described as follows:

Transference is especially knotty in the white-black dyad, because the black client brings to the relationship intense notions derived from his experience with and feelings toward whites in general, as Greenson points out. The Negro membership in an ostracized subcultural group tends to lead to certain habitual ways of relating initially to a member of the majority group . . . This is particularly true today.

Not only because Blacks still experience discrimination, insult, segregation, and the threat of violence, but also because they have become more sensitive and less adjusted to these affronts to human dignity. To them, the current problems and conflicts have much more significance than those in the past.[69]

Because transference is traditionally viewed as a response of the client to a worker in the present in a manner he/she has responded to a significant other in the past, the question on the relevance of current conflicts existing between inter-ethnic and racial minorities' relations creates a new dimension. Much of the dynamics that social caseworkers may attribute to an unconscious transference phenomenon in an inter/ethnic professional relationship may be the client's conscious reaction to the current tensions existing in interracial relations. Above all, this requires that the worker must develop self-insight and self-awareness into his/her own prejudices as they may affect his/her behavior and action in the therapeutic process.

It is detrimental to the casework process for the worker to inappropriately label current reactions of the client to deepseated transference phenomena when they are a conscious reaction to the current racial climate in the community or in therapy. In such instances, the worker focuses on the assumed, unresolved unconscious drives of the client as the core of the problem and will completely avoid the reality of the client's response. The worker's focus on unconscious causes for the client's behavior labeled as transference may be defined by the client as a defense mechanism of the worker. Secondly, there is a criticism that the social theory of psychoanalysis as actualized through transference places the blame of the client's psychopathology onto the client and deletes the current social system's impact on the individual. Such a disposition on the part of the social casework practitioner prohibits the understanding of the dynamics that current conflicts might play in inter-ethnic relations.

Consequently, social caseworkers of all racial and ethnic composition appear to be caught in an ambivalent situation in working with People of Color, but the difficulties are more paramount between white workers and People of Color. As one source puts it:

> While some white analysts seem compelled to overemphasize the effects of being Negro on their patient's personality difficulties, others have an apparent need to deny and sidestep any such effects altogether. Both overemphasizing and sidestepping seem fallacious in that they reflect a preconceived bias on the part of the analysts who should, instead, themselves be guided by what the material reveals.[70]

Continuing discussion on the role of the worker-minority client relationship, the author also states:

> One of the most disastrous results of too much race consciousness on the part of the analyst, for whom his patient's skin color obscures his view of the whole man, is his proneness to interpret too much in terms of racial conflicts and thereby deprive the patient of thoroughly reaching and working through whatever his basic difficulties may be. The analyst may thus unwittingly ally himself with the patient's resistance in failing to grasp the unconscious defensive uses to which the Negro patient may put race prejudice. On the other hand, the analyst's blinding himself to the racial factor may also play into the patient's resistance as well as deny some of the social realities of his current existence. Some white analysts stress the defense among their Negro patients of unrealistic denial of the psychological consequences of discrimination. While doubtless this occurs, it would seem dangerous and fallacious, in the aim of overcoming this defense, for analysts to perpetuate a new form of racial stereotype—the psychoanalytic stereotype—i.e., the Negro personality whose frustrated hostility toward whites must always automatically continue his central conflict and the core of his personality organization. Negroes, struggling against the standard racial stereotypes, are understandably alarmed by the threat of such a sophisticated new version of racial stereotypes under the aegis of psychodynamics.[71]

The author concludes by highlighting other important dynamics involved in the worker/minority client relationship.

> Both attitudes correspond to two rather frequently met defense patterns on the part of Negro patients—'All my problems are due to unfair racial discrimination,' i.e., the good excuse defense, and 'None of my problems have anything to do with being Negro and you're prejudiced if you think color made any difference in my life,' i.e., the magic denial defense.[72]

In spite of the many difficulties inherent in the worker/client relationship with People of Color, there are those who see racial and ethnic differences as a catalytic effect upon the treatment process relating to transference. As one resource states:

> Racial differences may have a catalytic effect upon the analytic process and lead to a more rapid unfolding of core problems.

> The catalytic effect of the analyst's race upon the development of transference occurs when the racial stereotypes are concerned with the same effects and conflicts as the transference.[73]

Although much of the discussion on the dynamics of the case-work relationship has focused on workers and clients of different racial and ethnic groups, there are many problems inherent in worker/client relationships of the same ethnic and racial group. The literature on transference and countertransference between worker and client of the same ethnic and racial group, however, is inadequate. Some of the variables on the part of the worker affecting the transference/countertransference interaction between members of the same race and ethnicity are as follows:

Worker denial of identification with in-group ethnic/racial consciousness.

Worker over-identification with in-group ethnic/racial consciousness.

Class and status differences between therapist and client.

Worker's view of clients within his/her minority group as low status.

Worker's view of relationship with clients within his/her minority group as an ego boost to his/her own identity.

Worker's correlation of working with minority client within the same ethnic/racial group as the solution to all the difficulties that his/her minority group faces.

Worker's identification of self as being the only one who can help such minority because he/she is a member of the same group.

Worker's view that 'I am the model' by having demonstrated 'I have made it,' and the client should adopt his/her mode of behavior if he/she is to make it.

Worker's attempt to compensate for the client's station in life compared to his/her own.

The following attitudes and disposition on the part of the client with a worker of the same ethnic and racial group may provoke countertransference in the therapist.

Client's view of the therapist as having 'sold out' to the white society due to his/her role in white society as part of the establishment.

Client's view of the therapist as being unable to understand, empathize or appreciate the Black, Red, Yellow, experience due to social and class differences.

Client's accusation that the therapist is attempting to convert him/her into the middle class standards and life styles of the therapist.

Minority client's view of the minority therapist as inferior or incapable of being able to help.

A few of the important factors that may have an impact on the transference and countertransference transaction between social caseworkers and People of Color are:

There is a negative impact of social and economic discrimination on the personality structure of Third World minorities.[74]

Suspicion and distrust of Third World minorities toward whites is a normal consequence of victimization by prejudice.[75]

Existence of a 'moral uneasiness' in workers who experience individual and collective guilt causes many workers to live in a constant state of conflict with People of Color.[76]

There is a need for the removal of the barriers of segregation to alleviate the psychological damage to People of Color.[77]

There is an assumption of innate inferiority of Third World minority culture and intelligence.[78]

There are a host of negative stereotypes regarding social and sexual behavior of People of Color.[79]

The assignment of negative social and psychological behavior to People of Color as being uniquely Third World.[80]

The view that Third World minority individuals are culturally deprived and do not have a culture.[81]

References

58. Sigmund Freud, (1905). "Fragments of an Analysis of a Case on Hysteria," *Standard Edition*, (London: The Hogarth Press, 1953), pp. 7–122.
59. R. Greenson. *The Techniques and Practices of Psychoanalysis*, (New York: International Universities Press, 1968), pp. 30–31, pp. 151–152.
60. R. W. White. "Motivation Reconsidered: The Concept of Competence," *Psychological Review* (1959) Vol. 66, pp. 297–333; I. Hendrix "Instinct and the Ego During Infancy," *Psychoanalytic Quarterly* (1942) Vol. 11, pp. 33–58.
61. D. Rapport. "The Theory of Ego Autonomy: A Generalization," *Bulletin Menninger Clinic*, Vol. 22, pp. 13–35.

62. C. R. Rogers. *Client-Centered Therapy,* (Boston: Houghton Mifflin Co., 1951).
63. H. S. Sullivan. *The Interpersonal Theory of Psychiatry,* (New York: W. W. Norton and Co., 1953).
64. F. Fromm-Reichmann. "Recent Advances in Psychoanalytic Therapy," *in* D. M. Bullard, (ed.), *Psychoanalysis and Psychotherapy,* (Chicago: University of Chicago Press, 1959).
65. F. Fromm-Reichmann. *Principle of Intensive Psychotherapy,* (Chicago: University of Chicago Press, 1950).
66. Thomas Szasz. *The Myth of Mental Illness: Foundation of a Theory of Personal Conduct,* (New York: Hoeber-Harper, 1961).
67. J. Ruesch. *Therapeutic Communication,* (New York: W. W. Norton and Company, 1961), p. 175.
68. Erwin Singer. *Key Concepts in Psychotherapy,* (New York: Basic Books, Inc., 1970), pp. 290–291.
69. Clemmont Vontress. "Racial Differences: Impediment to Rapport," *Journal of Counseling Psychology,* Vol. 18, (1974), pp. 7–13.
70. Viola W. Bernard. "Psychoanalysis and Members of Minority Groups," *Journal of the American Psychoanalytic Association,* I, (April, 1953), p. 262.
71. *Ibid.* p. 262.
72. *Ibid.* p. 262.
73. Judith S. Schachter and Hugh F. Butts, "Transference and Countertransference in Inter-Racial Analysis," *Journal of the American Psychoanalytic Association,* Vol. 16, No. 4, (October, 1968).
74. Abram Kardiner and L. Ovesey. *The Mark of Oppression,* (New York: W. W. Norton and Company, 1951).
75. William H. Grier and Price M. Cobbs. *Black Rage,* (New York: Basic Books, 1968).
76. Gunnar Myrdal. *The American Dilemma,* (New York: Harper & Brothers, 1944).
77. See "The Negro in American Life and Thought: The Nadir, 1877–1901," First published in 1954 and revised in paperback as *The Betrayal of the Negro,* (New York: Collier Books, 1965).
78. Eldridge Cleaver. *Soul on Ice,* (New York: McGraw Hill Book Company, 1968). Calvin Hernton. *Sex and Racism in America.* (New York: Grove Press, 1966).
79. William H. Ryle. "The Mind of the Negro Child," *School and Society,* Vol. 1, (March 6, 1915).
80. Daniel P. Moynihan. *The Negro Family: The Case for National Action,* (Washington, D.C.: U.S. Department of Labor, Office of Planning and Research, March, 1965).
81. *Ibid.*

VI. IMPLICATION FOR ETHNIC AND RACIAL AWARENESS

Racial, ethnic and cultural sensitivity must begin with the infusion of content on minorities in the education and curriculum of universities and colleges. Yet social work educators and scholars must first become sensitive to the racial and ethnic diversity before such content can become effectively incorporated into the curriculum. Dr. Matisushima in his article on "Resistance in infusing minority content in social work education" focuses on the need for sensitivity and self-awareness of human service educators. The one who is responsible for supervising and facilitating self-awareness must possess the potential capacity and experience of self-awareness and self-insight before they can be transmitted to the learner. Yet, self-awareness and self-insight are mostly an art and is not learned through academic exploration but acquired through experience. It is individual self-awareness and self-insight which is responsible for sensitivity to others.

Self-awareness and self-insight are not fixed and absolute but a process of continuous self examination, evaluation and assessment. The process of self-insight and self-awareness may be conceived of as the ability of a worker to take an objective and rationale view of the subjective and emotional aspect of his/her perceptions and feelings regarding self and others. This process of self-insight and self-awareness increases cultural, ethnic and racial sensitivity in that the worker will develop a potential for confronting negative stereotypes, myths and assumptions in self which may handicap the process of social intervention. The literature in this section will provide the reader with such a confrontation.

The skill of looking at self objectively is important in interpersonal relations particularly within interracial and interethnic relations because objective self-evaluation on the part of the worker is crucial to effective communication. Furthermore, sensitivity on

the part of the worker requires that the skills used in self-evaluation can be applicable to interpersonal interaction with others as
well as the profession.

As we look at the topic of racial ethnic and cultural sensitivity, the following themes are prevalent in the articles contributed.

> Theories of counseling and social work reflect white middle
> class norms and do not impact the cultural realities of minor-
> ity cultures.

> Standards and values of the predominant culture in America
> are used as the normative frame of reference for assessing
> Black behavior.

> Curricula of social work schools offer minimal content on
> minorities in America often perpetuating myths and ster-
> eotypes rather than destroying them.

> The social work and counseling profession must examine, re-
> examine and evaluate the relevance of particular theoretical
> frameworks with respect to the client's needs and values.

> Cognitive understanding of the unique nature of minority
> culture is crucial in helping the process as well as cultural
> sensitivity.

Given all the inherent difficulties involved in the dynamics of
the worker/client relationship with minorities, the first question to
raise is "which way is out" or how can the cultural, ethnic, and
racial barriers presented in the preceding sections be eliminated
or mitigated? It is the purpose of this section to get at those very
questions. One of the primary approaches is to provide more information and data on minority cultures while the other is to develop
sensitivity, insight, self awareness, and human relation skills. At
the same time, there is the clear need to include more minority
members as students, practitioners, and educators in the social
work and human services profession. Although the approaches
are identified as possible strategies there is another which indicates that they must be exclusive of each other. All three approaches, as well as the others mentioned in the literature, may be
used simultaneously.

At the same time, the need for the above approaches is not only for European ethnics but is applicable to minorities as well. In other words, there is a reciprocal need between People of Color and European ethnics. In fact, some of the literature suggests that People of Color must first address the problems they face with white America within their own separate ethnic groups before entering into sensitivity awareness with members of the European ethnics group. By the same token, it is suggested that European ethnic group members should engage in human relation and sensitivity experiences with members of the other ethnic and racial groups. The premise seems to be that before authentic relations can be developed across ethnic and racial lines, authentic relations must be developed within racial and ethnic groups. This is one philosophical approach and there may be others as well (as indicated by the readings), but the fact remains that finding solutions to the ethnic and racial dilemma we face in America is a continuous evolving process with the need for a multitude of approaches and strategies.

MINORITY CONTENT IN SOCIAL WORK EDUCATION: A QUESTION OF OBJECTIVES*

Enola K. Proctor and Larry E. Davis

As a result of social work's historic value commitment, many practice activities occur with persons whose ethnic, economic, racial, or political group may be different from the practitioner's. Hence, a major task of social work education in a pluralistic society is the preparation of practitioners to work with persons of different cultures.[1] In recent years, the development of knowledge and skills related to practice with ethnic minority groups has become an increasingly visible priority for social work.[2] In the early 1970s the Black Task Force of the Council on Social Work Education (CSWE) recommended that schools of social work move toward the inclusion of minority content into all required, basic curriculum.[3] Subsequently, the requirement that schools make "special, continual efforts" to include racial and cultural content into its instruction became a standard for accreditation by CSWE. According to CSWE, "the purpose of this standard is to provide students with the awareness and knowledge that ours is a pluralistic society and the implications of this for sensitive and effective social work intervention."[4] The National Association of Social Workers recently affirmed the importance of requiring that "undergraduate and graduate social work curricula and continuing

*Reprinted by permission of the authors and *Journal of Social Work Education* 19:2 (Spring 1983) 85–93; copyright © 1983 Council on Social Work Education.

education programs . . . include relevant and meaningful content related to racial and ethnic groups of color."[5]

Although the salience of race as an issue in professional education may be clear, and although the accreditation requirements have generated broad-scale efforts toward the inclusion of minority content into curricula across the country, a number of unresolved issues are apparent. This article identifies some of the issues educators face in their attempts to include minority content in the curriculum and concludes that a basic yet unresolved issue is that of specifying objectives. That is, the effects on students that are presumed to occur as a function of their exposure to minority-relevant content have not been clearly identified. The article aims to stimulate efforts among social work educators to identify such objectives and to stimulate the development of educational training models by which those objectives may be attained. Issues for research are identified, and the need for empirically evaluating the attainment of educational objectives is argued.

CURRENT ISSUES

Horner and Borrero report that faculty and administrators frequently convey to accrediting site visitors their uncertainty about how to incorporate minority content into their curricula.[6] The "strain and struggle [which] has attended efforts to incorporate the study of ethnic and minority group life into the social work curriculum" is further reflected in recent volumes of professional journals, in task forces appointed by CSWE and individual schools, and by discussions at professional conferences.[7]

One major issue facing curriculum planners is the question of *what* content should be emphasized in curricula. Mandates from professional and accrediting organizations offer no clear guidelines as to what content should be included, requiring only that "relevant and meaningful" content be delivered. Examples of content relevant to minorities that is frequently seen in curricula include the history of minority groups, patterns of minority family or community interaction, the consequences of public policy for minority groups, and professional responses to racism.[8] Yet, because the effect of these content areas on students has not been adequately investigated, decisions about their inclusion in curricula have not been made on the basis of empirical evidence.

Another issue facing curriculum planners is *where* minority-related content should be placed; that is, should the content be integrated into basic existing courses or should separate courses focusing exclusively on minority issues be instituted?[9] These two approaches have been characterized as the "everywhere and nowhere" and the "here and nowhere else" approaches, respectively.[10] These characterizations aptly reflect the potential weaknesses of each approach: Minority content that is incorporated into existing courses becomes the responsibility of all faculty, and hence that content may become diffused and absorbed by other priorities; yet if concentrated in particular and separate courses, minority content may become isolated and ignored in the remainder of the curriculum and by faculty who do not teach those particular courses.

These issues are central to the profession's efforts to include minority content in its training programs. However, decisions regarding these issues are often made in the absence of professional consensus regarding the desired objectives or effects of minority content on students. Until such objectives are more clearly identified, debate about what content to deliver and how to deliver that content may be premature.

IMPLICIT OBJECTIVES

The ultimate goal in professional social work education is the preparation of students for effective work with their clients. (For purposes of this paper, effective social work is considered to be interventive activity that assists clients to reach goals that have been mutually agreed upon by worker and client.) We may presume that schools of social work and CSWE believe that the inclusion of content relevant to minorities will contribute to the overall goal of helping students become more effective practitioners. More specifically, we may assume that the inclusion of minority content will *affect students* by producing certain changes related to the effectiveness of their eventual practice. That is, most educators probably expect their inclusion of minority content to produce desirable changes in the practice behaviors of their students.

Yet there appear to be relatively few instances in which educators actually prescribe specific practice behaviors and strategies for working with minority-group clients. Instead, educators generally provide normative content, descriptive of minority culture and life. It seems to be widely assumed that this new information will lead students to have more accurate beliefs and more positive attitudes toward minority clients and that these changes will in turn enhance their practice. Changes in attitudes and beliefs, then, may have served as the objectives—although frequently implicit—toward which the provision of minority-relevant content has been directed.

IMPORTANCE OF ATTITUDES AND BELIEFS

A number of writers have suggested that the attitudes of professional helpers are related to the effectiveness of their work with clients. For at least three decades, workers' feelings and attitudes toward minority clients have been identified as a potential interference to effective interracial practice. Brown suggested that workers' lack of association with blacks, their learned and ingrained negative attitudes toward minority-group members, or their personal need for a sense of racial superiority may result in uneasiness in interracial contacts and diminish their effectiveness with black clients.[11] More recently, Banks wrote that the attitudes of the white helpers often "constitute a serious detriment to a positive interpersonal relationship."[12]

Social workers, as members of the larger society and culture, are likely to bring preconceived ideas and attitudes about minority group members to their practice.[13] Such attitudes, beliefs, and social norms are presumed to be potentially detrimental to professional practice.[14] At least one study has demonstrated that counselors' ethnocentric or racial attitudes are linked to the duration of their treatment relationships with black clients.[15] And Cole and Pilisuk conclude that the differential treatment accorded black clients may be viewed as evidence of workers' negative attitudes and behavior toward minority-group clients.[16]

Although it is frequently suggested that racial attitudes affect practice, the manner in which these attitudes manifest themselves in practice behaviors has not been adequately discussed or explored. One author who addressed this issue suggested that white workers may convey socially conditioned emotional distance toward their black clients.[17] Sattler has also suggested that interviewers may unintentionally reveal their own attitudes.[18] Clearly, additional research is needed to clarify the bearing of racial attitudes on practice behaviors.

Another factor widely identified as potentially affecting the effectiveness of practice with minority-group clients is the worker's knowledge, understanding, and familiarity with minority culture and lifestyle. Professionals are often trained and educated with little exposure to or understanding of the meaning of the black experience as it relates to the behavior of black clients.[19] Perhaps this is due, in part, to the fact that traditional psychological and developmental theory has not dealt adequately with the developmental experiences of blacks.[20] Cole and Pilisuk estimate that 90 percent of black clients are treated by white workers who received no particular training for their work with the black population.[21] As a consequence, white workers are often attempting to treat clients "whom they 'think' they know, but in reality they have been miseducated or simply not educated about blacks."[22]

According to Hankins-McNary, white workers may have learned, from their involvement with larger society, to view minority groups not as culturally different, but as culturally disadvantaged, deprived or underprivileged.[23] This may have adverse consequences for the accuracy with which workers evaluate and diagnose problems experienced by black clients.[24] Moreover, without an understanding of and familiarity with minority culture, it is very difficult for workers to accurately empathize with, understand, and establish a rapport with black clients.[25]

A particular area of knowledge viewed as having important consequences for interracial practice is the worker's conceptual framework or theoretical perspective on problem resolution. Many practitioners hold an individualistic orientation in which environmental and social influences are minimized; that is, individual action is viewed as the best recourse for dealing with problems.[26] The inappropriateness and possible dysfunction of such an orientation for many black clients has been frequently identified.[27] Thus, it is important that social work educators and practitioners examine and evaluate the relevance of particular theoretical frameworks in relationship to the needs of minority-group clients.[28]

MODELS OF TRAINING

Once the field had thoroughly addressed the issue of objectives—that is, has explicated the changes in students that are desired as a result of their exposure to minority content—there remains the issue of exploring the best ways to attain those objectives. In addition to stimulating debate about the objectives for inclusion of minority content, this article hopes to generate efforts among social work educators to develop and empirically test various models of training students for effective practice with minority clients. Toward that end, the article will identify two possible training models that draw on and are consistent with the literature that has been reviewed on racial attitudes, beliefs, and their presumed implications for practice behavior.

The task of affecting students' attitudes, beliefs, or practice behaviors with minority-group clients is very complex. Indeed, attitudes, beliefs, and behaviors are often viewed as interrelated. The practice literature reviewed here, for example, contains many references to the presumed impact of attitude and belief on behavior. It seems to be frequently presumed that the process of influencing interracial behaviors also involves influencing beliefs or attitudes. In addition to being reflected in the practice literature, this assumption is consistent with some social-psychological approaches to interpersonal change.[29] Both now and in the past, racial attitudes have been the most frequently examined dependent variable in business, industry, the military, and education in race relations training programs.[30] These programs presumably view change in attitude as mediating and generalizable to behavioral changes. In a similar vein, although not related substantively to the issue of minority content, Patterson describes a social work training program in which students' knowledge of elderly persons is assumed to change their attitudes toward the elderly and, in turn, improve their helping behavior.[31]

Intrapersonal Training Model

If the premise is accepted that changes in attitude and/or belief mediate and generalize to behavioral change, what are the implications for social work training? Such a premise might logically lead educators to what we label the *intrapersonal training model.* This model is based on the assumption that one type of change in a student will lead to or result in subsequent changes in that student. For educators who accept these premises, change in students' attitudes or beliefs about minority-group persons serves as the objective toward which minority-relevant curriculum content is directed (see Fig. 1), with subsequent improvement in practice behaviors also expected or assumed. However, the changes in practice behavior might not be an objective whose attainment would be observed or evaluated by the instructor. Although this model is consistent with the literature on race relations training, and may be implicitly accepted by many educators, it should be noted that evidence supporting this model is limited.

Although Fishbein and Ajzen view attitude as a general predisposition to behavior, they caution that the performance or nonperformance of specific behaviors usually cannot be predicted from knowledge of a person's attitude alone.[32] The nature of causal relationships among attitudes, behaviors, and beliefs remains a central issue for social psychologists. Some contend that attitudes generally lead to, or cause behaviors.[33] Others believe that in certain situations behavior change will lead to attitude change.[34] Wicker's conclusion from a review of several studies was that it is considerably more likely that "attitudes will be unrelated or only slightly related to overt behaviors than that attitudes will be closely related to actions."[35]

Figure 1
Events Assumed in the Intrapersonal Training Model

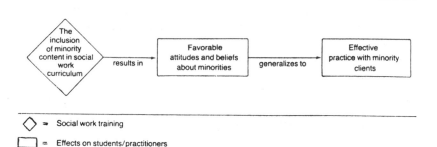

◇ = Social work training

☐ = Effects on students/practitioners

Figure 2
Events Assumed in the Prescriptive Training Model

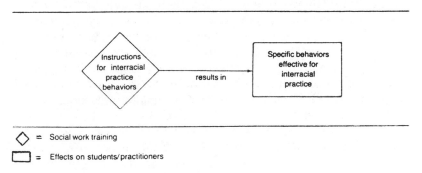

◇   =   Social work training

▢   =   Effects on students/practitioners

Fishbein and Ajzen's cautions regarding the prediction of behaviors from attitudes may be especially important in the area of
racial attitudes. Focusing on race related attitudes and behaviors
among northern white college students, Weitz found a significant
negative relationship between positive attitudes and friendly behaviors.[36] That is, students who expressed the most positive attitudes toward Blacks were found to communicate to Blacks in
less friendly voice tones and to be less willing to engage in future
contact with a Black subject.

Recent consensus on these issues among social psychologists
is that these relationships are now understood to be more complex than they were earlier presumed, due to possible differences
in the specificity of criteria (attitudes and actions) that are measured, differences in times of measurement (that is, specific acts
or repeated observations), and differences in the range of intervening factors considered. Recent studies point to the possibility
that an individual's intentions to perform behaviors may be an
important, though frequently overlooked, mediator of relationships between attitudes and behaviors.[37] Given this apparent
complexity between attitudes and behaviors, social work educators accepting or acting upon the intrapersonal training model
should note that there is no conclusive evidence to suggest that
changes in students' beliefs or attitudes are causally associated
with or generalize to changes in practice behaviors.

Prescriptive Training Model

If the interrelationship between change in attitude and/or belief and subsequent change in practitioner behavior is not assumed, then a different training focus may be implied. Educators may focus directly on students' practice behaviors and approach professional training from what we label the *prescriptive training model.* The goal within this model would be to prescribe for students behaviorally specific skills viewed as important for practice with minority group persons. Hence, practice skills would be viewed as directly modifiable rather than as a consequence of cognitive or attitude change (see Fig. 2). Educators following this model may view it to be parsimonious in that the focus of change is the ultimate objective—the skills needed for effective interracial practice.

Since the middle 1960s, literature on professional education has provided evidence of both the acceptance and effectiveness of what we have labeled the prescriptive training model for certain limited areas of practice behavior. Training models have been developed to teach three main types of practice skills, according to Matarazzo:[38] (1) skills related to client-centered facilitative variables as developed by Truax and Carkhuff;[39] (2) interviewing skills such as attentiveness, reflection, and summarization of feelings;[40] and (3) operant conditioning skills. In addition, focusing on skills for enhancing helping relationships between practitioners and culturally different clients, Rosen and Cohen developed a training model that they found to be effective in teaching social work students.[41]

In her extensive review of professional skill training, Matarazzo concluded that the teaching of advanced practice skills remains much less developed. In addition, insufficient empirical study has been directed to the question of whether, once skills are acquired in training situations, they are used and maintained over time. Spooner and Stone concluded from their research that direct skills training can be viewed as successful in establishing and maintaining certain practice behaviors, although more complex skills are less likely either to occur in the first place as a function of training or to be maintained over time.[42]

According to Matarazzo, selection of a skill training method is less of a problem than determining which skills are beneficial to clients and, hence, which skills should be taught. This issue is even more complex when the training is for interracial practice. Nearly a decade ago, CSWE's Black Task Force cited the importance of providing social work students with skills to enhance their effectiveness with black clients, as have researchers in the areas of counseling and psychotherapy.[43] Yet researchers have identified a very limited number of interventive skills known to have either detrimental or positive effects with minority group clients.[44] Perhaps as a result of the complexities of the issues for both practice and training, there appear to be few graduate training programs developing prescriptive models of training students for practice with minority-group clients.

As is apparent with even this brief review of the extensive literature bearing on training issues, the empirical support for either the intrapersonal or prescriptive models is inconclusive. This may reflect the fact that training practitioners for interracial practice has not been fully conceptualized or investigated. Whatever the reasons, the choice between these models currently remains largely a function of educators' philosophy or personal preference. If, indeed, the intrapersonal model is more frequently accepted, it may be due to the relative ease with which attitudinal change, in contrast to change in practice behavior, may be measured.

The training models identified here are only two of many possible ways of conceptualizing the task of training for practice with minority clients. The intrapersonal and prescriptive models were offered for the purposes of demonstrating their implications for education, identifying the host of questions they raise for future research, and stimulating the development of other models by persons engaged in professional training.

CHALLENGES FOR TRAINING AND RESEARCH

Although there are widespread efforts to include content relevant to minorities in social work curricula, most attention to date has centered on the issue of curriculum inputs. Schools have demonstrated concern with identifying and placing in their curricula content areas that are relevant to practice with minority group clients; accreditation teams have focused on whether schools' curricula contain "sufficient" minority content. These efforts reflect a commitment to quality professional training and they should be continued. However, this article has argued that a number of additional challenges must be faced if social work education is to ensure that students can work more effectively with minority-group clients.

First, it has been asserted that the question of objectives must be addressed; that is, social work educators must define what changes they hope to attain in students. Is the objective to increase the favorableness of students' racial attitudes? Is it to achieve an understanding of minority culture and lifestyle? Is it to provide students with specific skills and behaviors for practice with minority clients? If multiple objectives are sought, their presumed interrelationships need to be carefully considered. It is the thesis of this article that objectives need to be explicated and clearly identified by each school, for each curriculum area, and for each course.

Once objectives are established, the most effective means of achieving those objectives must be identified and/or developed. A review of innovations in curriculum development and classroom design is beyond the purposes and scope of this article. However, two possible models of professional training have been proposed and discussed. Educators should continue to explore various instructional approaches that are appropriate for attaining whatever objectives they have selected. As the discussion here has suggested, different objectives may require different models of training.

Finally, the attainment of educational objectives should be subjected to empirical evaluation. Serious concern about social work practice with minority clients requires that evaluation efforts move beyond quantifying curriculum inputs to questions of effectiveness. The specific approaches to evaluating professional training would, of course, depend upon the objectives sought and the training model applied. For example, those accepting the intrapersonal model of training would first evaluate the effects of social work training on students' attitudes and beliefs; once those changes were confirmed, the subsequent changes in practice behaviors would be evaluated. For educators adopting the prescriptive training model, evaluation simply would focus on the effect of training on changes in students' practice behavior.

We presume that the basic objective in social work education is to enable practitioners to work more effectively with clients of various racial and ethnic groups. Therefore, all curriculum content should be examined for its potential bearing on practice effectiveness. If the field is to address this important task, then there must be increased reliance upon assessment of the changes in practice skills, assessments that might optimally be conducted in the field or in actual practice situations.

There is no question that social work education should remain firm in its commitment to improve students' skills for practice with minority clients. This commitment has, thus far, led to considerable debate over how best to include minority-relevant content in social work curricula. The danger, it seems, is that exclusive attention to issues of curriculum inputs may deflect attention and efforts from even more fundamental and crucial issues. Thus, this article has aimed to stimulate efforts within social work education, first, to define its objectives—that is, to identify desired changes in students' knowledge, attitudes, and practice skills for minority clients—and, second, to demonstrate ways to best accomplish these important goals.

Notes

1. Delores G. Norton, *The Dual Perspective: Inclusion of Ethnic Minority Content into the Social Work Curriculum* (New York: Council on Social Work Education, 1978).
2. John B. Turner, "Education for Practice with Minorities," *Social Work*, 17 (May 1972), pp. 112–118.
3. J. R. Dumpson, "Education for Practice with and for Black Americans: An Historical Perspective," paper presented at the Council on Social Work Education Annual Program Meeting, Boston, Mass., March 1979.
4. "Guidelines for Implementation of Accreditation Standard 1234A" (New York: Council on Social Work Education, 1973).
5. "1979 Delegate Assembly Actions," *NASW News*, 25 (January 1980), p. 30.
6. W. Horner and M. Borrero, "A Planning Matrix for Standard 1234A," paper presented at the Council on Social Work Education Annual Program Meeting, Boston, Mass., March 1979.
7. Elfriede G. Schlesinger and Wynetta Devore, "Social Workers View Ethnic Minority Teaching," paper presented at the Council on Social Work Education Annual Program Meeting, New Orleans, La., February 1978.

306 Social Work Practice with Minorities

8. Sophie F. Lowenstein, "Integrating Content on Feminism and Racism into the Social Work Curriculum," *Journal of Education for Social Work*, 12 (Winter 1976), pp. 91–96; Norton, *op. cit.*; and Louis H. Carter, "The Black Instructor: An Essential Dimension to the Content and Structure of the Social Work Curriculum," *Journal of Education for Social Work*, 14 (Winter 1978), pp. 16–22.
9. Norton, *op. cit.*
10. R. R. Boltz, J. L. Erlich, and J. F. McClure, "Poverty and Minorities: Graduate Concentration and Core Course," paper presented at the Council on Social Work Education Annual Program Meeting, New Orleans, La., March 1978.
11. L. Brown, "Race as a Factor in Establishing a Casework Relationship," *Social Casework*, 13 (1950), pp. 91–97.
12. W. M. Banks, "The Black Client and the Helping Professionals," in R. L. Jones, ed., *Black Psychology* (New York: Harper & Row, 1972).
13. M. Bloomingbaum, J. Yamamoto, and Q. James, "Cultural Stereotyping among Psychotherapists," *Journal of Consulting and Clinical Psychology*, 32 (1968), p. 99; C. Vontross, "Racial Differences—Impediments to Rapport," *Journal of Counseling Psychology*, 18 (January 1971); and J. M. Siegel, "A Brief Review of the Effects of Race in Clinical Service Interactions," *American Journal of Orthopsychiatry*, 44 (1974), pp. 555–562.
14. A. D. Curry, "Negro Worker and the White Client: A Commentary on the Treatment Relationship," *Social Casework*, 45 (1964), pp. 131–136; and Julia B. Block, "The White Worker and the Negro Client in Psychotherapy," *Social Work*, 13 (March 1968), pp. 36–42.
15. J. Yamamoto, M. James, M. Bloombaum, and J. Hattem, "Racial Factors in Patient Selection," *American Journal of Psychiatry*, 124 (1967), pp. 630–636.
16. J. Cole and M. Pilisuk, "Differences in the Provision of Mental Health Services by Race," *American Journal of Orthopsychiatry*, 46 (1976), pp. 510–525.
17. E. Filbush, "The White Worker and the Negro Client," *Social Casework*, 46 (May 1965), pp. 271–277.
18. J. M. Sattler, "Racial Experimenter Effects in Experimentation, Testing, Interviewing and Psychotherapy," *Psychological Bulletin*, 73 (March 1970), pp. 137–160.
19. D. K. Cheek, *Assertive Black . . . Puzzled White* (San Luis Obispo, Calif.: Impact Publisher, 1976); and Lula D. Hankins-McNary, "The Effects of Institutional Racism on the Therapeutic Relationship," *Perspectives in Psychiatric Care*, 17 (1979), pp. 25–54.
20. P. L. Townsel and A. C. Jones, "Theoretical Considerations for Psychotherapy with Black Clients," in R. L. Jones, ed., *Black Psychology* (2d ed.; New York: Harper & Row, 1980).
21. Cole and Pilisuk, *op. cit.*
22. Cheek, *op. cit.*, p. 27
23. Hankins-McNary, *op. cit.*
24. Ibid.; and Sattler, *op. cit.*

25. M. S. Griffith and Enrico E. Jones, "Race and Psychotherapy: Changing Perspectives," in Jules H. Masserman, ed., *Current Psychiatric Therapies*, Vol. 18 (New York: Grune & Stratton, 1979); and Filbush, *op. cit.*
26. D. W. Sue, "Eliminating Cultural Oppression in Counseling: Toward a General Theory," *Journal of Counseling Psychology*, 24 (1978), pp. 419–428.
27. Banks, *op. cit.*; and W. A. Hayes and W. M. Banks, "The Nigger Box or a Redefinition of the Counselor's Role," in Jones, ed., *op. cit.*
28. D. W. Sue and D. Sue, "Barriers to Effective Cross-Cultural Counseling," *Journal of Counseling Psychology*, 24 (1977), pp. 420–429; and Townsel and Jones, *op. cit.*
29. M. Fishbein and I. Ajzen, *Belief, Attitude, Intention and Behavior: An Introduction to Theory and Research* (Reading, Mass.: Addison-Wesley, 1975).
30. E. Bogardus, "Social Distance and its Origin," *Journal of Applied Sociology*, 9 (1925), pp. 216–226; and Susan B. Strober and Milton Grady, "Effects of Race Relations Training on Racial Awareness," *Social Work Research and Abstracts*, 14 (Summer 1978), pp. 12–20.
31. S. L. Patterson, "Using Naturalistic Research on the Elderly to Change Student Attitudes and Improve Helping Behavior," *Journal of Education for Social Work*, 17 (Spring 1981), pp. 12–18.
32. Fishbein and Ajzen, *op. cit.*
33. J. M. McGuire, "The Concept of Attitudes and Their Relations to Behaviors," in H. W. Sinaiko and L. A. Boredling, eds., *Perspectives on Attitude Assessment: Surveys and Their Alternatives* (Champaign, Ill.: Pendleton, 1976); and L. R. Kahle and J. J. Berman, "Attitudes Cause Behaviors: A Cross-Lagged Panel Analysis," *Journal of Personality and Social Psychology*, 37 (1979), pp. 315–321.
34. See, for example, J. D. Bem, "Self-Perception Theory," in L. Berkowitz, ed., *Advances in Experimental Social Psychology*, Vol. 6 (New York: Academic Press, 1972).
35. A. W. Wicker, "Attitude versus Action: The Relationship of Verbal and Overt Behavioral Responses to Attitude Objects," *Journal of Social Issues*, 25 (1969), pp. 41–78.
36. S. Weitz, "Attitudes, Voice and Behavior: A Repressed Affect Model of Interracial Interaction," *Journal of Personality and Social Psychology*, 24 (1972), pp. 14–21.
37. Fishbein and Ajzen, *op. cit.*; and K. H. Beck, "The Effects of Positive and Negative Arousal upon Attitudes, Belief Acceptance, Behavioral Intention, and Behavior," *Journal of Social Psychology*, 107 (1979), pp. 239–251.
38. R. G. Matarazzo, "Research on the Teaching and Learning of Psychotherapeutic Skills," in S. L. Garfield and A. E. Bergin, eds., *Handbook of Psychotherapy and Behavior Change: An Empirical Analysis* (New York: John Wiley & Sons, 1978).
39. C. B. Truax and R. R. Carkhuff, *Toward Effective Counseling and Psychotherapy: Training and Practice* (Chicago: Aldine, 1967).

40. See, for example, A. E. Ivey, *Microcounseling: Innovations in Interviewing Training* (Springfield, Ill.: Charles C. Thomas, Publishers, 1971); and N. S. Mayadas and W. D. Duehn, "The Effects of Training Formats and Interpersonal Discriminations in the Education for Clinical Social Work Practice," *Journal of Social Service Research*, 1 (Winter 1977), pp. 147–161.
41. A. Rosen and M. Cohen, "Closing the Gap: A Training Program in Techniques for Relationship Management with Diverse Populations," paper presented at the Council on Social Work Education Annual Program Meeting, New Orleans, La., March 1978.
42. S. E. Spooner and S. C. Stone, "Maintenance of Specific Counseling Skills over Time," *Journal of Counseling Psychology*, 24 (1977), pp. 66–71.
43. E. Aracelis Francis, ed., *Black Task Force Report* (New York: Council on Social Work Education, 1973). See also R. R. Carkhuff and G. Banks, "Training as a Preferred Mode of Facilitating Relations between Races and Generations," *Journal of Counseling Psychology*, 17 (1970), pp. 413–418.
44. Banks, *op. cit.*

RESISTANCE IN INFUSING MINORITY
CONTENT IN SOCIAL WORK EDUCATION*

John Matsushima

Race and ethnicity have long been familiar themes to social workers, but the social revolution of the 60's mandated an accelerated
and not universally welcome equalitarianism for our society. The
equal employment and affirmative action laws stemming from the
Civil Rights Act of 1964 designated several minorities for com-
pulsory attention (Kandel, 1977).

While the rights of any minority can be acknowledged in the
abstract, it is quite another matter to institute tangible preferential
practices. For those minorities that may not have been mentioned
in civil rights legislation, it was as if their relative deprivation had
not been severe enough to acknowledge, or they were being penalized for having "risen above" their circumstances. And members
of the majority group, despite their recognition as to the plight of
the minorities, could not help but rue the relinquishment of special advantage. It is not hard to understand that these persons
might look askance at the price of justice delivered. Our collective
adherence to principle is more recently being subjected to heightened stress with the influx of Vietnamese, Koreans, Haitians, and
Cubans, so that our commitments will be tested anew.

Social work educators and practitioners are intimate participants in the ferment of our times, much more so than the lofty
social reformers of an earlier era. The time has long passed when
social workers were members of the privileged upper classes bent

*Reprinted by permission of the author and *Smith College Studies in Social Work*
51:3 (June 1981) 216–225; copyright © 1981 Smith College School for Social Work.

on uplifting the poor. We are of the middle class, much more a peer in the struggle for economic survival, and vulnerable to any special advantages granted potential competitors. It is this vulnerability of the ordinary citizen, together with the equalitarian ideals of social work, that presents special problems to us as professionals and as Americans.

The idealism of the 60's extracted advantages from the majority society. Educators as well as practitioners were not spared the many powerful and conflicting feelings associated with those shifts. Faculties recall all too clearly the anti-establishment and anti-authoritarian activism of the students; and certainly racist sentiments were manifested and engaged within the classroom. Where faculty were much more accustomed to educating students about how to work with the prejudices of socially distant others, they often found themselves the targets of role, racial, and generational stereotypes—and scrambled to retain their objectivity while under attack.

While the social tumult of the 60's and 70's appears to have subsided, it would be folly to assume that perspective has now been restored or that entrenched resistances do not linger and continue to separate us. If reactions today are more subtle than in recent years, the hurt and bitterness attendant to dramatic social changes remain fresh in the memories of minority and majority groups alike. Social work educators and students are no exceptions. Formal statements of support for affirmative action, flexibility in admissions criteria, and financial assistance earmarked for minorities arouse neither enthusiasm nor resistance. But provisions for and insistence upon visible accountability are not popular.

A most recent example common to all schools of social work was the accreditation requirement 1234A of The Council on Social Work Education (1971). In essence, the standard decreed that education regarding specified minorities was required *throughout* the curriculum (and not only in separate, discrete courses). It further stipulated that a school "must demonstrate the operational linkages between its stated goals and its plan for implementing Standard 1234A," and that "A school must create a mechanism that provides for a continual self-evaluation of the implementation of its plan for meeting Standard 1234A (1973,

1978)." Not only was affirmative action needed in hiring, admissions policies, and financial aid—the curriculum as a whole needed to incorporate demonstrable content on specific minorities.

RESERVATIONS AS TO INFUSING MINORITY CONTENT

Because of the difficulty in adding material to existing courses, it might have been anticipated that any externally-imposed requirement, no matter how justified, would not be welcome. For a part of the attraction of teaching is the challenge of extemporizing to suit the composition and tenor of the learning atmosphere of the moment, however committed one is to the core of knowledge that must be imparted in any course. To then be bound to introduce content according to some externally-ordained criteria introduces vexing constraints. And, given the controversial nature of the content on race, ethnicity, and women's rights, cries of outrage and opposition might have been expected. Instead, there seems to have been little overt reaction, and one wonders if infusion of minority content has indeed proceeded so smoothly—or whether pious platforms may have been adopted in principle and implementation overlooked.

At a time when collective dialogue and airing of differences is once again needed, there seems a marked reticence about revealing positions or engaging objections. It is hard to know if quiescence means acceptance or a polarization of positions, but communication problems within a profession committed to problem-solving among people cannot remain unaddressed. Social work practitioners have encountered similar circumstances when planning in-service training workshops on racial and/or ethnic minorities, and the citizenry as a whole appears wary for fear of re-arousing conflict. Schools of social work, however, that purport to teach professionals how to operationalize their social concern and work with the emotional crises of others must be in the vanguard of problem engagement. It is uniquely incumbent on social work educators to practice what we teach about facing those issues that seem so troubling to us.

UNRESPONSIVENESS AS RESISTANCE

Given that the CSWE accreditation standard would be approved
by a faculty and steps would be initiated to insure compliance, a
logical beginning would be an informal survey of existing minority
content in the curriculum. To the extent that a school sought
specifics beyond an abstract endorsement of the standard, one
could anticipate an accumulation of difficulties (at least, in the
writer's experience, this was so. Informal inquiries elsewhere indicated parallels at other institutions as well).

Typical were minimal responses to the most abbreviated
questionnaire, ignoring of follow-up requests, procrastination, and
an eventual response from a small proportion of the faculty. It
would be misleading to conclude that unresponsiveness mirrors
only prejudice, for these are persons whose careers are committed to the alleviation of ignorance such as is inherent in racial
prejudice. Certainly arbitrary and discriminatory behavior would
not be sanctioned in such a group. How, then, might one explain
the spotty response to the inquiries aimed at simple monitoring
procedures and quantitative guidelines? It was a frustrating and
perplexing situation that seemed totally contrary to the expected
stance, and we searched for a plausible explanation.

REALISTIC REASONS FOR RESISTING
ACCOUNTABILITY

We began by seeking the most apparent explanations among our
colleagues. Some were offered, while others needed to be inferred.

First consideration was given to the fact that all faculty are
overloaded with other obligations, including requests for replies
to an endless supply of questionnaires. Such forms, in their ano-
nymity, tend to be shunted aside in deference to other demands.
Still, the call for infusion of minority content was a topic of much
interest among students and faculty alike, so that prudence if not
enthusiasm would place a priority on such inquiries. Only three
questions were asked in the form that was initially sent to our
faculty: (1) about what percentage of class time included content

on minorities, (2) did the instructor anticipate less, the same, or more such content when the course was offered again, and (3) was the content introduced by the instructor or the students?

Objections did arise as to why only certain minorities (Blacks, Hispanics, Native Americans, Asian Americans, women, and the handicapped) were included. Weren't the mentally ill and the delinquent also minorities? And children as well as the aged? The answer seemed obvious, as the groups were designated by accreditation rules and federal law.

Related to the "Why some and not others" question was the predilection of some instructors to profess a "color-blindness" that avoided content on specific minorities. There is a valid point, of course, that the basic educational aim is that of understanding human beings—and that race, sex and physical handicap are subsidiary to a focus on the common humanity of us all. But literal adherence to such a stance would overlook any variables at all— such as age, stage in development, occupational and marital status, etc., as definitive classifications affecting human behavior, too, and would obviously be untenable.

Some instructors felt that the infusion of minority content was contrived, and that they needed to stretch and manipulate the reluctant flow of class discussions in order to meet some preordained quota. Such efforts seldom engaged the students, as the infusion may have been ill-timed and/or overlooked the considerable resistance of the majority group.

The sheer weight of potential content was mentioned as an obstacle by some faculty. They felt that any additional content would displace more essential material. Those teaching in technical areas, e.g., use of statistics, data analysis, computers, were especially concerned. They felt it would be a contrivance to infuse minority content into such courses, as such content was not relevant! One response was that reliability and validity of data were central in any such courses, as well as the differential impact and measurement of such variables as sex, race, age, and ethnicity. Many examples of ratings based on behavioral observations would be most appropriate to illustrate research technique as well as minority content. In point of fact, research seemed especially suited to a natural and current interest concerning minorities, e.g., intelligence testing, bilingual education and its effectiveness, Head

Start, desegregation and its impact on the quality of education, as evaluative research is so integral to the accountability requirement in so many programs intended to benefit minority groups.

STUDENTS' RESISTANCE TO MINORITY CONTENT

Perhaps the avoidance of discussing minority content as stated by some faculty did serve a protective function. For if the faculty felt some hesitation about its own lack of first-hand expertise, students of minority and majority groups also combined to support that avoidance for their own reasons.

One might anticipate that most of the White students would be empathetic and receptive to content on minorities, based on the predispositions of those who would be attracted to a human service profession. But there were variations, of course. As civil rights, equal employment opportunity, and affirmative action programs had come directly to impinge on students' vital interests, e.g., loans, scholarships, admissions criteria, employment opportunities—the students' dogmatic liberalism was challenged. As financial realities are paramount to all but the most fortunate of graduate students, obvious threats to self-interests were present. Under such stresses, the impact of their own socialization in a racist society was exceedingly difficult to overcome, and it was a struggle in which much help from the instructor was needed if education toward professionalism was to proceed.

The minority students, particularly the Black students, were also under severe pressure. They thoroughly recognized the covert resentment of the White students, but they may have been even more cognizant of the identity conflicts relative to the other Black students. A conciliatory attitude might be misinterpreted as passivity by some of one's own peers, while an assertiveness tended to arouse puzzlement among many White students who wanted to understand. Trapped by the power of one's own feelings, resenting the stereotyping that placed him/her in the position of speaking for generations of Blacks, many of the minority students would silently simmer and withhold their own opinions during class discussions.

Outright challenges to the instructor's content on minorities were rare, and any inaccuracies were generally overlooked. On the one hand, the instructor was reluctant to invite responses from minority students as some reacted defensively—wondering why they had been called upon for comment, or demurring on the basis that there was no way they could speak for another minority person (disregarding the fact that only his/her individual response was being solicited). And those minority students who might otherwise have volunteered did not wish to hazard possible peer disapproval by expressing anything but a predictably assertive position.

It was a classic "no-win" situation for even the most earnest of faculty and individual students, and many found it much simpler to rationalize their avoidance of minority content. It took an unusual sensitivity, assuredness, and rapport for an instructor to help the students engage these feelings—not only for the sake of the content, but as prime examples of the emotionally-charged situations that they must be able to handle as professionals. More common were didactic efforts by the instructor that left the students listening politely while setting their feelings aside, or ill-advised excursions into encounter group phenomena where unfettered emoting shattered rather than built communication bridges. All of these students, vulnerable to those aroused feelings based on a lifetime of socialization, needed the help of the faculty who were struggling with their own ambivalence.

THE EDUCATOR AND PROFESSIONALISM

For the educator to offer effective help, a first area of concern must be the cautiousness of communication that typifies discussion of majority-minority relationships. Many of the possible reasons have been mentioned in the preceding material, but the main stumbling block involves our personal feelings, i.e., we are participants as well as educators in these major issues of our times. The civil rights movement, equal opportunity laws, affirmative action programs, and the illumination of institutionalized racism—all have spotlighted us as members of minority or majority groups. We have been responded to as stereotypical members of such groups at times, so that personal, professional, and educational roles have been mixed and confused. It is especially critical for social work educators to rediscover the role played by our own feelings as they affect our perceptions, attitudes, and behaviors. For it is only in this way that we can help our students as they struggle to grow from socially-conscious lay persons to professional social workers.

Of serious concern is the difficulty in confronting obvious constraints to discussion. Where cautiousness grows to persistent avoidance, the educational enterprise suffers grievous harm. Conversely, where bridges of communication can be buttressed, they stand as evidence of our profession's core tenet, i.e., that highly-charged issues can be discussed toward constructive ends.

An imponderable is the depth and extent of conflicting feelings that exist among the majority group (faculty as well as students). The price of justice and equality has been rising steadily for members of the majority group; they cannot help but feel anxiety that those rights being won by others are at the expense of their own accustomed prerogatives. There is a point where even the most generous become wary as to the moment when lessened advantage passes over into supporting an alliance against one's own immediate interests. This natural human reaction cannot be denied, and surely it need not be condemned. It is, rather, to the credit of the majority group that they would accept the hope of longer-term advantage for *all* by relinquishing immediate advantage over minority groups. It is that positive eventual outcome, as well as the realistic vacillation of the majority person that needs to be acknowledged without apology.

It is a formidable task, for, if the faculty with its professional background and life experience needs to struggle to work out its conflicting feelings, the students literally can be paralyzed by the turbulence among the stresses of peer pressure, racial identification, and the concentrated demands of developing a professional identity and a new reference group.

THE HAZARD OF ETHNOCENTRICITY

The impassioned search for a heightened pride and identity among minorities, particularly Blacks in the 1960's, left a legacy of bitterness as well as victories. The process of advocating pride temporarily involved a wholesale rejection of Whites as an entity—and a blanket acceptance of all Blacks. If the reaction was understandable, the stereotypy was nevertheless limiting. There is a distinct hazard of confusing aggressive advocacy on behalf of one's own minority group with the task of social work education. Where the focus is on advocacy, one narrowly looks for content only on specified minorities, proselytizes students and faculty, and chides them for their ignorance and personal callousness. And one reacts confrontatively to real or imagined slights from any source. In such an atmosphere, loyalty to one's own minority group becomes primary, and any individual variations in attitudes even within one's own minority are suppressed. It is an atmosphere in which the "us" against "them" mentality prevails; and, in trying to combat racism, one practices it.

In a broader sense, the racial issue and difficulties in ensuring accountability that are being described here are not exclusive to the educational setting. Agencies that struggled to design inservice training programs in work with racial and ethnic minorities certainly have encountered all of these resistances—from polite restraint to intra-staff crises. The passions of the period seemed to obliterate the distinctions between staff and clients, inservice training and intra-staff racial feelings, and a polarizing of positions on the basis of race. Representatives of minority groups on staff planning committees experienced special pressures from their peers, and those not perceived as having sociological, psychological, or physical characteristics sufficiently "representative" may have received as much bitterness as the Whites on the committees. Impassioned issues are ever with us, and it seems likely that sexism may already have replaced racism as a prime issue, with agism patiently waiting to come to the forefront.

Whatever the crises of the moment, any human service professional must rely on his/her identity as a professional person—one whose identity in that capacity overrides components such as one's own race, or sex, or age, or any other variables that may still represent our other reference groups. That identity as a social worker carries with it the learned capacity and the responsibility to act with self-discipline and self-awareness of the deeply personal feelings experienced by us all. The factor that differentiates the professional from the lay person is not the *absence* of preconceptions, but the courage to recognize their presence within ourselves and to move toward constructive social solutions despite those feelings. It is this demonstrated commitment to act in pursuit of desired social goals—and a refusal to rationalize, deny, or to be otherwise deterred by our own prejudices—that remains our most powerful example to our students and our colleagues. To this end, a straightforward and highly visible program of accountability is most persuasive.*

THE CONTINUITY OF MINORITY CONTENT IN SOCIAL WORK

Our interest in minority group content has to do with the same reasons social work has always been interested in their plight—whether such minorities were immigrants, racial, or religious minorities. The impact of minority status, the personal and socioeconomic effects of difference, institutionalized stereotypy, role ascriptions based on sex, age, ethnicity are the priorities in social work education—and any number of minority groups lend themselves to cogent illustrations on the dynamics of visual differences.

The history of discrimination is as long as the history of humankind, and it surely did not begin with the most recent groups that have been specified. In fact, illustrative examples might well focus on the "boat people," or migrant workers from Mexico, or the Soviet Jews. Norton's *Dual Perspective* (1978) provides a theoretical framework for understanding any number of minorities, not only the examples cited by the contributors to the book.

A spirited objection may come from those minorities who are concerned that proliferation means dilution of content, and that generalization has been used in the past to divert and stifle rather than to engage and enlighten. It is precisely to guarantee against neglect that certain minorities have been designated for content

*The faculty at The School of Applied Social Sciences, Case Western Reserve University, approved an accountability plan whereby students rated type and adequacy of course content on each of the designated minority groups. Because each course is rated anonymously by students every semester (including ratings of instructors' competence), and such ratings are utilized by the Dean in matters of promotion and tenure, the accreditation standards could be implemented in a straightforward manner.

infusion in the curriculum, but the educational objective remains the same. "Except for a few people, religion, race, and ethnicity are only a component of identity and do not exhaust it. . . . The pertinent question is not whether America has cultural pluralism . . . but rather this: Under what circumstances do what kinds of people fall back on their ethnic consciousness? And under what circumstances does an ethnic heritage affect attitudes, values, and behavior? . . . Correlations between ethnicity on the one hand and attitudes and behavior on the other are all relatively modest—of about the same order of magnitude as social class. Ethnicity, in other words, is important, but not all important (Greenley, 1976, 7)."

In sum, we do need to require accurate information to supplant those stereotypes associated with the most neglected minorities in our country. And this needs to be done in a societal atmosphere rife with scapegoating, blaming the external environment, and jealous seeking of special advantage, where relationships within academia itself seem vulnerable to distortion and misperception.

But the aims of social work education have not changed, and this is not a new endeavor. It is a continuation of the effort that has characterized social work since its beginnings, and it needs to be viewed from that perspective. Professionalism may be especially difficult to maintain in view of our recent history and our collective vulnerability, but it is only by again giving priority to understanding our own motivations that we can be effective educators.

References

Council on Social Work Education. 1971. *Manual of accrediting standards for graduate professional schools of social work.* New York: Council on Social Work Education.

Council on Social Work Education. 1973. *Guidelines for implementation of accreditation standard 1234A.* February (mimeographed).

Council on Social Work Education. 1978. *Guidelines for implementation of accreditation standard 1234B.* December (mimeographed).

Greeley, Andrew M. 1976. "Why study ethnicity?" in P. S. J. Cafferty and L. Chestang, eds., *The diverse society: implications for social policy.* Washington, D.C.: National Association of Social Workers, 7.

Kandel, William L. 1977. "Introduction to EEO laws and regulations," in R. Freiberg, ed., *Manager's guide to equal employment opportunity.* New York: Executive Enterprises Publications, Inc.

Norton, Dolores G. 1978. *The dual perspective: inclusion of ethnic minority content in the social work curriculum.* New York: Council on Social Work Education.

BLACK AWARENESS AND AUTHENTIC BLACK/BLACK RELATIONS

David R. Burgest

DEVELOPMENT OF BLACK AWARENESS AND AUTHENTIC BLACK/BLACK RELATIONS

Since the decline of the Black liberation movement of the sixties, there has been a de-emphasis and decline on the creation and maintenance of Black awareness, Black identity and Black consciousness in the Black community. There are Blacks who are quick to refer to the concept of Black consciousness and Black identity as a time in the past with Blacks being forced into a new day with different approaches and attitudes. There are those who believe that we (Blacks) have outgrown the heyday of the sixties and must move to another level. It is not clear yet what that new level to which they refer really is, but it rests somewhere between the notion of individualism (get it on your own merit and skills) and a heavy religious orientation which hearkens back to the fifties and the years preceding. Black awareness and Black consciousness which permeated the dress, hairstyle, speech, and total lifestyle of many Blacks during the sixties are limited now to the study of Black and African History and cultures. However, many Blacks who experienced the sixties and the upsurge of pride, dignity, and identity continue to maintain the assumptions which emerged during that time even though they do not overtly manifest signs of the handshake, dress, and hairstyle. Most of those Blacks are parents today and they are attempting to develop Black awareness, Black consciousness, and Black identity in their children.

On the other hand, there is a group of Blacks who were not

ASSUMPTIONS OF BLACKS TOWARD THE DEVELOPMENT OF BLACK AWARENESS

Assumptions Blacks make

I happen to be Black

I am Black first and educator second

I am different from other Blacks because. . . .

All Blacks don't deserve respect because they don't respect themselves.

I am Black and proud of it.

Black is Beautiful but White can be beautiful.

I am Human first and Black second.

No Black person is free until all Black people are free.

Blacks are individuals

All Blacks are oppressed

Anything that is all Black is usually no good.

We need to "off" all Uncle Toms.

Some Blacks are racist toward whites as well as Blacks.

People are people regardless of the color of their skin.

I can't help it because I'm Black

I am pro-Black

The problem with us (Blacks) is Black self-hatred.

All Whites are racist*

Blacks really don't have much of which they can be proud.

The Black militants are the cause of most of the problems.

I believe in "every man for himself"

affected by the sixties. They continue to maintain the assumptions of race awareness which was prevalent during the forties and fifties. They maintained the notion that it was better to be light-skinned, curly haired, and imitate whites. Much of the reason that the notion of Black awareness and Black consciousness has gone underground could rest with the fact that no one has come up with a definition which is agreeable to all other Blacks. What is Black consciousness and Black identity to one person may not be Black awareness and Black identity to another. In other words there is no agreement on what it is to "think Black," "act Black," and "live Black"; yet, "thinking Black" or "thinking from a Black perspective" is a component which is seen as real.

BEHAVIORS OF BLACKS

Behaviors of Blacks

Avoidance of contact*

Treating Blacks and whites on an equal basis.

Showing annoyance at behavior which differs from your own.*

Black is Beautiful and we don't need to prove it.

Treating Whites on an individual basis.

Identifying with the positive qualities of Whites.

Proving that we are Black.

Being concerned about what white society thinks of us.

My approach in handling whites as superior.

Talking to other Blacks about white behavior rather than talking to the whites concerned.

Act as though we are as good as whites.

Viewing self as better than other Blacks because. . . .

Assisting other Blacks in developing Black consciousness.

Race is important in interpersonal relations between Blacks and Whites.

Seeing self as Blacker than other Blacks.

If I were white I'd have it made.

A Brother will let you down when things get tough.

Assisting whites in understanding unaware areas of racism.

We are no better or worse than the least of our brothers.

Going an extra mile to help someone Black.

---

*Taken from Lee, Betram M. and Warren H. Schmidt, "Toward More Authentic Interpersonal Relations Between Blacks and Whites," *Training News*, NTL Institute, Washington, D.C., Vol. 13, 1972.

One may never develop an adequate definition of Blackness which will be acceptable to all but we can identify the assumptions, myths, and stereotypes which Blacks hold about other Blacks, Blackness, Black culture, whites, whiteness, and white culture which may block the development of authentic interpersonal relationships between Blacks and Blacks. At the same time, we can identify the necessary assumptions, myths, and stereotypes that Blacks should possess to *facilitate* the development of authentic interpersonal relationships with other Blacks. It is safe to say that the assumptions Blacks hold about Black people,

Blackness, and Black culture provides an indication as to how they see themselves.

This Black awareness self examination exercise is based on the general premise that in order for Black individuals to truly accept themselves, their identity, their culture, and other Black people, they must destroy all of the negative myths, stereotypes, and assumptions regarding Blackness, Black people, and Black culture which have been created by white America. At the same time, they must do away with all the racist positive myths, stereotypes, and assumptions about whiteness, white people, and white culture. In other words Blacks must do away with the "what white is" and "what Black isn't" syndrome that is prevalent in all facets of American society. By the same token, this article is based on the premise that Blacks must develop authentic interpersonal relationships with other Blacks prior to engaging in the development of authentic relations with whites. Much of this has to do with the fact that the difficulties Blacks experience in relating to each other are directly related to the problems of racism and white supremacy in the American society. Therefore, they must purge themselves of the effect that Blackness has on them before they can attempt to engage in authentic relations between Blacks. It is not suggested, however, that this self-examination exercise on Black awareness cannot be useful as a tool in getting whites to look at their perceptions of how they assume Blacks should think.

This self-examination is divided into two topics, 1) assumptions Blacks make and 2) behavior of Blacks. In each case, one has to choose whether the statement indicated either blocks and/or facilitates the development of authentic interpersonal relations between Blacks and Blacks by placing (F) or (B) in the box indicated. This process of identifying the assumptions and behaviors which may block or facilitate the development of authentic relations between Blacks will stimulate an exchange between Blacks which will increase their sensitivity and awareness. However, there will be an analysis and interpretation of each statement indicating the appropriate assumption Blacks should hold. In addition to the above, it is important to note that all behavior is based on assumptions. The assumption may be either conscious or unconscious but the fact remains that assumptions predict behavior. By the same token, there are behaviors which Blacks manifest in their relationships to other Blacks which are detrimental to the development of authentic interpersonal relationship between Blacks and Black awareness. (See charts on pages 322–23.)

ASSUMPTIONS

I Happen to be Black (block). Too often Blacks view themselves as "happening to be Black." Usually, the comment is in reference to a noted Black scholar, figure, or individuals with achievements considered worthy. In such instances, there is a blatant apology for the color of one's skin and a subsequent acceptance of the racist premise that "white only" is worthy, good, or valuable and Black is unworthy, bad, and valueless. At the same time, there is a de-emphasis on color or race. The other side of the coin is "I happen to be Black" thus I "could have been white." By the same token, such Black individuals have accepted the negative definition of Blacks and Black culture as defined by white racist America. Above all, there is a view that the color of one's skin and race is accidental or circumstantial.

The other side of the coin on "happening to be Black" is used by Blacks who consider themselves worthy in reference to excommunicated Blacks who are considered unworthy. That is, they will say that this person "happens to be Black." Such an approach is taken because many Blacks view the negative behavior of other Blacks as reflecting on the entire Black community or Black race.

Seldom, if ever, do whites abdicate the positiveness attributed to whiteness by stating that they "happen to be white." The rare occurrence of such verbal comments from whites is limited to conversations in the presence of Blacks in an attempt to express apologies for the negative treatment of Blacks by whites. The purpose of the statement at that time is to identify with the humanness in Black people and to imply the possibility of "having been Black." In this instance to be Black is to be human and to be white is to be non-human and the white person is identifying with the qualities in this situation to make him look favorable. However, there are no other given circumstances where whites view being white as a misfortune or happenstance whereas Blacks are attempting to escape all of the negativism implicit in the concept "Black." This is not to imply that since whites do not abdicate their whiteness, Blacks should not abdicate their Blackness. This is to suggest that once an individual or person is able to accept one's culture, lifestyle, customs, and color, there is no need to apologize for race for one's racial identity is God-given.

I am Black first and Educator second (facilitate). It is not infrequent that we hear Blacks who say "I am a Doctor first and Black second" or "I am a Social Worker first and Black second." In most cases, Blacks identify with their profession more than they identify with their Blackness. In essence, Blacks are placing the greatest emphasis upon their acquired professional skills and de-emphasizing color or race. The fact of the matter is many such Blacks have assimilated the negative myths, stereotypes, and assumptions about Blackness, Black people, and Black culture created by white racist America. Consequently, in an effort to move closer to a white orientation, they identify with their profession first and their race second. At the same time, such Blacks do so because they have a need to be identified with a league of white professionals. By the same token, many Blacks de-emphasize color and race out of a fear that to limit themselves to being *Black first* is to limit the scope of their contribution. Many Blacks take this to the extreme that they prefer not being looked at as a *Black doctor* but as simply a *doctor* or *lawyer* or *teacher.* There is a fear that their identity will somehow be diminished by being identified as Black.

On the other hand, whites do not experience the ambivalence of being identified as *white* and *educator* or *white* and *teacher* because it is generally assumed that the two are equivalent. That is, white America set the standards and parameters of education in this society and there is no disassociation of being *white* and being an *educator, doctor,* or *lawyer.* To the extent that many Blacks perceive their professions to be white oriented and dominated, they prefer to be more closely identified with their profession than their racial origin. However, there should not be a dichotomy between being Black and being a professional. If such a distinction is to be made, Blacks should identify with their God-given identity first and their acquired profession second. In this way, it is clear where the Black person places his/her greatest emphasis and commitment.

I am different from other Blacks because. . . (block). Each person is a unique individual and differs from other individuals in some aspects. However, it is the view of many Black individuals that they differ *from the masses of other Black people.* The emphasis here is being placed on the notion that one Black person feels as though he or she possesses unique qualities which somehow are not attributable to "other Black people" or the masses of Black people. In other words, some Blacks feel that they have liberated themselves from behaviors and attributes which are identified as being Black and thereby they are different from other Blacks. This is not to suggest that they are not different from other individuals. However, it does imply that all the behavior manifested by Black people, negative as well as positive, must be viewed in the context of Black behavior. This includes the behavior of Blacks who have adopted and assimilated in the white culture as well as the behavior of Blacks who maintain ties with the Black culture and community. This includes Blacks who are lazy/smart, prostitutes/ministers, pro-black/anti-white, Uncle Toms/militants, and others. Given the impact of racism/white supremacy upon Blacks' behavior, as well as the domination by a western world-view culture, the range of Black behavior is varied. The point being made, nonetheless, is that some Blacks view themselves as differing from other Blacks, have identified themselves as being superior in quality from what has been identified as Black behavior. Such a view is destructive to the notion of Black unity as well as the development of Black consciousness.

All Blacks don't deserve respect because they don't respect themselves (block). There is a prevailing premise that there are more Blacks who do not respect themselves than whites who do not respect themselves. The truth of the matter is that all individuals are deserving of respect regardless of their race or position in society. One should not assume that another individual, because he is Black, does not respect himself/herself. The other part of the assumption that Blacks hold is that Blacks are not worthy of respect. This view is held by whites as well as Blacks and such a view is destructive to the development of Black identity, Black consciousness, and Black awareness.

Black is beautiful but white can be beautiful (facilitate). It is a popular idiom in the Black community that "Black is beautiful." Many Blacks have come to accept this as reality more than a slogan. This is good. On the other hand, there are many Blacks who have adopted the view that "Black is beautiful" but "white isn't." There are anti-white feelings existing under the assumption that *only*

Black is beautiful. Yet, anti-whiteness is still no indicator of pro-Blackness. In other words, "everyone who hates white people does not necessarily love Black people," even though there may be slogans and clichés utilized to express anti-white sentiment and feelings. We must move to the level of consciousness where we can recognize that "Black is beautiful" but "white can be beautiful." In this way *Black* pride is not existing and thriving on the negative assumption of another race for the beauty of Blacks can stand alone on its own merit. Too often, the love of self is dependent on the hate of someone or something else. This is not authentic love of self. Consequently, we as Black people must recognize the same potential of beauty in white that exists in Blacks. In this way, there is truly the possibility of developing Black awareness and authentic interpersonal relations between Blacks and Blacks.

I am human first and Black second (block). In the usual context of the statement "human first and Black second" there is a blatant apology for the color of one's skin or the race of an individual and a de-emphasis on color or race. At the same time, there is a concentration on the "humanness" or "humanity" of the individual. Yet, to become "legitimized" into the human race is equivalent to becoming white—given the white society's definition of whiteness and blackness. In the Euro-American culture, to be Black is to be nonhuman and to be white is to be human. Therefore, many Blacks see a contradiction in being Black and being human. In an effort to resolve the contradiction, they view themselves as being human first and Black second. Yet, there is no physical or psychological process by which one can separate their *humanness* from their *Blackness*. Yet, by identifying with being "human" first, Blacks see themselves as being able to align themselves with a core that encompasses the attachments of whites. Nonetheless, a dichotomy between being Black and being human need not be made. A Black individual is a *Black human being*.

No Black person is free until all Black people are free (facilitate). There are many Black individuals who hold the view that "I am free." That is, they do not recognize any barriers created by the white society that in any way prohibit their growth and development as individuals based on their color. They may have the financial resources, education, home, care and other material values and social contacts with whites and other Blacks which may suggest to them that they are free individuals. They may feel that they have not experienced racial prejudice or discrimination based on color or race. Nonetheless, there are Black people who have been and are currently victimized by racism, racial prejudices, and discrimination. The individuals who view themselves as being "free" reply that such Blacks can overcome those obstacles through either education, assimilation, or integration. They do not recognize that the threat or perpetuation of racism, racial prejudice, or discrimination against any Black person in the world based on color is an indictment against all Black people. In other words, so long as racism is alive no Black person is free. Consequently, no Black person is free until all Black people are free. This is the proper attitude and assumption to possess for the maintenance and development of Black consciousness, Black identity and Black awareness.

Blacks are individuals (facilitate). There are those (both Black as well as white) who wish to look at Blacks as a group rather than as individuals. Thus, many whites developed the concept "all Blacks look alike" to suggest that there is no individuality. On the other hand, many Blacks during the height of the Black identity regeneration of the sixties suggested that Blacks must not look at themselves as individuals but as members of a group. That is, they must not act as individuals or think as individuals but should always think about themselves as members of a group. In most instances, it is good to be group-conscious but the fact remains that Blacks are individuals with their own unique qualities, style, personality, and functioning. In this way, it is impossible for stereotyped behavior to be applied to Blacks. Blacks must be looked at as individuals even though they may possess group unity.

All Blacks are oppressed (facilitate). In the same manner that no Black person is free until all Black people are free, no Black person is free from oppression until all Black people are free from oppression. Consequently, all Black persons are oppressed whether they recognize it or not. There are many Blacks who prefer to believe that they are not victims of oppression. Even though a Black individual may be a millionaire in the American system with the purchasing power to buy and go where she or he pleases, the fact remains that such persons are subject to the same elements of racism, prejudice, and discrimination based on his or her color and race. I can recall Black politicians and judges who were subjected to the same search and seizure tactics applied to all Blacks of the Black community as they attempted to enter the Black community to negotiate with the Black looters and rioters of the sixties. Once a Black millionaire is removed from his or her immediate environment and moved into Black and white society, that person is subject to the same racial oppression that any other Black person may be subject to.

There may be Blacks who do not recognize, based on their personal experience, that all Blacks are oppressed. That is, they have not encountered any experiences which would indicate that they are oppressed, therefore, they do not assume that all Blacks are oppressed. Nonetheless, if the least one of us (Blacks) is oppressed based on color anywhere in the world it is a threat to the welfare of Blacks everywhere. When a Jew is being oppressed in Russia, Germany, or any other place or country in the world, the Jews all over the world become upset and attempt to negotiate to resolve the difficulty because they clearly recognize the implication that all Jews are oppressed when one Jew is subject to oppression. We must become similarly aware and conscious that our relationship and existence are dependent upon the survival of all Blacks.

Anything that's all Black is usually no good (block). There is an assumption in the Black community that anything that is all Black is not any good, therefore Blacks do not frequent all Black stores, shops, restaurants, schools, or organizations. If whites are not present in some capacity, usually with a share in defining the direction of the facility, Blacks as well as whites assume that there are deficits within the structure of that facility. Much of this has to do with the fact that Blacks are considered inferior by the white society and many Blacks have assimilated the definition in the American culture of "what Black isn't" and "what white is." For example, an all Black school is considered innately inferior to a school where there are white teachers and students. Many Blacks will not send their children to an all Black school for this reason. This is not to suggest that an all Black situation is innately superior to an all white situation but it does suggest that Blacks, as well as whites for that matter, should do away with the assumption that "just because something is all Black," it is inferior in quality and service.

We need to "off" all "Uncle Toms" (block). There is a view within the Black community that "Uncle Toms" are responsible for all of the difficulties Blacks experience in their effort to gain liberation as well as bearing responsibility for all the difficulties inherent in Black-white relations. This is not true; for it is white racism which is responsible for the difficulties inherent in Black-white relations as well as the difficulties Blacks experience in their efforts toward liberation. However, "Uncle Toms" may be destructive in that they ingratiate themselves with whites, create a false stereotype in the minds of whites as to how Blacks should respond, and carry information to whites on the planned activities and strategies of Blacks. The ultimate goal of the "Uncle Tom" is to gain favoritism from whites based on his/her behavior. The goal of the "non Uncle Toms" is similar in that they are attempting to affect the behavior of whites, but based on the principles of equality in the relationship rather than subordination of oneself. Both "Uncle Toms" and "non Uncle Toms" want primarily the same thing but their approach is different. It should become the responsibility of the "non Uncle Toms," therefore, to develop self-awareness in the "Uncle Toms" by showing them another more human approach to affect the behavior of white society. As the Black militants used to say during the heyday of Black awareness in the sixties, "every Uncle Tom is a potential revolutionary."

Some Blacks are racist toward whites as well as Blacks (block). There is no such entity as "Black racism" whether it is supposed to be geared toward other Blacks or whites. Yet there is the opinion existing that Black racism exists in relationships between Blacks and in relationships between whites. First of all, whites (Europeans/Greeks) are the creators and perpetuators of racism. American racism is based in the coming of African slaves to white America and continues through the process of segregation and discrimination based on color and race. Consequently, it is the natural response of a people who are oppressed, victims of prejudice, segregation, and discrimination, to react negatively to that experience. Those negative reactions are real and have resulted in the destruction of property and lives of white people. Nevertheless, they cannot be interpreted as racism, even though the same elements may be present in the Black behavior and assumptions that are present in the white behavior and assumptions that contributed to white racism. Instead, the Black behavior must be viewed as a reaction to the historical and contemporary treatment received by Blacks.

Many whites are ready to define the reactions of Black revolutionaries and militants to white oppression as Black racism. It is easy to see how individuals both Black and white are able to make this mistake. However, there is no mistaking the behavior of an individual who is bound and gagged and struggling for freedom as a reaction to his/her oppression as contrasted with the same behavior on the part of the person who gagged and bound him or her.

On the other hand, there is the view that Blacks demonstrate racist behavior toward other Blacks. That is, Blacks discriminate, segregate, and have feelings of racial prejudice towards members of their own race. This is true. Many Blacks have the same stereotypes and negative assumption of Black people, Black culture, and Blackness that Whites hold. There are Blacks who prefer to live in an all-White community, send their children to an all-White school, and refuse to rent or buy from other Blacks. In this instance, it is clear that such Black persons have been inoculated with the values of White society. Nonetheless, they can not be called Black racist even though the symptoms may be similar; the dynamics are different. Blacks must be viewed as victims of a White racist society in that they have bought the definition of "Whiteness" and "Blackness" created by White society and they have been successfully indoctrinated into the White culture. Consequently, they are responding to the racism of the American society rather than being racist. Racism must be viewed as a phenomenon which occurs between two different races rather than a phenomenon which occurs within races, although bias and prejudices exist within all races.

People are people regardless of the color of their skin (facilitate). There is no individual or race that is inherently evil or inherently good even though as we analyze the historical relationship between Blacks and Whites, many Blacks as well as Whites would think that about each other. There is good and bad in each and every individual and race. Therefore, people are people regardless of the color of their skin or racial identity. To think otherwise, one would be put in the position to assume that the destruction of a total race is necessary for the implementation of equality, humanness, and harmony within the universe. This is not true even though it appears that the White race is bent on the perpetuation of racial prejudice and disharmony between Blacks and Whites as well as other races and ethnic groups. By the same token, it appears that the exploitation of the minority groups is done even at the expense of capitalistic gains and technological advancements within the society. Nonetheless, the relationship between Blacks, Whites and other minority groups is relatively young and the potential of unity and harmony between races, colors and ethnic groups is real.

I can't help it because I'm Black (block). Living Black in White America has a way of causing Black individuals to think "I can't help it because I'm Black" as if to say I am not to blame for being Black; therefore, I should not be required to suffer the agony experienced as a result of being Black. It is certainly true that one has no control over his or her racial identity for this most surely must be predetermined by divine forces. Nonetheless, it is a negative and destructive view of self and the universe to adopt the notion that there is something wrong with being Black. This is the explicit assumption in the expression. The fact of one's Blackness is absolute and nonnegotiable in the same way that one's whiteness is absolute and nonnegotiable. Thus, there is no need to attempt to compromise one's Blackness by stating that one "can't help it." Such dialogue is indicative of hopelessness and despair.

I am Pro-Black (facilitate). Many Blacks resist the notion of being pro-Black and consider pro-Blackness as negative. There is the assumption that there is something wrong with being pro-Black. There is the view adopted that people should be pro-human and do away with any distinctions relating to color or racial identity. This would be ideal in a society where all is equal; however, all is not equal. On the other hand, there are many Blacks who hold the view that to be pro-Black is to be anti-White which is not necessarily true. There are some Blacks who do feel that being pro-Black is directly equivalent to being anti-White. It is necessary for Black people to operate out of an assumption of pro-Blackness, that is, buying Black, supporting Black functions, operations, and organizations for Black survival. This is not to say that one is anti-White for supporting Black pride, Black consciousness, and Black awareness. It is the same behavior which is manifest among

Jews, Germans, and other ethnic and religious groups. Yet, it is probably among the Black American groups that the awareness to develop Black institutions and Black causes functions least.

The Problem with us (Blacks) is Black Self-Hatred (block). There is an assumption existing in the Black as well as the White community that the major problem with Blacks is Black self-hatred. In other words, if Black people did not hate other Black people, they could make progress socially, economically, and politically. Crime in the Black community, drug addiction, suicide, breakup of the Black family, and all other social ills of the Black community have been attributed to Black self-hatred. Black self-hatred has even been blamed for the riots of the sixties and the existence of anti-White feelings in Blacks. Aggressive behavior as well as submissive behavior on the part of Blacks has been attributed in part to Black self-hatred.

Nevertheless, the major problem that Black people face is not Black self-hatred. While some Black people do hate themselves, to a very large degree the concept of Black-self-hatred, which emerged during the early sixties, is primarily a white society's interpretation of Black behavior. It places the burden of the social ills in the Black community upon Blacks and glosses over the role white society plays in creating the ills. Looking at the historical relationships between Blacks and Whites, we can find many such concepts to explain and interpret Black behavior. At first Blacks were considered savages/barbarians who were in need of socialization by White society. The "inferior" behavior of Black people was attributed to the fact that they were savages. However, after the so-called emancipation, Whites apparently could not justify co-existence with savages; consequently, Blacks were defined as innately inferior and this was attributed to the fact that they were unable to develop and progress within the American society. As time went on, segregation and discrimination were considered to be the cause for the "inferior" behavior of Blacks. Finally, the concept of Black self-hatred emerged. It is clear that the Euro-American's underlying definition of Black behavior has not changed: only the labels have changed. The problems Black people face stem primarily from the inability of white society to abolish the notion of white supremacy/Black inferiority and racism.

All Whites are Racist (facilitate). Many Blacks do not feel that all Whites are racist and most whites do not feel as though all

Whites are racist. There are both Blacks and Whites who reject the notion on the general premise that "all" is too inclusive. They hold the view that to say "all" invalidates the premise. In addition, there are Blacks who have come in contact with Whites whom they would not define as racist, prejudiced, or biased against Black people. By the same token, there are Whites who hold the view that they harbor no negative feelings, racist feelings, or prejudiced feelings against a people based on color. All of the above may very well be true. Nonetheless, White individuals are a product of a white racist society as well as benefactors of institutionalized and individual racism against Blacks and other minorities. Consequently, they are unable to be free of racism until the reality of racism has been abolished in the universe. It is one thing for Whites to be friendly with Blacks and not harbor any negative, racist or prejudiced feelings against Blacks, but the responsibility of whites does not end there. It is their responsibility to work with other whites for the total destruction of racism; they cannot be viewed as free from racism until the total job is done.

In many instances, it is easy for Blacks as well as whites to identify with the notion that "all" Blacks are victims of racism whether the individual Black recognizes it or not. In this case the question of invalidity does not occur even though "all" are included. Yet, when the premise that "all" applies to whites being racist, the notion of invalidity applies. Still it seems logical that if no Black person is free until all Black people are free (all Black people are oppressed by White racism in America) then it seems logical that "no White person is free of racism until all whites are free of racism." This is not to suggest that whites or Blacks should not establish relationships with each other and neither should this assumption alter any relationship already existing between Blacks and Whites.

Blacks really don't have much of which they can be proud (block). There are Blacks who feel as though there is little of which they can be proud. Much of this stems from the fact that there has been an inadequate interpretation of Black history in America and Africa. Black history has been distorted, "lost, stolen, and strayed." Secondly, Black people in America have generally limited their study of Black people to the continent of the United States and see themselves primarily as products of this continent. Thirdly, Blacks have been portrayed in the media, radio, and motion pictures in a negative sense. Fourthly, many Blacks highlight their victimization by white racism—as slaves and subordinates—as the major focus of their history.

Blacks in fact have a heritage of which they can be proud. To prove this, one need only examine their roots in Africa and analyze the many contributions that Africans have made to the development of the Eastern world, the many contributions which Blacks have made to America, as well as the contributions Africa and Blacks have made to the world. History informs us that civilization began on the Nile, in the Euphrates Valley of Egypt. In addition, Blacks in this country have had a major impact in areas as diverse as medicine, science, art, music, religion and politics. The fact that Black people have survived the oppression of white America is a tribute which can be made to every Black man, woman, and child today.

The Black Militants are the Trouble-makers (block). There are many Blacks who feel that it is the "Black militants" who are responsible for most of the difficulty inherent in Black-White relationships. There are Whites who hold the same views. The assumption seems to be that "everything would go along fine between Blacks and Whites if it were not for the 'trouble makers.' " Black militant behavior is considered disruptive because it further alienates whites from Blacks and may create a "White Backlash." At the same time such behavior supposedly alienates Blacks from other Blacks who hold different views on race relations. On the other hand, there are whites who are more readily able to compromise with Black moderates after a confrontation with Black militants. By the same token, there have been strategies of the sixties where the so-called militant and moderates cooperated to the advantage of all Blacks. The militants kicked down the door and the moderates followed with a milder approach to negotiate and compromise. Thus, Black militants as well as Black moderates play a significant role in Black-White relations. The Whites who retreat into a "backlash" due to militants could not have been very sincere and authentic with Blacks in the first place.

White society labelled and categorized the behavior of aggressive Blacks as "militants" and set them apart from other Blacks as a means of diminishing their effectiveness. Therefore, a negative image is created in the media of the "Black militant" as a means of discrediting them within the white as well as the Black community.

The Black militants are not "trouble makers" in that they are responding to the problems created by white society rather than having created the problems. It is the creator and perpetuator of racism who should be held responsible for the problems and if the concept troublemaker applies, it should apply to white racist America.

I believe in "every man for himself" (block). There is a prevailing assumption unique to Western (European) thought that persons can make it on their own unique individual qualities, skills, and talents. In the Black society where the access to the resources and benefits of white society are few, many Blacks have adopted this same notion. That is, they must not be concerned about the welfare of another less fortunate Black person because whoever is in that position is so because he or she has not been able to develop or utilize their skills and talents due to some inherent deficiency. This attitude may be partly true for individual whites who do not experience prejudice, bias, or discrimination based on their color but it is most definitely not true for Blacks. The white institutionalized system in America will only accommodate so many Blacks at one time irrespective of their qualifications. This is true in universities as well as in the job market where the quota system is in operation. Recently, a white individual (Bakke) felt as though he had been discriminated against (rejected) because of the quota system set up for Blacks and the U.S. Supreme Court upheld his position. Consequently, every man for himself should be abolished in the thinking of Black individuals.

Blacks should recognize that the survival of individual Blacks is intricately tied into the survival of Black people as a whole. Consequently, Blacks who have unique qualities, skills, talents, and resources should use those resources and talents for the enhancement of the Black community. We cannot afford to adopt the attitude of "I got mine, now, you have to get yours." During the bombing of Pearl Harbor, all Japanese in the U.S. were incarcerated. They did not differentiate between the militant, moderate, Uncle Tom, Christian or Muslim Japanese. The same is true for Black people in terms of their lives interlocking together and Blacks must respond to each other as though they are intricately interwoven. This is not to say that Blacks should not take advantage of the resources of white society because other Blacks may not be able to do so. But it is to say that Blacks must do what they can to assist other Blacks.

BEHAVIORS

In the same way that there are assumptions, stereotypes, and myths which Blacks operate out of that either block or facilitate the development of Black awareness, Black identity, and Black consciousness in self and within the Black community, there are behaviors of Blacks in Black/Black relationships which may block and/or facilitate the development of authentic interpersonal relationships. In this section we will look at such behaviors and their implications.

Avoidance of Contact (block). It is the behavior of many Blacks to avoid contact with other Blacks. Much of this has to do with the fact that there are Blacks who stereotype other Blacks in the same way that Whites stereotype them. The fact of the matter is that many Blacks accept the stereotypes and myths about Black people which have been created by whites. Such Blacks have not lost their physical identity as being Black but they have rejected what has been traditionally defined as "Black behavior" and have modified their own behavior accordingly. Consequently, they avoid contact with Black people.

On the other hand, there are many Blacks who hold the view that they are not to congregate or assemble in a group consisting of white people. They do not want to be labelled as segregationist, anti-white, or separatist. Consequently, Blacks in the midst of a large group of whites oftentimes speak to each other but spend their time mingling and mixing with whites. In this way, they avoid being labelled or categorized in a negative sense. It is true that there are whites who view the congregation and assemblings of Blacks in a large group of whites as separatist, anti-social, and possibly anti-white. The notion of separatism and anti-social behavior is not equally distributed in that most whites present in the large group of Blacks do not hold the view that they must disperse and mingle with the Blacks present in order to avoid being considered separatist. By the same token, it is commonplace to see whites sitting or standing together in a large group of Blacks. It appears from the prevailing assumption on the part of whites that it is the responsibility of Blacks to demonstrate and prove that their motives are pure.

Treating Blacks on a One-to-One Basis (facilitate). It is necessary for Blacks to treat other Blacks on a one-to-one basis. Too often Blacks react to other Blacks on the basis of stereotypes developed by white America as well as the stereotypes they have created on their own. In the eyes of many whites, all Blacks are the same; many whites say that "they all look alike." To suggest that Blacks relate to Blacks on an individual basis is not to imply a de-emphasis of unity. Blacks are individuals as indicated previously and just because Blacks are of the same race, this is not to imply that all Blacks are going to be able to get along with each other. By the same token, the existence of differences and personal preference among Blacks in developing and establishing relationships is not to suggest that some Blacks are better than other Blacks. The matter of personal choice in selecting friends, acquaintances, and associates within the race of Black people is a phenomenon which cannot be overlooked. By the same token, Blacks as well as whites must relate to Blacks on an individual basis.

Showing Annoyance at Behavior Which Differs From Your Own (block). Oftentimes individuals show annoyance at behavior which differs from their own. They feel that their behavior is the more acceptable, and behavior contrary to theirs must be put down and destroyed. This is true in Black/Black relationships. In the eyes of many Black people, the definition of what is considered proper and improper Black behavior is directly related to what is considered proper or improper behavior in white society or based on white society's definition of what is proper or improper for Black people. In other words, there are many Blacks who adapt their behavior according to what white society thinks. I can recall the reactions of many Black politicians and social scientists to the many motion pictures which were created by Blacks during the seventies. One Black man indicated that he was ashamed after viewing one motion picture created by Blacks which he thought perpetuated the image that all Black females were prostitutes. His greatest fear was that whites would begin to think of all Black women as being prostitutes. My response is that the Black individual should know the realities of what Black women are based on experience in the Black community; therefore, what he knows to be reality should not be determined or dictated by what whites may think. Too often, Blacks respond to each other based on what whites think as opposed to what the realities might be. Consequently, behavior which differs from their own becomes a threat as to how all Blacks might be viewed by whites.

As Black people, we must recognize that there are individual differences among Blacks and it is the prerogative of Blacks to respond as individuals. Once this is understood, Black individuals can more appropriately respond to other Blacks whose behavior differs from their own. It should not be the burden of Blacks to try to abolish the stereotypes of whites by accommodating their behavior accordingly.

Black is Beautiful and We Don't Need to Prove It (facilitate). There are many Blacks who "jump on the bandwagon" to demonstrate and illustrate that "Black is beautiful." They respond as though this is a new-found revelation of which they have just become aware. They feel they have to prove that "Black is beautiful." That is, they have to convince themselves as well as "prove" this to whites. The fact of the matter is that it is not really pertinent whether whites think Black is beautiful or not. Black society does not need to seek approval from white society that "Black is beautiful" before it is able to accept this fact. Yet many Blacks may unconsciously see this as necessary. Secondly, "Black is beautiful" does not necessarily mean that white isn't, even though there are many Blacks who have adopted this attitude. Finally, any efforts to "prove" the obvious is an indication of insecurities about the matter. Yes, Black is beautiful and we do not need to prove it to ourselves or to anyone else.

Treating Whites on an Individual Basis (facilitate). There are many Blacks who look at whites in the same way that many whites look at Blacks. That is, Blacks look at whites as one large mass of people without individual differences and uniquenesses. Whites differ in attitude, disposition, and behavior to the same degree that Blacks do. All whites are not the same in regard to their views of Black people. This is not to say that all whites are not racist because they differ in their approach to Black people nor is this to suggest that all Blacks are not oppressed even though their behavior, attitude, and disposition may differ. The fact that one Black individual is discriminated against due to race suggests that no Black person is free until all are free. By the same token, as long as white racism is alive and well within our society no one white individual is free from it until all whites are free. The above is not to suggest that you should not treat whites on an individual basis in the same way that you treat Blacks on an individual basis.

Identifying with the Positive Qualities of Whites (block). There are Black individuals who adopt the view that they can "improve themselves" by identifying with the positive qualities of whites. They see this as an indication of cultural growth and awareness. The problem with this approach is that there is an underlying assumption that "positive qualities" are somehow associated with white people and white culture. This implies that "positive qualities" are unique to white society and does away with the notion that "positive qualities" are a human phenomenon that cuts across all racial, ethnic, and religious grounds. There are qualities which people admire but these qualities must be associated with human qualities and not the white race.

It seems logical that many Blacks adhere to the notion that they must adopt the positive character of whites given the definition in the American culture of "what white is" and "what Black isn't." Given this definition, there are many Blacks who do not see Blacks as possessing any positive qualities. On the other hand, there are many Blacks who identify certain behavior in Black people as "white." By the same token, Blacks will say to other Blacks that now you are acting like a "nigger" (*nigger* in this sense is defined as behavior which is uniquely "Black"). The fact of the matter is that Blackness/whiteness are both real issues but are not the basis on which to determine behavior. This is not to suggest that Black people do not have a culture or do not have a lifestyle which is uniquely theirs nor that whites do not have a culture and lifestyle of their own. It is true that each has a culture of its own; however, there is a thin line between behavior/culture and the instinctive forces which dictate and determine behavior. Nonetheless, the major premise here is that Blacks should not accept the notion that they must receive the positive qualities of life by identifying with whites thus placing themselves and their culture in a subordinate position. They should identify with the qualities they deem as necessary for their survival and the survival of their children. Those qualities are universal and not specific to a racial group.

Proving that We are Black (block). Blacks should not be put in a position where they feel they have to prove that they are Black or prove their Blackness. Similarly, whites should not be put in a position to prove that they are nonracist or free from racism. It's similar to being put in a position of "proving that you are human." Once Blacks engage in the process of proving that they are Black, it is very likely an indication of their uncertainty and insecurities about the issue. Once you are sure where you stand, you do not have to prove anything.

For Blacks who engage in the above process, it is destructive in that the boundaries and parameters are not clear-cut and one can always suggest that the behavior being manifested is not Black enough. Such dialogue and interaction is debilitating in group meetings among Blacks. Such behavior is also destructive of Black-White relations. Blacks do not need to prove to whites how Black they are or the fact that they are Black. First of all, the fact is obvious and any interpretation beyond that point is fruitless.

Being Concerned About What White Society Thinks of Us (block). There are many Blacks who are acutely concerned about how they may be viewed by the white community as individuals and there are Blacks who are concerned about what the white society thinks about Black society. The Black individual's concern supersedes how he or she may be viewed as an individual but relates to what he/she is thought of as a *Black person*. That is, they are concerned as to whether they are projecting the proper images and attitudes as a *Black person*. Much of this has to do with the fact that many Blacks have a need to seek the approval of whites on anything they may do. Ultimately, they request approval to be Black with an Afro and with a dashiki. If whites say they like it the Blacks are satisfied. On the other hand, if whites disapprove the Black person is hurt and modifies his/her behavior.

Likewise, there are Blacks who are concerned about the images of the Black community from the white perspective. I have often heard Blacks who expressed grief when a Black person rapes someone white, or commits mass murder because they are fearful of the images that white society will get. That is, they fear that whites are going to generalize that "they are all like that." However, Blacks must come to realize that they cannot be responsible for the individual and/or collective behavior and actions of other Blacks. Above all, they cannot control what white society may think about Black people. The fact of the matter is that what white individuals and society think about Black people tells one more about that particular white person than it does about Black people. Yet we do have the responsibility to try to sensitize whites in areas of unaware racism when the situation arises. This is different from being overly conscious about what they think about us as individuals and/or collectively.

My Approach is the Best Approach in Handling Whites (block). Oftentimes, Blacks are encountered with other Blacks who feel as though they have the best solution to the problems of Black-White relations. They adopt the view that their approach in handling whites is the best approach and no other approach is feasible or workable. This is not to suggest that Blacks cannot learn from each other in their approach to handling difficulties in race-relations. At the same time, some strategies may be more appropriate at a given time than other strategies but the fact remains that no one individual Black has a monopoly on the best approaches to handling whites. An individual with such an egocentric view is not open to learning other possibilities and other options. Above all, there is no fair exchange of ideas which can facilitate learning.

Talking to Other Blacks About White Behavior Rather Than Talking to Whites Who Are Present (block). Blacks are able to discuss, analyze, and interpret the behavior of whites but find it difficult oftentimes to confront whites on an individual basis or collectively about issues. Many Blacks fear that their behavior or motives may be misinterpreted or they feel inadequately prepared to defend themselves in case the white individual refutes the arguments being raised. Nonetheless, those fears are not present while in the company of other Blacks who show approval as well as disapproval of the analysis and interpretations being made.

It is necessary that Black individuals undertake to spend less time ventilating with other Blacks and spend more time dealing directly with what they perceive to be the source of their problem. In many instances, there are Blacks who can given a vivid description of what they should do or what they in fact are planning to do but much of what is discussed is often not realized. In the company of other Blacks, there are many Black individuals who are able to "move motivations" in regard to their treatment of Blacks but oftentimes such Blacks are "morse" in the presence of whites. This is not to suggest that Blacks are not supposed to converse with other Blacks about their relationships with whites or their analysis of white behavior; but it is to imply that Blacks are not to limit their concern with ventilating to other Blacks.

Act As Though We Are As Good As Whites (block). There are many Blacks who adopt the view that they are as "good as whites" or that they can "act as though they are as good as whites." Implicit in this assumption is the view that whiteness is associated with being good while Blackness is associated with being bad. By the same token, there is the ever-present assumption that white behavior is to be emulated because such behavior is equivalent to goodness and superiority. Black behavior is to be rejected because it is equivalent to inferiority; consequently, many Blacks see it as appropriate to "act like whites." Once Black people liberate themselves from the negative stereotypes and myths about Blackness and Black people in the American culture and abolish all of the racist positive myths and assumptions about whiteness and white people, the more realistically can Blacks look at each other as well as at whites. At the same time, whites will be better able to look more realistically at themselves and at Black people and Black culture.

Viewing Self As Better Than Other Blacks Because . . . (block). Once Blacks begin to look at themselves as being "better than other Blacks because . . ." they are using the same tactics to discriminate and justify their prejudices that they complained about in whites. This is not to imply that all Blacks are the same or that Blacks should view their behavior as similar even though there are distinct differences in Black behaviors. However, those behaviors which differ from your own should be looked at as being merely different and neither inferior nor superior. In this assumption there is no need to attempt to persuade all Blacks to be the same nor is there an attempt to eliminate or discriminate against the behavior of Blacks which is not similar to your own. Nevertheless, it is quite appropriate to recognize differences. At the same time it is true that likeness attracts and Blacks gravitate to other Blacks who hold similar goals, aspirations, and behaviors but it is inappropriate to separate one's self from other Blacks who may differ in behavior, aspirations, or values.

Assisting Other Blacks in Developing Black Consciousness (facilitate). In the same manner that Blacks should make white individuals aware of subtle areas of racism, Blacks have a responsibility to assist other brothers and sisters in their development of Black consciousness, Black awareness, and Black identity. It is the process of sharing between Blacks that continues to lead to the development of Black awareness and Black consciousness. It would be ideal if Blacks developed their Black identity and Black awareness mutually. However, it does not always operate in this manner.

Black scholars, educators and social scientists should be developing Black awareness kits for use in elementary schools, high schools, colleges and the community as a whole.

Race (Color) is Important in Interpersonal Relationships Between Blacks and Whites (facilitate). There are many Blacks as well as whites who hold the view that color (or factors of race) is unimportant in interpersonal relationships between Blacks and whites. As a result of an informal survey (Discussions in Classroom Situation Between Blacks and Whites) I have conducted, there are more whites than Blacks who hold the notion that color is unimportant in interpersonal relations. Blacks seem to want their color to be recognized as important while whites prefer to ignore color. At the same time, Blacks tend to want to recognize whiteness as a factor in establishing a relationship with whites and they see the whiteness of the individual as being significant.

As we analyze this situation further, it becomes apparent that whites wish to ignore color or see color as unimportant because they say that "they look at the individual." When the point is made that they are looking at a Black individual, they ask why that is important. Further interpretation of this fact will reveal that whites wish to ignore color because in the minds of many whites the mere act of identifying color somehow implies discrimination or prejudice. At the same time, there is a fear on the part of some whites that to identify race or color as important is to generate all of the negative myths, stereotypes, and assumptions existing about Black people. Therefore, in order to avoid this outcome, many whites avoid looking at color as being important. By the same token there are some whites, who are able to deny color because they see this Black person as being just another "white" individual.

However, race and color of the individual is important because it demonstrates acceptance of the other person's total identity. It implies the recognition and acceptance of differences and not the need to create or develop sameness in order to develop or maintain a relationship. This is true for whites as well as Blacks for there are many Blacks who prefer to ignore color in their relationships with whites. Much of this has to do with the fact that Blacks attempt to make such whites into "Blacks" as a means of accepting them. The recognition of color as important implies that each individual is comfortable with his or her racial identity and comfortable with the race or color of another whose physical appearance and culture happen to be different. In conclusion, however, color should not be important in relationships with members of the same race.

Seeing Self As Blacker Than Other Blacks (block). The "Blacker than thou" syndrome is destructive to the unification of Black people in the same manner that proving you are Black is destructive. Such rhetoric and verbal exchange among Blacks is merely an indication of their insecurities in the area of their Black awareness. If one is secure with one's identity, there is no need to engage in fruitless dialogue such as being "Blacker" than another Black individual. Yet the practice was widespread during the sixties and is prevalent today. In addition to individuals, there are Black organizations and institutions which engage in the same dialogue. If a Black person feels that he or she has some expertise or knowledge to offer the Black community, they should make this knowledge known. However, if their expertise is no needed or required then such Black individuals should find the organization or institution which can best use their services.

If I Were White I'd Have It Made (block). There are Blacks who would prefer to be white, given what appears to be a privileged position that whites have within this society. Thus, they feel as though they would be really "getting over" as whites given the talents, skills, and energy they possess as Black individuals. On the other hand, there are Blacks with undeveloped skills and talents who adopt the view that they would have it made as a white person because of the readily available resources for white people. Yet Blacks with such an attitude place the greatest emphasis on the acquisition of material goods in society and they equate material wealth with "having it made" and de-emphasize the quality and essence of their individual identity as a persona. In other words, they have identified with the benefits accorded white America based on the white American's exploitative nature and racism. There is no inherent quality relating to white humanity which Blacks do not have, for ultimately the oppressor is as oppressed as the individuals whom he oppresses. They are both captives. If the analogy of the white man standing with his foot on the Black man's back is an indication of racism, then it takes as much energy if not more for the white man to keep the Black man down as it does for the Black man to attempt to get up.

A Brother Will Let You Down When Things Get Tough (block). There is a particular assumption in the Black community that a Black man will let another brother down in the crunch, particularly when the situation involves confrontation with whites. Thus Blacks operate out of fear and paranoia when they work with other Blacks in planning strategies against white society. This view is also held when Blacks operate within groups among themselves. This is not to suggest Blacks have not let other brothers down when the going gets tough; however, this myth is not reality and it is destructive to the development of Black awareness and Black consciousness. Instead, Blacks should look at Blacks on an individual basis and not perpetuate stereotypes which are destructive to Black unity.

Assisting Whites in Understanding Subtle Areas of Racism (facilitate). During the sixties and the height of Black consciousness-raising, many Blacks held the view that it was not their responsibility to educate, teach, or sensitize white people. However, much of this view changed with the decline of the Black liberation struggle. Nonetheless, there are still many Blacks who hold this point of view.

Once we accept the fact that being Black is not directly equated with being anti-white and for that matter, being anti-white is not necessarily equated with being pro-Black, then we can accept the fact that we have a continuous responsibility to make whites conscious of unaware areas of racism. This is not putting one's self in the position of being a test tube or guinea pig as expressed by the Blacks who refuse to make whites aware, for it should be the responsibility of any individual to make other individuals aware. This is no more than the communication which should take place between two authentic adults. Yet, the view remains that the whites who claim to be aware should make other whites aware. This is true; however, the only way that most whites can get to the point that they can educate other whites is through contact with, and sensitivity to, Blacks.

We Are No Better or No Worse Than the Least of Our Brothers (facilitate). It is a fact that Black people have thought of themselves as being better than other Blacks for various reasons. Some Blacks have considered themselves better than other Blacks because they may have been lighter in complexion, more educated, had more money, because they associated with whites, live in a certain neighborhood and many, many more. The fact is, however, that no Black person is better or worse than the least Black among us. Our lives are intricately tied into the lives of all other Blacks. Consequently, Blacks cannot engage in the better/worse paradigm. This is not to suggest that Blacks are not different or that they do not possess individuality but the fact remains that we are no better or worse than the least among us. Ultimately, in the eyes of white America this is true. The FBI's suspicion and surveillance of the N.A.A.C.P., S.N.C.C., and the Black Panther party is a clear-cut indication of this. In *The Man Who Cried I Am*, by John A. Williams, the author revealed a plan whereby all Blacks would be incarcerated if a full-scale Black revolution emerged. This plan included the "best" and "worst" of the Black community.

Note

This article, in a slightly different form, appeared in Molefi Asante and Abdulai S. Vandi's *Contemporary Black Thought: Alternative Analysis in Social and Behavioral Science* (Beverly Hills, Calif.: Sage Publications, 1980).

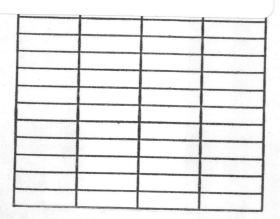